GW00363558

Channel Hopper's Wine Guide

by Henry Konigsberger

Berlitz Publishing Company, Inc.

Princeton   Mexico City   Dublin   Eschborn   Singapore

Although we make every effort to ensure the accuracy of the information in this guide, changes do occur. If you have any new information, suggestions or corrections to contribute, we would like to hear from you. Please write to Berlitz Publishing at the above address.

Original text: Henry Konigsberger
Editors/additional text: Nicole Irving, Hilary Hughes
Cover design: Mostra
Front cover photograph: Peter Zownir
Cartography: Visual Image

Thanks to Julian Parish for his suggestions for the Loire chapter

Contents

Introduction

A holiday in France has always been about enjoying the pleasures of the food, the wine and the romantic ambience, returning with a few bottles of wine, some *pâté* and cheese. In January 1993, the lifting of limits on bringing wine into the UK meant that instead of bringing back the odd bottle, you could now load up your car! The downside was the weekend away changed; the pleasure of buying a few bottles of wine vanished into just another supermarket trip, and you filled your trolley with wines whose quality, or lack of it, you might only discover when you opened them at home.

It is hoped that this book will help bring back the pleasure of a trip to France with practical advice on where to buy wine (in the Channel ports and in the wine regions of the Loire, Alsace and Champagne); exactly what to look for and how much to pay (especially in the 15 to 30F range); where to stay in comfort at a reasonable cost (between 275F and 375F); and where to eat well for under 100F. Of course there are exceptional wines, wonderful hotels and superb restaurants that will cost much more; these are mentioned simply because they are so good and you may decide to treat yourself.

So, whether you're planning a quick weekend hop to buy wine in a Channel port, or a more leisurely visit to some vineyards, all the facts you should take into account are set out in the Practicalities section. This gives advice on getting across the Channel, driving in France and planning your route. If you are daunted by the idea of visiting vineyards, the last chapter, More about Wine and Food, gives information and includes advice on the étiquette of winetasting in a shop or vineyard.

Buying wine

The main focus of this book is on buying wine. The savings possible when comparing French and UK prices are about £1.50 per bottle – mainly UK excise duty that you no longer pay when you bring in wine yourself.

5

The cheapest buys are in the big hypermarkets at the ports, where you can buy wine for as little as 8F, and where you'll find a wide choice under 30F. The wine merchants recommended are those who are friendly and helpful. You will enjoy shopping more if you know what you want – is it to be two cases of red; *vin ordinaire* or more expensive wine; a combination or maybe a case of inexpensive champagne?

If you travel to the vineyards you can taste wine where it is made, and buy wine that may never otherwise get further than the local area. The vineyards recommended produce good quality, good value wine, and the proprietors will make you feel welcome and put no pressure on you.

The Loire has everything: beautiful countryside, châteaux, delicate wines and welcoming winemakers. Although there are some cheaper wines in the west (Anjou from 18F a bottle), Loire wine can be a touch expensive, particularly Sancerre and Pouilly-Fumé (over 45F a bottle), sparkling or sweet Vouvray and the sweet wines of Coteaux du Layon, Bonnezeaux, Quarts de Chaume and Savennières. For mid-price wines from 25–40F, the Loire is unbeatable.

Go to the Champagne region to visit the grand champagne houses, as well as the small houses whose wines you are unlikely to find in the UK. You will find few champagnes under 70F, so for cheaper ones go to the supermarkets or the ports.

Alsace is a bit more than a hop across the Channel at 1000 miles for the return journey; it is an expensive part of France, but it is also remarkably beautiful. Bear in mind that apart from Sylvaner, you will not find many good wines under 30F.

Hotels and restaurants

This book is also about enjoying a country that lives for food and wine. Recommended hotels are reasonably priced (generally between 275 and 375F for two per night). A few more expensive hotels are included because they offer greater comfort, as well as good value.

Eating out can be great value in France, particularly at lunchtime, with a choice that goes from *menus ouvriers* (workers' menus) at 60F to fine restaurants offering lunch from 80 to 100F. Some of France's finest chefs have restaurants in the wine regions, offering a splendid night out.

PLANNING YOUR JOURNEY

Getting to France

Your choice of route and carrier may be influenced as much by cost as by convenience. Watch out for special fare promotions, particularly out of season (September–June). The Channel Tunnel really is comfortable and fast (35 minutes) and can be worth the premium. However, delays have been known, and you do have to sit in your car all the way, with no opportunity to take a stroll on deck, or have a drink or a bite to eat, which does make a difference if you have driven for hours to the port.

Details of how to get to the various Channel ports are given at the start of the relevant section. Useful telephone numbers:

Brittany Ferries, tel: 0990 360 360
Brittany Ferries (Cork, Ireland), tel: (00 35) 321 277801
Hoverspeed, tel: 01304 240241
Irish Ferries (Cork, Rosslare), tel: (00 35) 1661 0511
Le Shuttle, tel: 0990 353535
Sally Line, tel: 0800 636465 (freephone)
Seafrance, tel: 01304 204204
Stena Line, tel: 0990 70 70 70
P&O European Ferries, tel: 0990 980 980

When to go

April, May and June, and mid-September to the end of October are good times to visit France, though autumn is *vendange* time and growers will be very busy. There are fewer tourists at these times, the weather is mild and cross-Channel fares reasonable.

You may have to go in the summer holidays, when the carriers kindly raise their fares, the roads are crowded, accommodation is at its most expensive, and some shops, restaurants and indeed winemakers take their summer holidays too. All of France takes to the roads on the first and last weekends of August. The July weekend nearest the 14th, Bastille Day, and the mid-August weekend should also be avoided. But if you have to travel then, take the signposted holiday routes (*itinéraires touristiques*), which take diversions around congested areas.

Practicalities

Accommodation

There is a wide variety of accommodation available in France. Phone ahead to make a reservation to avoid looking for a hotel after a long day's drive. You'll rarely be asked to pay a deposit or give your credit card number over the phone. Always call if you are not going to take up your reservation.

Hotels. These are officially classified from one to four star (luxury). Prices, fixed according to amenities and the number of stars, are posted at reception and inside each room.

Châteaux-Hôtels de France. These converted châteaux and country houses command high prices for luxurious surroundings – a treat if you can afford it, especially in the Loire. In addition, some privately owned châteaux take paying guests. Expect to pay a lot, and bear in mind that you'll be staying in a private home.

Logis de France, Auberges de France. These are government sponsored character hotels, often outside towns. You can obtain a free directory from the French National Tourist Office (see page 16) before leaving the UK – on the spot you'll have to pay for one. *Logis* are in the one and two-star bracket; *auberges* (inns) are smaller and simpler.

Chambres d'hôtes. This is bed and breakfast accommodation. Some owners offer evening meals as well as breakfast.

Gîtes de France, Gîtes ruraux. These are officially sponsored, simply furnished holiday cottages or flats, often in out-of-the-way locations, always self-catering. Rental includes all charges. Sleeping might be in dormitories (the norm in *gîtes d'étape*, which offer hostel-type accommodation).

Camping and Caravanning. There are many officially approved campsites, graded one to four star. Look out for *camping municipal* (the town campsite), often superb value; and *camping à la ferme*, which will be a field on a farm or vineyard, with basic amenities, and often well off the beaten track.

Communications

Post offices *(La Poste)*. All the usual postal services; you can also make phone calls, buy *télécartes* (phonecards) and send faxes. Phonecards and *timbres-poste* (stamps) can be bought from *tabacs* (tobacconists) and souvenir shops.

Telephones *(téléphone)*. Most public phones take phonecards, not coins. For an international call, dial 19, then the country code (44 for the UK), the area code (less any initial zero), and finally the number. For international inquiries, dial 19 33 and the country code. For the operator, dial 12.

For calls within France, all numbers have ten digits: eight digits preceded by a two digit regional code, which must always be dialled. There are five regional codes: 01 for Paris and the surrounding Ile-de-France; 02 for the northwest; 03 for the northeast, 04 for the southeast, and 05 for the southwest. If you make a call from your hotel room, you'll pay a supplement.

Customs

There is no limit to what you can bring into the UK in the way of goods purchased in France, duty-paid, provided that the goods are for your personal use, and not intended for resale. No questions should be asked up to the following amounts per person: wine 90 litres, beer 110 litres, fortified wine (port and sherry) 20 litres, spirits 10 litres, cigarettes 800, cigars 200, tobacco 1kg. Acceptable reasons for bringing in more are holding a party, a wedding reception or stocking your private cellar. Some proof such as an invitation would be helpful.

Driving in France

Take a valid UK driving licence; car registration papers; insurance cover (a green card is no longer obligatory but comprehensive cover is advisable); a red warning triangle and a set of spare bulbs. The minimum driving age is 18. Driver, front- and back-seat passengers must wear seat belts. Make sure your headlights are adjusted for driving on the right with opaque tape over the area between 2 and 3 o'clock on your headlamps, or you can buy specially designed stickers.

Driving regulations. Remember to drive on the right; watch out particularly on roundabouts. Give way to the right, even if you think you should have right of way. The more important road with right of way may be indicated by a yellow diamond.

Drink driving. Watch how much wine you taste. Random breath tests are frequent and the alcohol limit is very low (corresponding to one small drink). Drink nothing if you're driving.

Speed limits. The limit is 31mph (50km/h) in built-up areas. Elsewhere it is 55mph (90km/h); 70mph (110km/h) on dual carriageways; 80mph (130km/h) on *autoroutes* (toll motorways). In rain, limits drop by 6mph (10km/h), and by 12mph (20km/h) on motorways. In fog, the limit is 31mph (50km/h). Speed traps are common woth on-the-spot fines.

Road conditions. For information, Radio France-Inter's Inter-Route service operates 24 hours a day, tel: (33 1) (02) 48 94 33 33, from the UK; (02) 48 94 33 33, in France (English spoken).

Breakdowns. Take out international breakdown insurance. Ask for an estimate before authorizing any repairs; expect to pay TVA (value-added tax) on the cost. 24-hour breakdown services are offered by Automobile Club Secours, tel: (01) 05 05 05 24 (toll-free) and SOS Dépannage, tel: (01) 47 07 99 99.

Fuel and oil *(essence, huile)*. Fuel is available as *super* (98 octane), *normal* (90 octane), *sans plomb* (lead-free, 98 or 95 octane) and *gasoil* (diesel). Many garages shut on Sunday. A supermarket fill up can be up to 15% cheaper.

Distance

km	0	1	2	3	4	5	6		8		10		12		14		16
miles	0	½	1	1½	2		3		4		5		6		7	8		9	10

imp. gals	0					5					10
litres	0	5	10		20		30		40		50

Road signs. Most signs are the standard pictographs used throughout Europe, but you may encounter these signs as well:

Déviation	Diversion
Péage	Toll
Priorité à droite	Yield to traffic from right
Vous n'avez pas la priorité	Give way
Ralentir	Slow down
Serrez à droite/à gauche	Keep right/left
Sens unique	One way
Rappel	Restriction continues

Route planning

'A' roads (*autoroutes*) are privately-run motorways. Many are only two lanes in each direction, but they're pleasant to use, with wide lanes, good quality surfaces and landscaping; they're fast, comfortable, and well worth the high tolls you have to pay.

'N' roads (*routes nationales*) often have heavy traffic, particularly trucks avoiding tolls; a good proportion are single lane in each direction, so the going can be slow and tiring, especially for British drivers who may find overtaking difficult. Many also run through town centres, although this is improving with new bypasses (*rocade, périphérique*).

'D' roads (*routes départementales*) are similar to 'N' roads, but without the heavy traffic. They can be quite relaxing, are often more scenic and are reasonably fast.

'C' roads (*routes communales*) are small country roads generally in very good condition and almost devoid of traffic.

Electric current

Supplies are 220 volt. French sockets are for two round pins, so you'll need an adaptor for British plugs. Shaver outlets are generally dual voltage.

Embassy and Consulate

If you lose your passport, all your money or are involved in a major accident, have trouble with the police or find yourself in any other serious predicament, you can contact the British Embassy at 35 rue du Faubourg-Saint-Honoré, 75008 Paris; tel: (01) 42 66 91 42; or the British Consulate at 16 rue d'Anjou, 75008 Paris; tel: (01) 42 66 06 68; fax (01) 40 76 02 87. They can also supply a list of English-speaking doctors.

Emergencies

For 24-hour assistance anywhere in France dial:

Police (police secours)	**17**
Fire brigade (pompiers)	**18**
Ambulance (SAMU)	**15**
Police!	**Police!**
Fire!	**Au feu!**
Help!	**Au secours!**

Food and Eating out

Breakfast. This is the most variable meal in France, and often the worst value in a hotel. If breakfast is charged separately, why not go to a café; coffee and croissants won't be any cheaper, but they will be good.

Lunch. Considered the best value meal in France, prices start from about 48F for a *menu ouvrier* (worker's menu), which might include up to four simple courses, including a glass of wine or coffee.

Look out too for *menu à prix fixe* or *menu touristique* (fixed price menus, typically offering three alternatives for each of three courses), *plat du jour* (dish of the day), or set price *for-*

12

mule, all of which are usually excellent value. Eating *à la carte* (*carte* is menu) can be an affordable option, particularly if you only want one course.

Remember that lunch is at lunchtime and not at any other time. French restaurants take orders for lunch strictly between noon (or 12.30) and 2pm. *Le déjeuner est terminé* is a phrase you will come to understand quickly. A *brasserie* (a cross between a restaurant and a café) may keep less strict times.

Dinner. In the evening, hours are just as inflexible, with orders normally taken between 7.30 and 9pm. Eating early (say at 6pm) can be as difficult as eating after 9.30pm. But fast food outlets and shopping malls now offer all-day eating, maybe not of the highest quality, but certainly good value.

Reservations. It's worth reserving a table for a special meal or if you've set your heart on a particular restaurant. Public holidays and Sunday lunchtimes tend to be the busiest times.

Buying food. To buy food for picnics or an al fresco breakfast, go to a *boulangerie* (bakery), *pâtisserie* (cake shop, which may sell savoury pies and quiches), *charcuterie* (delicatessen specializing in *pâté*, ham, *saucisson* (French salami) and so on), *traiteur* (sells ready-made food), a supermarket (small ones might be called *libre-service*, bigger ones are *supermarchés*, and huge ones *hypermarchés*), or best of all a lively *marché* (street market).

Language

Even if your French isn't perfect, don't feel inhibited. It's better to make an effort; and never assume that people will be able to speak English.

The Berlitz French Phrase Book and Dictionary covers most of the situations you're likely to encounter; it's also available as part of the Berlitz French Cassette Pack. The Berlitz French-English/English–French Pocket Dictionary contains 12,500 terms, plus a menu-reader supplement. (See also page 256 and Useful Expressions on the cover.)

13

Maps

Michelin produces superb maps. The most useful are the 1:200,000 series, which also indicate scenic routes. Any sizable bookshop will stock them.

Medical care

Take out travel and health insurance before you leave the UK that covers you for any illness or accident while on holiday.

As a British national, you are entitled to medical and hospital treatment under the French social security system. Before leaving home, pick up a form E111 from a post office. Doctors who belong to the French social security system (*médecins conventionnés*) charge the minimum.

Money

The French franc (abbreviated F, Fr or FF) divides into 100 centimes (c or ct). Coins (*pièces*) come in 5, 10, 20, 50 centimes (marked 1/2F); 1, 2, 5, 10 and 20F, and bank notes (*billets*) in 20, 50, 100, 200 and 500F.

Banks and currency exchange offices (*banques; bureaux de change*) (see Opening Hours). Always take your passport when you go to change money or travellers' cheques. Large hotels, shops, tourist offices and restaurants may also offer an exchange service, though at a less favourable rate.

Credit cards are widely accepted as payment at the motorway tolls, hotels, supermarkets, restaurants and petrol stations. You may also be able to use your card to withdraw cash from automatic teller machines (DAB, *distributeurs automatiques de billets*), but some machines only respond to French-issued 'smart' cards. If your card is rejected by the machine, you can get cash from some bank exchange counters. Visa cardholders can call freephone 05 90 82 81 (no prefix) for assistance.

Travellers' cheques (with identification) and **Eurocheques** (with encashment card and ID) are widely accepted.

14

Sales tax. Value-added tax (TVA) is added to almost all goods and services, and is usually included in the price. In hotels and restaurants, this is on top of a service charge (also included).

Opening hours

Banks. Open 9am–5pm weekdays. Closed 12–2pm; Saturday or Monday; national holidays.

Post offices. Open 8am–7pm weekdays; 8am–12pm Saturday. Small post offices close 12–2pm or 2.30pm, and at 5 or 6pm.

Grocers, bakeries, tobacconists, food shops. Open from 7 or 8am–7pm (or later), Monday–Saturday. Food shops often open on Sunday morning. Small shops usually shut 12.30–2pm.

Supermakets. Typically 9am–12pm and 2–5pm. Many don't close for lunch and stay open later. The largest open 9am–8pm Monday to Saturday. Closed Sunday and public holidays.

Other shops, department stores, boutiques are open from 9, 9.30 or 10am to 6.30 or 7pm (or later in summer), Tuesday to Saturday. Closed Monday morning or all day Monday.

Vineyards should be visited between 9am and 12pm and 2.30–5pm, Monday–Saturday. Respect their lunchbreak. Specialist wine shops and vineyards may close on public holidays.

Public Holidays

1 January	*Jour de l'An*	New Year's Day
1 May	*Fête du Travail*	Labour Day
8 May	*Fête de la Victoire*	Victory Day (1945)
14 July	*Fête nationale*	Bastille Day
15 August	*Assomption*	Assumption
1 November	*Toussaint*	All Saints' Day
11 November	*Armistice*	Armistice Day (1918)
25 December	*Noël*	Christmas Day
Movable dates:	*Lundi de Pâques*	Easter Monday
	Ascension	Ascension
	Lundi de Pentecôte	Whit Monday

Time difference

France keeps to Central European Time (GMT + 1hr). Clocks are put one hour ahead (GMT + 2hrs), from late March to end September. Thus in summer when it's 12 midday in France it is 11am in the UK.

Tipping

A service charge is included in the price of a drink or a meal, so no tip is necessary or expected. It is customary, however, to leave any small coins in your change at the bar or on your table, and if you are really happy leave 5–10%. Elsewhere, tip with a 5 or 10 franc coin.

Toilets

All cafés have toilets. If you're not a customer, leave 2 or 3F in the dish provided or at the bar. On the motorways, service areas with toilets are denoted as *aire de* followed by the place name.

Tourist Information Offices

These range from proper offices, with knowledgeable staff and plenty of maps and brochures, open throughout the day, to simply someone at the *Mairie* (Town Hall) who, if they happen to be there, will answer queries. Ask for the *Bureau d'Information*. Many close 12–2pm. The French National Tourist Office (178 Piccadilly, London W1V 0AL) has an expensive premium telephone number: 0891 244 123 and fax (0171) 493 6594.

Travellers with disabilities

Access is often awkward at the vineyards with steps to cellars and tasting rooms, but telephone ahead to ask about accessibility and assistance. The bigger supermarkets have specially wide cashier points, especially the really large, modern ones such as those at Cité Europe in Calais.

16

The Channel Ports

Boulogne-sur-Mer

The old town in Boulogne is particularly attractive with its mediaeval walls still largely intact. Philippe Olivier's cheese shop is an absolute must for foodies; Wednesday and Saturday are market days.

How to get there

Most cross-Channel services now go to Calais, but the drive down the coast to Boulogne-sur-Mer from Calais is very pleasant and scenic. Hoverspeed operate their high-tech Seacats direct to Boulogne-sur-Mer from Folkestone, taking only 55 minutes to cross the Channel.

Where to buy

The Grape Shop
Gare Maritime, 62200 Boulogne-sur-Mer
Tel: (03) 21 30 16 17
Open every day 9am–9pm
and
85 rue Victor Hugo
62200 Boulogne-sur-Mer
Tel: (03) 21 33 92 30
Open 10–7
The outlet at the port is by far the easiest for parking, and is comfortable and spacious. The shop in town is small, crowded and parking is less easy. Don't be put off by the customs' barrier at the port – they will wave you through.

The Grape Shop's reputation is impeccable: Martin Brown's buying is first class and is driven by quality as well as price. If you are unhappy with any of the bottles you have bought, you can take them back to The Grape Shop in Battersea for exchange or refund (tel: 0171 924 3638).

17

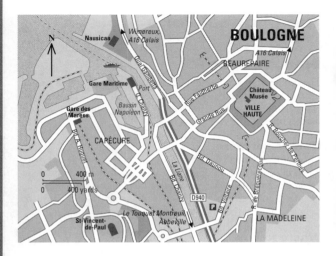

The range of wines is vast. One of the best things about The Grape Shop is that most of the less expensive wines are available for tasting to help you choose. There is, however, a downside to this practice: some bottles may have been uncorked for several days, so what you taste may not be as good as the wine in a freshly opened bottle.

Of wines under 30F, Château de Brussac Bordeaux Sauvignon 94 has the edge on a similarly priced Bordeaux Sauvignon 94 from Château Bois de Favereau, which is bottled by the same *négociant*. Of the inexpensive red bordeaux, the Bordeaux Supérieur 92 from Château La Grave Singalier is certainly worth tasting.

The range of champagnes includes a few interesting small winemakers that you are unlikely to see anywhere else unless you drive down to Champagne itself; though they are obviously on sale here at somewhat higher prices than at the vineyard gate. A good selection would be wines from Guy Larmandier,

Michel Gonnet, Henri Goutorbe and Michel Loriot (all at around 100F). The best value of the champagnes available here is probably Champagne Maurice Lasalle, from Chigny-les-Roses.

There are some lovely wines from the Loire Valley, particularly a Pouilly-Fumé 93 from the excellent vineyard of Domaine Châtelain (56F) and a Saumur Blanc 93 Clos de l'Abbaye (Aupy) at 26F. In the Loire reds, go for Domaine Ogereau's Anjou-Villages 93, a fresh and pleasant Chinon 93 by Domaine des Rouet (both around 37F), a complex and elegant Saumur-Champigny 93 from Domaine des Roches Neuves, and a Saumur 93 Clos de l'Abbaye from one of my favourite winemakers, Jean-Luc Aupy. Saumur is a distinctive wine, and Jean-Luc Aupy is a leading winemaker in this district of the Loire Valley.

From Alsace, the Gewürztraminer Coteau du Haut-Koenigsbourg 93 by Claude Bléger (from one of the oldest families in Orschwiller) is a wine that should be kept for a few years. Equally fine is his classic aromatic Riesling Coteau du Haut-Koenigsbourg. Both these wines were only produced in small quantities, so full marks to Martin Brown for obtaining them (and at under 52F).

The South African range is particularly good, but the prices will come as a bit of a shock to anyone who has visited the vineyards themselves in South Africa, and is aware of how inexpensive good wines are out there. There are excellent wines on sale here from Thelema, Kanonkop, Mulderbosch, Le Bonheur and Buitenverwachting, none of which sell here for under 56F a bottle.

The selection of Australian and New Zealand wines is one of the best I have seen in France. From New Zealand, Cooks' Winemakers' Reserve Sauvignon and Nautilus Marlborough Chardonnay 93 both cost between 55 and 60F. The Australian sparkling wines are also competitively priced, Seppelt's Great Western Brut is priced at 24F; Killawarra or Seaview Brut are at 27F.

Milles Vignes
90–94 rue Carnot
62930 Wimereux (2.5 miles/4km north of Boulogne-sur-Mer)
Tel: (03) 21 32 60 13
Closed Monday
This bright shop with its stripped wood floors is easy to find on a corner along the main street, although parking close by may be difficult. Nick Sweet, the manager, could not be more pleasant and helpful. The shop sells only French wine and it would be nice if there were more winemakers represented.

Top end clarets are much less expensive than in the UK: a Médoc 90 from Château Patache d'Aux (good year, good wine) costing 60F is £8.50 at Philip Ayres in Amersham. A St-Julien 86 from Château Gruaud-Larose (one of the best years ever for this château) at 230F is sold in the UK at the same price, between £25 (from Thos Peatling in Bury St Edmunds) and £30 (from Lay & Wheeler in Colchester or Robersons on Kensington High Street).

An inexpensive Bordeaux Supérieur 93 from Château de Parenchère may be a volume prduction wine, but it is well made and sensibly priced. Minervois from Château de Gourgazaud is usually reliable, go for the Réserve 93.

Where to stay in town
La Maison de Flore
32 rue St-Martin
62200 Boulogne-sur-Mer
Tel: (03) 21 91 70 12
Open all year (book ahead)
Double 300F
This designer bed and breakfast is in the heart of the mediaeval old town, unmarked and seemingly known only to the select few who keep the five rooms constantly occupied.

A beautiful conversion in stone and timber, it is in a superb location with the late night Vole Hole (see below) only a few yards away.

Boulogne-sur-Mer

What to see
Château-Musée
rue de Bernet
62200 Boulogne-sur-Mer
Tel: (03) 21 10 02 20
Open 15 May–15 September 9.30–12.30 and 1.30–6.15;
Sunday 9.30–12 and 2.30–6.15. 16 September–14 May
10–12.30 and 2–5; Sunday 10–12.30 and 2.30–5.30.
Closed Tuesday
Admission: adult 32F, child 13F
Thirteenth-century Boulogne castle is the main feature of
the walled old town, with its moat and drawbridge intact.
The Castle Museum collection is wide and various, and the
Boulogne Gallery has examples of works by local artists
Tattegrain, Cazin, A. Delacroix and Gil Franco.

Nausicaã (Centre National de la Mer)
boulevard Ste-Beuve
62200 Boulogne-sur-Mer
Tel: (03) 21 30 98 98
1 June–14 September 10–8;15 September–31 May 10–6;
weekends and public holidays 10–7; closed two weeks in
January
Admission: adult 50F, child 35F
An experience of sealife in all its glory, from reconstructed
tropical lagoons to the unfathomable depths of the oceans.
There is also a restaurant overlooking the sea, a swimming
pool, gift shop and 'meet the fish' sessions.

Where to stay out of town

Hôtel Cléry
rue du Château
62360 Hesdin l'Abbé
Tel: (03) 21 83 19 83
Double 390–550F
Closed mid-December to early January

Five and a half miles (9km) southeast of Boulogne, just off the
N1, this elegant 18th-century château is approached along a
crunchy gravel driveway through an avenue of mature trees and
12 acres of lovely gardens. The décor is neutral international
four-star, but this does not detract from the handsome building.
Public rooms have vast ceiling heights, stripped wood floors
and huge windows looking out onto the lawns. I did miss a
burning log fire in the morning and during the day when I visited in winter – it was only lit in the evenings.

Rooms vary in size and price, the smaller ones with plastic
cabin shower and toilet cubicles. The least expensive rooms are
in the annex – the 'large cottage'. A light dinner is available on
weekday evenings, perhaps fish soup served from a grand
tureen, goat's cheese soufflé, seafood quiche or warm scallop
salad, or stroll down to the Auberge de Manoir for a fuller meal.

The grounds are large enough for a pleasant stroll and the
terrace perfect for tea or an early evening *apéritif* in summer.

Where to eat in town

L'Huîtrière
11 place de Lorraine
62200 Boulogne-sur-Mer
Tel: (03) 21 31 35 27
Menu 80F

Fabulous value in this small restaurant in the centre of town, offering the freshest quality shellfish and seafood. Three tables by
the bar in the front and seven tables in the back room, with blue

lino on the floor, part panelled yellow walls, bright lighting and paintings of fishermen that would be unlikely to sell quickly. Forget the 80F menu and enjoy the brilliant *à la carte*, prepared in a tiny kitchen, with a total staff of three. Huge servings, so be warned. Start with a hearty authentic fish soup, with *rouille* of course, or half a dozen oysters; for main course mussels of every description, huge succulent prawns bathed in garlic and Mediterranean herbs or fish in season – red snapper, turbot, monkfish or sole. A truly delicious, unpretentious meal.

Warning: the restaurant is bright, cheap and only a stroll from the day-trip coach pick-up point, so to avoid groups clamouring for instant service in order to get back to the coach in time for the 9pm departure, arrive just after 9 for a calm, civilized meal.

Where to eat out of town
Hostellerie de la Rivière
17 rue de la Gare
62360 Pont-de-Briques
(3 miles/5km southeast of Boulogne-sur-Mer)
Tel: (03) 21 32 22 81
Closed Sunday evening and Monday; and mid-August to early September; menus from 160F
There is a bridge and there is a stream, but it is not quite the rural idyll conjured up by the romantic name and address. This is, however, a very comfortable and cossetting restaurant. Rooms available upstairs for just under 300F.

The no-choice 160F menu (the least expensive) offered *rillette de cabillaud* with salad to start, a *filet de truite rôti, fond de poireau et jus de lapereau* as the main course, and a *tarte fine à la nougatine mignardise* to finish. This is cooking of a high standard.

For a complete contrast, drop into the absolutely authentic **Café de la Gare** next door for a drink at the bar, before or after your dinner.

L'Atlantic

Digue de Mer
62930 Wimereux (2.5 miles/4km north of Boulogne-sur-Mer)
Tel: (03) 21 32 41 01

This restaurant has just been bought by Alain Delpierre, who owned the highly regarded La Liègeoise in Boulogne. His entire team has moved with him, so it will be well worth visiting. It is right on the beachfront with views across the Channel from the first floor dining room. Rooms available upstairs.

L'Epicure

1 rue de la Gare
62930 Wimereux (2.5 miles/4km north of Boulogne-sur-Mer)
Tel: (03) 21 83 21 83
Closed Sunday evening, Wednesday; Christmas

There is quality cooking in this delightful small restaurant with imaginative menus: the 140F menu offered *persillé de cuisse de canard, jus de celeri vert* to start, *crépinette de lotte*, haddock, *chou frisé* as main course, *fromage blanc en sorbet*, and *gâteau de riz* as you have never known it, with *abricots secs macérés aux épices*.

The 230F menu was even more exquisite: *foie gras de canard, tomate verte confite* or *ravioles de saumon, potiron et jambon sec*, followed by *cabillaud rôti, céleri-rave, jus de volaille au thé*; as main course *noisettes d'agneau sautées, rattes au saffran, ail rôti*, followed by cheese and *médaillon de chocolat, coulis d'orange, sirop de cacao*. Sublime.

Where to drink

The Vole Hole

rue de Lille
62200 Boulogne sur-Mer (old town)
Open 11.30am till late; evening only Monday. Closed Sunday.
Boulogne's trendiest and smallest wine bar in the heart of the mediaeval old town. Owned by Englishman Roger Young, one

24

of the pioneers of the cross-Channel wine business who managed the first Grape Shop in Boulogne, and his partner. Offers about a dozen specialist beers – Kriek, Bitburger, l'Angélus on tap – and about 20 wines by the glass (10–14F). Great atmosphere at its wooden tables on wood floors, stone walls and arches, and a ceiling covered in hessian coffee sacks from Brazil, Ethiopia and Cameroon. Boulogne's British ex-pats gravitate here in the evenings.

Caen

Caen lies inland a few miles (kilometres) from the port of Ouistreham, and is one of the main ports of entry for Normandy. It is well placed for driving down to the Loire: Caen to Angers, using the motorway between Le Mans and Angers, takes three hours.

How to get there

From Portsmouth with Brittany Ferries. The monopoly on this route means expensive fares but being a French-run company, the on-board food is very good.

Where to buy wine
Normandie Wine Warehouse
12 quai Charcot
14150 Ouistreham
Tel: (02) 31 36 05 05
Open daily 10am–10pm
Chris Bullimore, formerly manager of Maison du Vin in Cherbourg, opened this shop in 1995. It is a bright, basic, warehouse-style shop on the road a couple of hundred yards away from the port.

The best value wines in the shop happen to come from some of my favourite winemakers: Jean-Luc Aupy's Saumur rouge

25

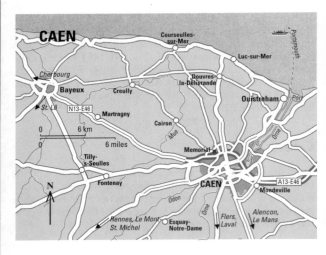

93 Clos de l'Abbaye (27F) is a lively, full wine made from Cabernet Franc, very typical of the *appellation*. Remember that every vintage will taste distinctly different, but here is a consistent winemaker who will deliver quality every year.

The Muscadet de Sèvre-et-Maine sur lie 93 from Domaine de la Tourlaudière Cuvée Première (24F) is made by Roland Petiteau-Gaubert, not to be confused with the many other winemaking Petiteaus in the region. This Muscadet will restore your confidence in this *appellation* as a pleasant, fragrant and refreshing summer wine. This one had a flowery nose, was slightly grassy, and tasted of green apples – a well made, well balanced Muscadet. You'll find the 94, when it's in stock, is particularly pleasing.

The label on the back of a bottle of a Côtes du Ventoux 90 from Château Pesquié (44F), with a smudgy laurel and Médaille d'Or Concours AOC Ventoux 1992, Coup de Coeur Guide Hachette 1993, Prix d'Honneur Vinalies 1993 and Médaille d'Argent Blaye-Bourg 1993 certainly tries to convince. But there is no need: this is a very nice wine, lighter than it looks and still young. It has gorgeous soft fruit, rounded flavours and is well made. If you hold the view that only good wines should be used in fine cooking, then its strong flavours would make it ideal for cooking a *coq au vin*.

A couple of other gold medal winning wines here lend credence to the argument that medals are not in every case a guide to the best wines. A 92 Lussac-St-Emilion from Château Croix de Rambeau (39F), sporting its 1994 Gold Medal in Paris (Concours Général) twice on its label, along with that seductive individual bottle numbering, although smooth and with some taste and bite to it, was certainly not exceptional. It would make a good house wine.

Another gold medal winner in Paris (1995) was the Vin de Pays de Terroirs Landais 94 from Noël Laudet's Domaine de Laballe, which also produces Armagnac. This is an inexpensive wine at 18F, but it was not as wonderful as perhaps a gold medal suggests. However, a co-op produced Merlot Vin de Pays des Coteaux de l'Ardèche 94, also at 18F, is a definite buy – velvety and a good colour, but it needs to be drunk quite soon.

Millesims

allée du Bac
cours Montalivet
14120 Mondeville (2 miles/3.5km east of Caen)
Tel: (02) 31 82 20 54
Closed Sunday, Monday morning and most Saturdays
This wine warehouse used to supply small restaurants: it is currently going through some major changes, with smaller premises and much reduced stock at the time of my last visit.

Of the wines I tasted, a red Bordeaux 94 from Château des Chapelains, although slightly musty, was substantial and good value at 23F. It certainly prompted some different comments: 'Good with bangers and mash', said one taster, 'A horsebox wine at a point to point', said another. The blanc sec 93 which I

27

tasted, however, had deteriorated.

Wines expected to be stocked soon are a Graves rouge 93 from Château Simon (31F), a much praised Crémant de Bourgogne Blanc de Noirs 92 from Caves de Bailly (42F) – this is an *appellation* well worth getting to know, there are some extraordinary wines at half the cost of champagne – and a Côtes de Duras 93 from Château La Petite Bertrande.

How to get there: If you are on the *périphérique*, or ring road, travelling in the direction of Cherbourg or Bayeux, take Exit 1 marked St-Jean, just before you drive onto the landmark bridge. The slip road leads to route de Colombes, which runs parallel to the waterway. Take a left onto this road, and then first left again into allée du Bac. In case you miss the sign for Millesim's, other easy-to-spot signs in this commercial complex are Zénith and Tabur.

Nicolas

10 rue Belivet
14000 Caen
Tel: (02) 31 85 24 19
Closed Sunday and Monday morning

The staff here are extremely friendly and helpful. This is an essential pre-picnic address. It has a fridge with chilled champagnes in it (a rarity in France): for example, they have a half-bottle of Henriot for 65F, or there is a half of Veuve Clicquot for 85F.

The range of bordeaux is extensive, and indeed expensive: 3550F for a Petrus 81 rang a bell, its postcode is 33500 Pomerol. Don't be fooled by the price, 81 was a good year, but the great year for Petrus is 82. The great year for Margaux from Château Dauzac is 1990, and here it is for only 185F, but be warned, it is *not* ready for drinking yet.

The wide range of wines includes some inexpensive Vin de Pays d'Oc at 11F and Côtes du Roussillon AOC 93 at 15F, but you should buy a bottle of these first and taste before purchasing more.

Caen

What to see
Le Mémorial: Un Musée pour La Paix
esplanade Dwight-Eisenhower, 14000 Caen
9–6 daily; 9–9 from end May–4 September; closed 25 December and first two weeks January
A visit to the Memorial should be a prelude to any tour of the Normandy landing beaches. It will give some understanding of how this area was occupied, destroyed and rebuilt as a result of two world wars.

Centre Guillaume-le-Conquérant
rue de Nesmond
14400 Bayeux (14 miles/23km northwest of Caen)
16 March–12 May and 18 September–15 October 9–12.30 and 2–6.30 daily; 16 October–15 March 9.30–12.30 and 2–6 daily; 13 May–17 September 9–7 daily
There is more here than the Bayeux Tapestry (a theatre, exhibitions, audio-visuals) but that is what draws the crowds. But this extraordinary mediaeval embroidery vividly describes the story of the Norman conquest of England and shouldn't be missed.

Côte Fleurie
To the east of Ouistreham
The coast road (D513) passes through several picturesque small resorts – Cabourg, Houlgate, Villers-sur-Mer, Blonville-sur-Mer, Bénerville-sur-Mer – which all have excellent beaches, and small hotels and restaurants overlooking the sea. Deauville and Trouville are grander but charming and well supplied with facilities for visitors.

Caves de Rosel

chemin du Clos Joli
14740 Rosel (4 miles/6km northwest of Caen)
Tel: (02) 31 80 05 75
Closed Sunday from noon until 10am Tuesday

This is the most delightful location of any of the wine merchants in Caen, with a rushing stream in shady grounds filled with the sound of wood pigeons. In the tasting room, Monsieur Coleaux offers a selection of a dozen new wines for tasting every month, most of them inexpensive. Some are available for sale *en vrac*.

How to get there: If you are driving from Caen towards Cherbourg, exit at Rots (Cora supermarket will be on your right), and then turn right on to the D170 to Rosel. In the village the D170 is crossed by the D126. Turn left here to Caves de Rosel, which is on the right just after you cross a small bridge.

Carrefour

Herouville-St-Clair (2 miles/3km northeast of Caen)
Open Monday to Friday 9am–9.30pm; Saturday 9am–8pm; closed Sunday

There are certainly some wines worth sourcing here. Whilst the cheap champagne stocked at all Carrefour outlets, Hubert de Claminger (53F), is, well, bubbly and, er, champagne, it does not offer the best value for money, even at this price, but would be just about fine for summer champagne cocktails. The bubbles do not last long in the glass, so best for a quick, one glass drink such as a toast. If you are not after a real cheapie, but a good one, there is tremendous value from Cazanove, a giveaway at 69F. Other champagnes at excellent prices include Marie Stuart, Mercier, Duval-Leroy, and the best of the bunch at this price, the 89 vintage Cazanove (84F).

In the 15–30F bracket there are some surprisingly good wines. A red Côtes du Marmandais 93 Le Vieux Cloître from Les Vignerons de St-Laurent (18F) is a good dry red, some tannin, slightly spicy, earthy, not bad at all at this price, a wine you would certainly enjoy in a local restaurant. A Bordeaux 94 from Château Cazeau is a rare example of a very drinkable cheap and young bordeaux. A silver medal (Paris 95) may be misleadingly displayed on a gold band, with three other medals (silver in Aquitaine, bronze at Blaye-Bourg and bronze at Mâcon), but you will not need convincing: it is a very pleasing wine, nice berry fruit nose, smooth, full bodied and very good value.

If you are looking for a cheap wine that is quite drinkable, the house Minervois 94 is worth tasting. It smells inviting, with a blackcurrant nose, it is smooth, and although it does not have any real depth of flavour, it is certainly worth considering at 10F. The Carrefour Muscadet sur lie 94 (17F) and a Médoc 93 from Château Tour Prignac, despite a smartish label and a bronze medal in Paris, were both disappointing. Other choices might include, from Alsace, Léon Beyer's Gewürztraminer 93 at 42F and a surprisingly good-value St-Emilion in the form of a 92 from Château Yon Figeac for 56F.

How to get there: Just off the *périphérique*, on the road from Caen to the ferry port (direction Ouistreham), but allow extra time for the spaghetti junction.

Cora

off the N13 (the road to Cherbourg)
Open Monday to Saturday, 9am–9pm; closed Sunday
Well worth the drive out of town, you can't miss Cora, the newest and most salubrious supermarket chain in northern France, which has its corporate flag flying along a kilometre of access road.

Apart from being shiny and new, it is well managed with an attention to detail that will win it many loyal customers. Decent loos, a café that would do well even without a captive market (witness the number of non-shoppers who flock here for lunch), and ancillary businesses, such as drycleaning, offer good value and fast service. Arrive before 11am and have a stand-up breakfast of juice, coffee, croissant, *pain au chocolat* and bread, butter and jam for 18F. At lunch, the pleasant cafeteria offers excellent value in the way of cold meats, cheeses and salads. And which other café would offer fine wines at supermarket prices? A St-Julien 92 from Château Teynac (73F), a Pessac-Léognan 90 from Les Hauts de Smith (77F), Haut-Médoc 92 from Château Camensac (69F) and a St-Emilion grand cru 92 from Château La Croix Figeac (60F). Quite extraordinary.

The wine department is the first aisle you enter, and starts with champagne. The cheap champagne here, Sire de Chalussay, was more dire than sire, but there is good value in the mid-range. Mercier was on sale for 82F (compared to a UK price of £15.50), Perrier-Jouet at 99F (saving at least £3 on the lowest UK price), and you might be lucky to find a bottle or two of the superb Jacquart 90 – part Pinot Noir part Chardonnay – a very elegant champagne.

Best of the inexpensive wines was a Bordeaux 93 from Château La Vieille Eglise, fairly soft, and half-bottles at 11F.

A half-bottle of 1993 Riesling from Dumoulin-Storch of Sigolsheim (19F) is an example of half-bottles having a shorter life than whole bottles. Whatever inspired the gold medal in Paris in 1993 was no longer clearly evident. It was still fairly fragrant, but otherwise rather dull and flat. Lost it, in other words. Watch out for half-bottles: they may not last as long as whole bottles, so this 1993 might still be fine in a full bottle.

The general rule that fine bordeaux are often better value in the UK than in France, given the strong franc, clearly does not apply here. A Haut-Médoc 89 from Château Larose-Trintaudon, last seen at John Harvey (of Bristol) for about £12 for a standard size bottle, is on sale here for an astonishing 99F for a magnum. It is a château with a reputation for consistently good winemaking. Another magnum on offer is from Château Carbonnieux, a Pessac-Léognan 90, a good year from a reputable château. On sale at 239F (for a magnum), this compares favourably with a 92 (not as good a year for this château) on sale at Victoria Wine for just under £13 for a 75cl bottle. Les Hauts de Smith, the second wine of the distinguished Château Smith Haut Lafitte, is available in the 90 vintage – a good year, but not yet ready for drinking (65F).

Dreams are made of Château Lafaurie-Peyraguey's magnificent Sauternes 90 (147F), a great wine, but closing up now from its wonderful youth; it should be laid down now for graceful ageing.

For price comparison, or if you trust a wine merchant's storage conditions more than those of a supermarket, get in touch with J.E. Hogg of Edinburgh (tel: 0131 556 4025), who has this particular vintage. Others who stock Lafaurie-Peyraguey include Barnes Wine Shop, Lea & Sandeman (Kensington Church Street and Fulham Road) and Roberson (Kensington High Street). As ever, watch out for the vintage: 91, 92 and 93 are inferior. A St-Julien 90 from Château Gruaud-Larose (in St-Julien-Beychevelle) is available at 150F, a good year from this château and considerably cheaper than in the UK. A Pauillac 88 from Les Forts de Latour, the second wine of Château Latour, is 130F, about £3.50 less than at home.

Where to stay in town

Le Dauphin
29 rue Gemare
14000 Caen
Tel: (02) 31 86 22 26
Double 370–440F

Well known to British visitors, this is an old favourite in the heart of the city. Better known as a restaurant (see below), it does in fact have 22 rooms. The reception area and dining room are stylish and characterful, the small rooms almost nondescript by comparison. They are, however, modernized and comfortable.

Breakfast is healthy, generous and of the highest quality: fresh juice, decent yoghurt, proper cereals, fresh fruit and of course croissants, jams, tea and coffee. Unfortunately the car park is small, and parking on the street is in demand because of the restaurants in the vicinity.

Where to stay out of town

Manoir des Tourpes

rue de l'Eglise
14670 Bures-sur-Dives (8.7 miles/14km east of Caen)
Tel: (02) 31 23 63 47
Open most of the year, but book ahead
Double with breakfast 280–350F

Manoir des Tourpes is a 17th-century manor, situated in a lush, gently rolling landscape by the River Dives, a 15-minute drive east of Caen. It is everything you could hope for: an elegant mansion, with four well kept, appropriately decorated and comfortable rooms. The owners are English speaking (Mike Cassidy is American), charming, friendly and helpful.

The guests' drawing room has great atmosphere with flagstone floors, booklined walls and a large stone fireplace ablaze in colder weather. The largest bedroom is my favourite, with views over the meadows, the church and the graveyard – perhaps it is because of the stone walls and floors, wicker chairs and pretty bathroom. The neighbouring room has its bathroom across the hallway, the other two have en-suite showers. One of these rooms is in the attic, with old beams and a bird's eye view of the river. The riverside garden is idyllic in the summer, perfect for reading or sipping a wine chilled in the river.

How to get there: Take the A13 towards Paris. Take Exit 30 to Troarn (have a 1F coin handy to use at the unmanned toll collection machine). Once in Troarn, take the D95 to Bures (signposted to the left); in Bures follow signposts for *Chambres d'Hôte*.

Chez Madame Hamelin

14430 Beuvron-en-Auge (18.5 miles/30km east of Caen)
200F for a double room, including breakfast
Closed from November to Easter
Worth the extra drive, this less expensive bed and breakfast is in one of Normandy's prettiest villages.

Where to eat in town

Le Dauphin

29 rue Gemare

14000 Caen

Tel: (02) 31 86 22 26

Closed Saturday lunchtime

Menus from 95F

This is one of the best looking dining rooms in Caen, with a quarry-tiled floor, beautifully crafted stone walls, ageing mirrors hanging on one wall, and pink and blue fabric on the others. There are a couple of gorgeous pieces of massive furniture in the room, and a fire blazing in cool weather. It is grand and intimate at the same time, immensely comfortable and has a gentle atmosphere.

The cooking is careful and exact, the ingredients of the finest quality. If this restaurant were in London, lunch would be booked out weeks in advance for the 95F menu (remember that this includes the service charge). The menu offered a *charcuterie* bursting with flavours or herring fillets with a potato salad, to start, a *méli-mélo des poissons* or *fricassée de volaille* (*Vallée d'Auge*) as main course, and either cheese from a magnificent cheese board or fruit tart to finish.

Remember that this part of Normandy is at the heart of some of the finest cheese production in France, so make sure that you sample at least one: Camembert, Pont l'Evêque, Livarot or Pavé d'Auge. The other great product of Normandy is apples – so apple tarts, cider and Calvados are sure to feature on menus throughout the region.

Hefty mark-up on the wine list here, though: the Jacquart which costs 83F around the corner at Carrefour is priced at 360F in the restaurant. Whilst the owner and chef appeared very friendly to all the other guests, spending some time chatting at their tables throughout the meal, I was aware that my table was studiously avoided. Was it my clothes, or was it the fact that I hadn't ordered wine?

Le Gastronome

43 rue St-Sauveur
14000 Caen
Tel: (02) 31 86 57 75
Closed Sunday evening
Menus from 86F

This is a very pleasant restaurant, quite formal and restrained, its cooking done with care and skill, and served with pride. During the week, the 86F menu offered a terrine of *gibier aux pommes*, a *cassoulet* of mussels with endives or six oysters as starters, a supreme of salmon *aux coques*, *civet de lièvre* or *gigolette de volaille* for the main course, and a *poire meringuée au Grand Marnier* or *sorbets* on red fruit *coulis* for dessert.

Le Boeuf Ferré

10 rue Croisiers
14000 Caen
Tel: (02) 31 85 36 40
Closed Saturday and Sunday lunch; part of July
Menus from 75F

A couple of blocks along the street from Le Gastronome, Le Boeuf Ferré is usually packed at lunchtime during the week, so make a reservation.

Certainly good value for the 75F lunch: snails in aneth and pastis, sauté of lambs' kidneys in a port sauce or *cuissot de canard confit*, *sauce aux cèpes*, and an apple mousse with Calvados to finish.

L'Assiette

2 place Fontelle
14000 Caen
Tel: (02) 31 85 29 16
Menus from 85F

A fun place, particularly at Saturday lunchtime. Bright, cheerful atmosphere, with decent cooking using good locally produced ingredients.

Where to eat out of town
Hostellerie du Moulin du Pré
route de Gonneville-en-Auge
14860 Bavent (8.7 miles/14km northeast of Caen)
Tel: (02) 31 78 83 68
Closed Sunday evening and Monday (except in July and August) and on public holidays; also part of March, and October
Menus from 250F
Rooms are available upstairs at 320F
The key element in the success of this restaurant is the charm of the owners: Claude Holst is not only a restaurateur, but also a poet and superb host. There are tranquil gardens in which to stroll or sit with a pre-dinner cocktail (the house champagne cocktail is unbeatable, with champagne, vodka, Grand Marnier, Campari, white rum, lemon juice and orange juice).

The dining room, although quite large, is warm and intimate, the fire burning all year, as this is where meats are grilled. The cooking is imaginative and well executed. Try the gazpacho with poached oysters or pretty courgette flowers stuffed with turbot and girolle mushrooms to start. Main courses range from meats grilled over the wood fire or hearty rabbit cooked in cider, to a navarin of lobster. For dessert have the mixed plate.

Le Pavé d'Auge
14430 Beuvron-en-Auge (18.6 miles/30km east of Caen)
Tel: (02) 31 79 26 71
Closed Monday, Tuesday; February and mid-November to mid-December
Menus from 130F
Regional cooking of a high standard in a gorgeous old building in the heart of one of the most beautiful villages in Normandy. Well worth the drive out. Allow some time for a walk around the village before or after your meal. The chef's wife is originally English, which will help you decipher the splendid menu. Great atmosphere.

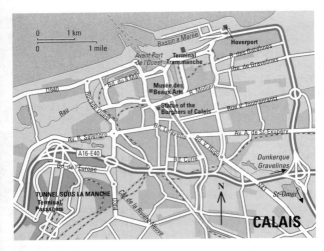

Calais

Calais happens to have the biggest selection of wine outlets of any of the ports and it is also a historic town with ancient British connections. Take time to wander round the Citadelle where parts of the old walls still stand.

How to get there

The cross-Channel journey time from Dover is short, just 35 minutes on some carriers, services are frequent, and the competition keeps prices lower than on other routes. There is a choice between the Seacat, hovercraft and conventional car ferries, operated by Hoverspeed, P&O, Stena and Seafrance. And, of course, there is now Le Shuttle. The terminal is on the Boulogne side of Calais town; on your return take Exit 13 from the A16 autoroute and follow signs for *Tunnel sous La Manche*.

Where to buy wine
Victoria Wine Company
Cité Europe (in the Channel Tunnel complex), 62100 Calais
9am–10pm; closed Sundays

A very pleasant shop – good looking, well organized, easy to work your way around, and brilliantly located. There is also an excellent range of wines here, from the very cheap (yet perfectly drinkable) to good quality at great prices.

Starting with the cheap wines, there are obviously plenty of customers who like the Alta Mesa Tinto 94, a red Portuguese wine from Estremadura made by Adega Cooperativa de Saõ Mamede da Ventosa. Perhaps it's the price, 10F (superb value against the UK price of £3 to £3.50) or perhaps it's the gold medal bestowed on it by a (respected) British wine writer. It is good value, with fine purple colour, an aggressive nose, and full fruity taste. Try a bottle first. Personally, I would either spend even less and buy the Leziria at 8F, another huge saving on the UK price of £2.90 (at Somerfield and Victoria Wine) or cross the border and splash out 17F on a bottle of Spanish Campillo Rioja 1989, fruity and well balanced, selling in the UK for £5.60 at Oddbins and Victoria Wine. Other cheapies under 18F worth tasting are a rich and spicy Syrah 94 from Galet Vineyards in Gard, in the south of France, and a sunny, ripe Vin de Pays du Gard 94 from Riverbed Vineyards (the same winemakers as Galet).

Also at a ridiculously low price is a 1993 Bulgarian white, Bear Ridge, made by Kym Milne, all apples at 8F. Not everyone is a fan of the commercial Californian vineyards of Ernest and Julio Gallo, but at 17F their white Sauvignon Blanc and Chardonnay, and red Cabernet Sauvignon are excellent value. The well known house of Calvet makes a pretty reasonable claret under the Victoria Wine label for 15F.

For good savings on Australian wines you might be buying normally in the UK, look out for Hardy's Nottage Hill Cabernet Sauvignon-Shiraz 93 and Jacob's Creek Shiraz-Cabernet 94 (under 20F), Deakin Estate's ripe fruit Cabernet Sauvignon 94 and Penfold's Rawson's Retreat Bin 35 Cabernet Sauvignon-Shiraz 94 at under 25F, and Koonunga Hill Shiraz-Cabernet 93 at just under 30F. Australian whites that are good value include Hardy's Nottage Hill Chardonnay 95 (under 20F), and Lindeman's ever so slightly spicy but peachy Bin 65 Chardonnay 94 at 28F. From South Africa, try the rather earthy Klein Constantia Shiraz 92 at 25F.

Interesting French wines are Fortant de France's Vin de Pays d'Oc Merlot 94 from Sète, in the south of France, lots of ripe fruit, splendid with a summer barbecue grill, at 17F. More sunny wines come in the form of a Corbières 93 from Domaine du Tauch (19F) and a Cahors 92 from Château de Léret at 28F. Also ripe and rich is a Gigondas 94 Les Perdrix from the local co-op at 30F. Sunny whites worth tasting include a Vin de Pays d'Oc 94 La Pérouse from the Franco-Australian partnership of Penfolds and Les Vignerons de Val d'Orbieu at Narbonne and James Herrick's Vin de Pays d'Oc Chardonnay 94 both at under 29F. From Chile, try Vina Casablanca's Sauvignon Blanc 94 from the Lontue Valley in Curico, a fresh, pleasant wine at around 25F.

And if you are looking for some fine vintage champagnes, here are a Bollinger 88 for 239F, Moët et Chandon 88 for 148F and Lanson 88 for 138F.

Tesco
Cité Europe
62100 Calais
Monday to Saturday 9am–10pm
Not the most imaginatively designed shop, and certainly not as pleasant as the wine section of any major Tesco back home. Good for standard brand name beers: Kronenbourg 26 x 25cl for 48F, Stella Artois 10 x 25cl for 18F, '33' 24 x 25cl for 42F, and German Holsten 24 x 50cl for 103F.

Australian wines are well represented with some very good winemakers such as Tim Adams and Château Tahbilk alongside

Calais

What to see
The Burghers of Calais
by the Town Hall
Rodin's famous bronze sculpture commemorates the English siege of Calais which started in 1346, and shows six of the city fathers offering themselves as hostages to save the city from the ruthless English king.

Musée des Beaux-Arts et de la Dentelle
25 rue Richelieu
62100 Calais
Open every day (except Tuesday) 10–12 and 2–5.30
Admission 10F, free on Wednesday
The city of Calais was founded on the lacemaking industry which has now largely died out, but there are displays here describing how machines took over from traditional methods. There is also a neat model of the old walled town.

standard cheapies such as Nottage Hill Cabernet Sauvignon-Shiraz 94 and Jacob's Creek Sémillon-Chardonnay 95 at under 20F. The fine bordeaux shelves include the less than fine vintages of 84 and 87, but the range of champagne is everything it should be. Whilst the Roederer Cristal 88 and Dom Pérignon 85 are unrealistic for most at 485F and 356F respectively, the Moët et Chandon 88 is a steal at 130F. Non-vintage Lanson Black at 97F and Mercier at 81F are very well priced, as is Tesco's own, made by the reputable Jeanmaire, at 80F.

If you haven't yet discovered how good South African wine can be, here is a good place to start. Many of the wines are not only well chosen, but value priced. Charles Back's fabled winemaking skills at Fairview are evident in the barrel fermented

Shiraz 94 (only 27F), and in his award winning Merlot 93 at 38F. Although Boschendal is a high volume producer, its Sauvignon Blanc is some of the best in the region – here their 94 is 31F. Also recommended are André van Rensburg's Stellenzicht Shiraz 93 and Danie de Wet's Chardonnay 95, both at around 30F.

If you have not tried a Vouvray or a Saumur, here are a couple of inexpensive examples: a Vouvray 93 from Bourillon in Rochecorbon is worth trying, and a Saumur 94 from the Cave des Vignerons de Saumur (both at around 25F). In the fine wine section, there is a Margaux at 70F that is just waiting to be discovered: the 92 from Château Cantenac Brown is a superb Margaux for the year, with a wonderful colour, lovely bouquet. A smooth, slightly peppery wine, keep it until 2000, but if you must, it is in fact drinkable now.

Carrefour
Cité Europe
62100 Calais
Open Monday–Friday 9am–9.30pm; Saturday 9–8
Closed Sunday
Convenient location at Cité Europe, brand new trolleys and a sparkling store. It does have to compete with Victoria Wine and Tesco in the same complex, but you are still likely to find yourself doing some food shopping here.

For details of the wines available here, see the write-up on the Carrefour in Caen (page 30).

Mammouth
On the N1 to Boulogne (about 2 miles/3.2km southwest of Calais)
What an extraordinary mix of wines there is in this store! Hidden amongst the pile 'em high wines, you will find some real gems.

One of the most stunning wines is a Pessac-Léognan 90 from Château La Louvière at 129F, simply the best year this château
42

has ever had. A Sauternes 90 from Château Suduirat (169F) is so fragrant, so elegant, and so delicious that you will have to exercise great restraint not to drink it immediately, though it really should be kept for another few years. What the splendid Margaux 92 from Château Margaux is doing here – a magnificent wine indeed, perfumed, smooth, elegant, refined – is extraordinary. You might also enjoy a good Haut-Médoc 90 from Château La Tour Carnet at 80F.

The range of Alsace wines comes mainly from Dopff au Moulin in Riquewihr, a respectable winemaker, although not to be confused with Dopff & Irion, also in Riquewihr. The wines are very reasonably priced, and the Riesling 94 at 33F is a good choice.

Of the champagnes, best value are Jacquart, Mercier and Germain.

Sainsbury's

On the N1 to Boulogne (about 2 miles/3.2km southwest of Calais), next door to Mammouth
Monday to Saturday 9am–8pm
This store should keep Sainsbury's own customers happy on the basis of price, although it does not have the pleasant atmosphere of Sainsbury's wine departments in the UK, nor are the staff as cheerful and helpful.

The range of French wines is disappointingly small, as is the range of champagnes, which could hardly be smaller, but Sainsbury's own brand at 77F, made by Duval-Leroy in Vertus, is excellent value.

At the cheaper end there are wines such as the Hungarian Balatonboglar's Chapel Hill Irsai Oliver at 10F, and well known standards such as Jacob's Creek Shiraz-Cabernet 94 or Sémillon-Chardonnay 95 at under 20F.

If you are prepared to spend more, there are two interesting New World wines in the form of Firestone's Chardonnay 91 from the Santa Ynez Valley in the States at 55F and a Chardonnay 94 from Boschendal in South Africa at 39F.

The Wine and Beer Company

route de Boulogne
62231 Coquelles (2 miles/3.2km southwest of Calais)
Tel: (03) 21 82 93 64
Open every day 7am–10pm

This is a bright and cheerful store with friendly, helpful staff. The stock is the same as it is in the stores in Le Havre and Cherbourg. For details of the wines available see page 78.

How to get there: From Calais take the N1 in the direction of Boulogne (or Exit 14 on the A16, then onto the N1; or Exit 12) and then on to the centre of Coquelles.

The Grape Shop

40 rue Phalsbourg
62100 Calais
Open every day 8.30am–9pm

The stock and the service here are the same, and of the same quality, as in the Boulogne store. For details see page 17.

Le Chais

rue de Phalsbourg
62100 Calais
Tel: (03) 21 97 88 56

Less well kept than The Grape Shop next door, this slightly dusty warehouse does have some champagnes at very competitive prices, with Bollinger and Roederer at 135F, Taittinger at 115F, Lanson Black Label and Bruno Paillard both at 100F, as well as sparkling wines, with Bouvet Ladubay's Saumur Brut and very good Saphir costing less than at Bouvet-Ladubay itself in St-Hilaire-St-Florent.

Château de Cocove

62890 Recques-sur-Hem (16 miles/26km southeast of Calais)
Tel: (03) 21 82 68 29

This is the cellar for the hotel at Château de Cocove, particularly convenient for its guests, who are welcome to visit the cellar at any time that the reception desk is open. Many of the wines are available in the restaurant, and some by the glass at the bar upstairs. Have lunch at the hotel, and enjoy a day out in the country. Easy parking.

The choice of champagnes is limited to three houses: Bauget-Jouette at 95F, Gardet Royal Brut at 58F a half-bottle, and Pol Roger Brut at 185F (or 95F a half).

The selection of burgundies and Beaujolais come mainly from two *négociants*, Maison Chanson, very solid and reliable, and Debeaune, whose pedigree is equally sound. Beaujolais start at 25F for a Beaujolais-Villages.

From the range of white wines, try the very good Saumur blanc 93 from Domaine de la Renière at 28F. This vineyard is located in Le-Puy-Notre-Dame, home also to Clos de l'Abbaye, a favourite. The Muscadet de Sèvre-et-Maine sur lie 93 from Château Plessis-Brezot comes from the vineyard taken over by the previous owner of Château Cocove. It is a well made, lively wine, with a wonderful floral nose (30F, or 17F a half-bottle). Try the Monbazillac 90 from Château Fontpudière, which makes consistently good wines. This sweet wine is luscious and costs 77F.

If you haven't tasted a Saumur rouge, René Gay's Domaine de la Renière 93 at 30F is very typical, and a well made example of this Loire wine.

Of the more expensive red wines, try the Haut Médoc cru bourgeois from Catherine Blasco's Château Hanteillan. The 90 is probably the best value of the vintages available here (58F). Château Loudenne is one of the most beautiful vineyards in the Médoc, with gorgeous views towards the Gironde. Their 89 is currently on offer at 51F. The Margaux wines range in price from 72F (Château Paveil de Luze 92) to Château Lascombes 88 at 158F.

Three châteaux from St-Estèphe are featured: the 88 from Château Phélan-Ségur (146F), an 89 from Château Franck (the second wine from Phélan-Ségur) for 68F and a 90 from Château le Crock at 82F.

The Sunday Times Wine Club Shop
(Tel: 01734 481713 in the UK, £10 annual membership)
La Ferme
quai du Haut Point (off place du Chrest, near the canal)
62500 St Omer (about 25 miles/40km south of Calais on the
N43)
Tel: (03) 21 38 43 95

Although this is a club, which enables members to order wine in advance in the UK, pay in sterling and arrange a guaranteed pick-up time, non-members can also walk into the shop and buy wine at the same prices as members. The risk for non-members is that a particular wine may not be in stock when they visit, whereas members are guaranteed that the wine will be awaiting them.

There are no tastings offered in the shop, because the club hopes to pick up orders in advance, and since the wines sold here are the same as those sold in the UK, members are likely to have tasted some from previous orders.

The range on sale is interesting, albeit fairly limited, and there is a reasonable selection of cheeses on offer as well.

PGs

On the N1 to Boulogne (about 2 miles/3.2km from Calais)
On the way out to Mammouth, you will see a small unremarkable supermarket with an even more uninspiring name, PGs. Watch your trolley, mine was pinched from under my nose for the 10F it yields on its return to the trolley park. An assistant said that this is not unusual.

The champagne selection includes Mercier at 77F, Canard-Duchêne at 92F, Lanson Black at 100F, Perrier-Jouet at 107F and Taittinger at 115F.

Chablis from the reputable Domaine Alain Geoffroy is available at 49F. You might like to try a rich, scented St-Emilion grand cru 91 made by Yves Blanc at Château Franc Bigaroux, an organic vineyard, for 48F, or another St-Emilion grand cru 93 from Château Rol de Fombrauge at 63F.

Match
place des Armes
62100 Calais
In the centre of Calais, this well-heeled shop has a small wine section with an interesting information booklet on individual wines which describes their characteristics, what food they should be drunk with, when and how to drink them.

Luc Gille's Bar à Vins
52 place des Armes
62100 Calais
Tel: (03) 21 96 98 31
You can drop in here for an espresso, a glass of wine or indeed a case of wine.

Where to stay in town

Meurice
5 rue E. Roche
62100 Calais
Tel: (03) 21 34 57 03
Double room 375–475F
Parking charge

A Calais institution, the Meurice is still well regarded locally, although in terms of facilities it has been overtaken by the newer hotels. Off the main shopping area, the hotel is quiet.

The public areas have a style of their own, plush and old-fashioned in the nicest sense of the word, with a cosy bar and pleasant, intimate restaurant. The older rooms have more character than the modern ones. If you are a single, budget traveller who can bear not having a shower at all (be warned, not even a communal one, a fact not always clearly spelled out) you might appreciate paying only 95F for the tiny room I had to take one evening. Check out its décor and size first.

The buffet breakfast looks quite normal, but help yourself to fruit juice or yoghurt and a charge will appear on your bill.

George V

36 rue Royale, 62100 Calais
Tel: (03) 21 97 68 00
Double 300–370F

A grand name, but this is not Paris. The Calais Georges V is a mid-range hotel in the centre of town. Its biggest asset is its secure and pleasant car park, easy to park in (at no charge) and locked overnight: there are far fewer spaces than there are rooms, but that is no problem because many of the rooms are taken by coach package holidaymakers. The George V has a formal restaurant and a brasserie, the **Petit Georges**. The brasserie can be quite lively, with a 68F two course supper menu. Have a café breakfast when the tour groups are in.

Holiday Inn Garden Court Hotel

boulevard des Alliés, 62100 Calais
Tel. (03) 21 34 69 69
Double 640F

The Garden Court does not feature in reports on romantic French hotels, but it does provide the highest standard of room in town, with up-to-date facilities. It is essential to book a room with a harbour view, and preferably one with a balcony. Immaculate, well equipped rooms, with large twin beds. Mini-bar there may be, but a mere Coke will set you back 21F. Pleasant bar area, and a bright and cheerful restaurant. The car park is free, and the location very central.

Lagrillardière

71 boulevard Victor-Hugo
62100 Calais
Tel: (03) 21 96 49 32

Budget travellers might find this one appealing. Simple rooms cost 130F for two, sharing a loo, and the café downstairs has character, although food prices might be above budget (65F for three courses, such as goat's cheese or herring salad to, grilled lamb chops or sautéed pork as main course, and dessert).

Where to stay out of town
La Grande Maison
62179 Escalles (10 miles/16km southwest of Calais)
Tel: (03) 21 85 27 75
Double 250F including breakfast
Follow the coast road from Calais to Boulogne on the D940 and enjoy magnificent views of the sea from rolling hills. In the village of (La Haute) Escalles, you will find reasonably priced accommodation at this friendly farmhouse. Sprawling and pretty, with lots of flowerbeds around the low lying stone building, the rooms upstairs are large and comfortable. No need to go out to a restaurant for dinner if you would like to stay in, especially after a long drive from the UK, dinner is available for 80F (at a communal table).

Maison de la Houve
62179 Audinghen (12.5 miles/20km southwest of Calais)
Tel: (03) 21 32 97 06
Double 170F, single 120F, including breakfast
An old farmhouse with eight rooms, this bed and breakfast offers terrific value. It has a huge amount of character, with Madame Danel's favourite colour pervasive, from the pink shutters and pink roses to a pink 2CV in the garage. There is as much character inside as outside, the ultimate in clutter in the nicest sense of the word with lots of lace and ornaments. Not the place for ex-smokers, who might be tempted by cigarette packets (with a choice of brands, no less) left on one table for guests' use. There are superb views of the Opal Coast from the main living room and several rooms, some of which have four-poster beds. The pleasant courtyard has tables and chairs for sitting out in fine weather. Madame Danel's latest venture is her children's shop in the barn, laid out in separate sections with gifts for Maman, Papa and Grand'mère – all gifts under 100F. No meals available in the evening. Exceptional value, so you will need to book ahead.

Château de Cocove
62890 Recques-sur-Hem
(16 miles/26km southeast of Calais)
Tel: (03) 21 82 68 29
Double 435–490F

The splendid cellar is reason enough to stay here (see Where to buy). Don't be put off by the grim wall to the property or the flags at the entrance proclaiming membership of Great Western Hotels: once you are through the front gates, there is a long crunchy driveway, copses of grand old trees, immense lawns and an elegantly ageing château. Parking is by the stables and the main entrance is across a gravel forecourt.

This is a romantic place. Sit at one of the white steel tables on the terrace with a drink before dinner and look across the lawns to the huge trees (the copper beech is particularly beautiful), listening to the white doves cooing in the dovecote, and watching the sun going down.

The bedrooms are rather ordinary in comparison to the stylishness of the rest of the building. Most spacious room is number 14 (690F) with two large windows looking onto the front lawns. Some of the rooms face the rear, and if you want a real double bed, as opposed to twin beds with a double sheet, you will need to stress your requirement, as most of the rooms are twin bedded (ask for *un grand lit*).

The dining room in the west wing is simple and understated with stone floors and walls, a few columns and old timber beams and a plain ceiling, all of which create a perfect room with the most peaceful of views across the front lawn (see Where to eat). The bar, too, is all stone, but intimate with only half a dozen tables and a wood burning stove.

On warmer mornings, have breakfast out on the terrace, otherwise it is served in the dining room and bar.

How to get there: To avoid the motorway (A26) take the N43 (direction St Omer) from Calais. At Ardres, follow the signs to Recques-sur-Hem. Alternatively, take the A16, and come off at junction 2.

Copthorne

62231 Coquelles (3.7 miles/6km southwest of Calais)
Tel: (03) 21 46 60 60
Double 630–730F, breakfast 60F per person

A newly built international-style business hotel, exceptionally convenient for the Channel Tunnel terminal; sited on a hill overlooking Cité Europe (and the motorway), the Copthorne is popular with groups and for seminars. It is well run with friendly and helpful staff.

Rooms are large, immaculately clean, and beds very comfortable (just love the walnut burr on the headboards). Whilst these are certainly the best rooms in the Calais area (and so they should be at 750F double with breakfast), seasoned business travellers will miss the little things that are the norm even in mid-range business hotels: no assistance with luggage on arrival, no complimentary newspaper to wake up to, no minibar in the 'classic' (that is, standard/630F) rooms, no central heating above a certain general hotel temperature when desired, and no mini-gym. Rooms 139 and all odd numbers to 159, similarly on the second floor, are best for least motorway noise and Eurotunnel announcements. No courtesy shuttle bus into town, so not really for those without a car.

Moulin d'Audenfort

62890 Tournehem-sur-le-Hem
(about 19 miles/30km southeast of Calais)
Tel: (03) 21 36 52 00
Double 550F including breakfast

This converted watermill obviously has its fans, and it is not difficult to see why. It has an idyllic rural location by the River Hem, very peaceful and romantic. The warm, welcoming, house-party atmosphere is generated by the owner, former airline pilot Hugh Hutton and his English speaking staff. Help yourself to cold drinks, beer and wine at no charge; indeed you can use the phone within reason as well. Whilst many of the rooms have lovely views over the river, I found them rather basic for the cost. It is a fun, sociable place, but even with the cost of wine and beer taken into account (not that much in France), it is difficult to see why it should be so much more expensive than other bed and breakfasts, such as the Manoir des Tourpes (in Caen), which offers the highest quality for 280F double, or La Maison de la Houve (see below) which offers double rooms at 170F with breakfast. Dinner is available at 150F if you do not feel like driving out at night. Good maps and suggestions about where to drive to for an evening meal are offered to guests.

Where to eat in Calais

Au Côte d'Argent
1 digue Gaston Berthe
62100 Calais
Tel: (03) 21 34 68 07
Menus from 95F
Closed Sunday evening and Monday; one week early March, and one week at the end of September–early October
Almost on the beach (just a car park in between) with views of the Channel through large windows. Charming welcome, and a very relaxing place. The cooking is skilled and very precise, with good quality ingredients and dishes full of flavour. Deliciously fresh seafood and fish dishes. Desserts were a shade old fashioned, which will no doubt delight many.

Le Channel
3 boulevard Résistance
62100 Calais
Tel: (03) 21 34 42 30
Closed Sunday evening (except holidays) and Tuesday; two weeks at the end of July, beginning August
Menus from 95F
A Calais institution, only a few yards from the main square and overlooking the port. The staff at Le Channel treat every guest as though they hope to see you again soon, and as a result they
52

do – this is a courteous and professional team.

Although there is an 85F menu (except on Sundays and public holidays), the 135F menu is much more interesting. Start with *langoustines mayonnaises*, a dozen snails, or a quail mousse *glacée a la grande champagne* served with warm *brioche*. For main course, there is always a choice of fish, perhaps *escalopes* of monkfish in a curry sauce or a *pavé* of salmon with a red pepper sauce. I passed over the *confit* of duck with sautéed apples for grilled lamb cutlets in a *girolle* mushroom and garlic sauce, with tiny roast potatoes. The cheese selection is from the famous Monsieur Olivier.

The wine list is a good read, with grand wines such as a Château Petrus 85 at 3,800F or a Château d'Yquem 79 at 2,400F. Of course there are also many less expensive wines, with a decent selection of half-bottles. *Négociants* include Kressmann and Louis Jadot. Full marks to Le Channel for charging reasonably for champagne, with Jacquart, for example, at 190F.

Straightforward food, even if not quite 90s, at average prices, and with a very pleasant staff. Very brightly lit on the evening I ate here.

Aquar'aille
255 rue Jean Moulin
62100 Calais
Tel: (03) 21 34 00 00
Menus from 98F
Closed Sunday evening
On the top floor of a beachside residential apartment building, the Aquar'aille has the most splendid Channel views in Calais. The international style décor, complete with reflective ceiling, is not what you come here for. Come for the unsurpassed views, and simply good cooking. The 98F menu offers six oysters or a *terrine de canard* to start, a *filet de cabillaud au coulis de crevettes* or a *jambonette de canard* as a main course, and some brie or a warm apple and almond tart to finish.

Where to eat out of town

Château de Cocove
62890 Recques-sur-Hem
Tel: (03) 21 82 68 29
Menus from 120F

For a relaxing lunch in the country drive 16 miles (26km) south of Calais to Château de Cocove (see Where to stay for directions). Arrive early for a drink on the terrace and a stroll through the grounds, and leave time for a browse through the cellar. The restaurant is elegant and understated with stone floors and walls. Sit comfortably on bamboo chairs at tables laid with crisp white linen and a small vase of fresh flowers, looking out onto the extensive lawns. The 120F menu offered slices of salmon *cuites à l'assiette* or terrine of young rabbit to start. For the main course poached cod on a white onion *compote*, or supreme of chicken. To follow, cheese or dessert such as luscious profiteroles or caramel mousse.

Try a bottle of Médoc 88 from Château Laborde at 98F (not to be confused with Château Labarde, the second wine from Château Dauzac, whose Margaux 92 is available in the restaurant for 278F, and the 89 for 127F from the cellar). The mark-up on cellar prices is high: a Crémant de Loire is 39F in the cellar, 140F in the restaurant, and a St-Julien 92 Léoville Barton 125F in the cellar, 318F in the restaurant.

Cherbourg

Cherbourg is a busy commercial and naval port which was almost completely destroyed in the last war. Consequently a great deal of the centre is new, but nevertheless it has character and is pretty in parts. Market days are Tuesday, Thursday and Saturday at place Général de Gaulle. From the Fort de Roule there is a wide view of the town and the port, and a museum about the last war and the liberation of Cherbourg.

How to get there

From Southampton (Stena, 5 hours), Portsmouth (P&O, day crossings 5 hours, night crossings 9 hours) and Poole (Brittany Ferries, day crossings 4–5 hours, night crossings 6 hours). From Ireland Irish Ferries have sailings from Cork and Rosslare (around 18 hours).

Where to buy wine

La Maison du Vin

71 avenue Carnot, 50100 Cherbourg

Tel: (02) 33 43 39 79, open every day 10–7

Easy to find with plenty of parking and friendly staff, this store is owned by Richard Harvey Wines of Wareham (tel: 01929 480 352) and is managed by Rebecca Sutherland (and if she is not there, by Andrew Gordon). The warehouse is simply a concrete floor, white walls and an exposed asbestos roof. Avoid the

55

pre-ferry rush that occurs an hour before departures if you want to taste wines in comfort and be able to discuss them at leisure with the manager or other staff.

Take full advantage of the tastings offered, but check how long open bottles have been uncorked. In the under 30F bracket, we enjoyed the Bordeaux Supérieur 93 from Château Bauduc, made by David Thomas in Créon: fruity, fragrant and very drinkable. His Bordeaux Clairet 94 and Bordeaux blanc sec 94 are also pleasant drinking. A Côtes de Bergerac 93 (a red wine) from Château Richard (owned by Richard Doughty) is very good value, slightly spicy with a hint of vanilla and well made. Taste the Bordeaux blanc sec 94 from Château Sercillan to see if you like it. Recommended are the Saumur rouge 93 and the blanc 94 from Château Beauregard. A (red) Minervois 93 from Château du Donjon (M.L. Panis-Mialhe at Bagnoles) was a pleasure to drink and gives the lie to the old story that Minervois is a not-very-well-made, cheap wine. Good value too are the Australians: Penfold's Rawson's Retreat Bin 35 Cabernet-Shiraz 93 (28F) and the Chardonnay 94 from Penfold's Koonunga Hill, with a peachy vanilla aroma, but fresh and zesty in drinking, at 32F (about £5 in the UK).

A Muscadet sur lie 94 from Domaine du Vieux Chai (Bideau-Giraud in La Haye-Fouassière) was delicious, and a fine example of a well made Muscadet: fresh, bright and fragrant. More expensive, but still good value, is the Pouilly-Fumé 93 from Domaine Masson-Blondelet (49F).

Disappointments included Peter Hawkins' Vin de Pays des Côtes de Gascogne 94 at Domaine de Papolle, in Mauléon d'Armagnac, and both the red and white Vin de Pays d'Oc 93/94 from Domaine de la Ferrandière.

The burgundies are not cheap, but there are some interesting wines. From the Côte de Beaune, a red Saint-Aubin 92 premier cru Les Frionnes from Henri Prudhon is particularly fine, which is why you are paying 69F for it. From the Côte de Nuits comes a Gevrey-Chambertin 92 from Domaine Thierry Mortet (89F). Wait, however, for his 93 Clos Prieur.

Cherbourg

What to see
Musée Thomas Henry
quai Alexandre II, 50100 Cherbourg
9–12am and 2–6pm daily except Monday (from 10am on Sunday)
There is a good collection here of work by Jean-François Millet, who was born in the nearby village of Gruchy and studied in Cherbourg, as well as work by other artists inspired by this area.

Château de Tourlaville
(3.5 miles/6km east of Cherbourg)
10–12am and 2–5pm daily (to 6pm from March to 31 October)
A turreted Renaissance château in a beautiful park laid out with formal gardens, lakes and waterfalls, Tourlaville is infamous for an incestuous love affair between Marguerite and Julien de Ravalet which led to their execution in Paris.

Frédéric Duseigneur made so little of his Lirac Blanc 93, that it's a surprise to find it here at all. This is a wine to be drunk young, and worth trying at 35F. Virtually all of the wine made for Châteauneuf-du-Pape is red, only the smallest quantity is white, and here is one from Château Simian (75F). Even more expensive is a Condrieu 92 from Guigal (149F), known for his commitment to quality.

The selection of wines from Alsace is all from one producer, Rieflé, a family who have a deserved reputation for making fine wines. 93 and 94 were not outstanding vintages in Alsace, but the 95 will be worth looking out for. Prices from 29F for the Sylvaner 93 to 39F for the Riesling 93, and their more expensive Gewürztraminer is always seductive.

A Saussignac from Château Richard (see above) is a sweet white wine from an area little known in the UK except to those with friends in the Dordogne, but which produces some fabulous *moelleux* wines. If you are ever in the Dordogne, try to buy a Saussignac from an up and coming winemaker in this area, Patricia Atkinson, an Englishwoman whose Saussignac 93 Clos d'Yvigne has tremendous promise.

The Wine and Beer Company

Continent supermarket mall
quai de l'Entrepôt, 51000 Cherbourg
Tel: (02) 33 22 23 22
Open Monday to Saturday 8.30am–8.30pm

The Wine and Beer Company have done a sufficiently decent shop-fitting job here to make your shopping pleasant in an otherwise unattractive shopping mall with a scruffy car park. For full details of the wines available at this store, see page 78.

Continent

quai de l'Entrepôt
51000 Cherbourg

This is the best supermarket in town for champagne, despite the grotty car park. Good value Castellane, Mercier, Germain, Lanson Black Label and Jacquart (83F), easily my favourite in this group, a light, quality champagne with a subtle nose. This one costs around £15 in the UK if you can find it. Look out for the brilliant 90 vintage, of which a few bottles may come up for sale here. Cheapest champagne is Charles Vincent at 55F, but frankly it is not as good value as the others mentioned.

InterCaves Geisler

27 avenue Aristide Briand, 50100 Cherbourg
Tel: (02) 33 44 48 03

Closed Sunday afternoon and Monday

Parking is on the street, but not too difficult. There is a range of 10 litre bag-in-the-box *appellation contrôlée* wines by La Fontaine, from 16F per litre for white Bergerac or 18F for red Bergerac to 21F per litre for AOC Bordeaux 94 and 27F per litre for Graves 93 AOC. Definitely taste before buying.

My favourite wine here is the Côteaux du Languedoc 93 from Château de Pech-Redon, perhaps slightly expensive at 36F for this *appellation*, but smooth and satisfying. A Côtes du Marmandais 90 Le Président, made by one of the major producers of this *appellation*, Cave (co-op) de Cocumont (30F), was another smooth well balanced wine, with a slightly peppery nose and a lovely colour. Less successful was a Bergerac 94 from Château le Grand Buisson (25F), which, although quite well balanced, smooth and dry, in the end promised more than it delivered.

La Cave du Roy
47 rue Tour-Carré
50100 Cherbourg
Tel: (02) 33 53 05 21

Closed from noon on Sunday until Tuesday morning

This shop in the old town has some interesting wines. The bordeaux are from reliable vintages, and there is a good selection of bourgognes from reputable producers. But the problem is knowing whether there is any saving on the UK price, or whether you can obtain a particular burgundy at home. Take, for example, a Fixin 92, a really superb intense wine by Domaine Pierre Gelin (76F), which is the same price as in the UK. But is it going to be possible to walk into a wine shop and buy it in the UK?

What did catch my eye were the champagnes. The Roederer 90 Blanc de Blancs (224F) is a wonderful wine, delicate, sophisticated and very difficult to find. From the same brilliant 1990 vintage, try a magnum of Ruinart (360F); and finally there is the beautiful Dom Ruinart 88 Blanc de Blancs at 189F.

Where to stay
Mercure
Gare Maritime
Cherbourg 50100
Tel: (02) 33 44 01 11
Double 590F including breakfast

The hotel may be an unattractive concrete box with small windows, narrow corridors and low ceilings, but it is the most comfortable hotel in Cherbourg. There is easy parking outside, self-service luggage trollies, and smiling, helpful staff at reception bode well.

Forget the smaller (less expensive) rooms that look into a warehouse, and take a larger room with a terrific view over the marina. Comfortable beds and good linen, a phone that stretches to the far side of the bed, decent lighting and CNN when you get bored with the twinkling late night view of the harbour. The minibar is useful for chilling your new-found wines, and the bathroom is large, with all mod cons.

Breakfast is a reasonably generous buffet, with cold meats and cheeses and squeeze-your-own juice.

Chantereyne
port de Plaisance
50100 Cherbourg
Tel: (02) 33 93 02 20
Double 320–360F (harbour view)

The décor is dull 70s, with orange carpeted walls in the corridors, brown formica-clad fitted furniture in the bedrooms, in neutral browns and beiges, which are impersonal but adequately comfortable.

The two-storey hotel looks across a large car park to the marina, and there is quite a lot of through traffic. There is no restaurant in the hotel, but it is just a short stroll to the Yacht Club dining room (see below). Could do with some fresh colours, but nonetheless comfortable, friendly and pleasant.

Where to eat
Le Faitout
25 rue Tour-Carré, 50100 Cherbourg
Tel: (02) 33 04 25 04
Menus from 110F

There is charm and character in this small, locally renowned bistro, pretty with deep maroon wood windows and lace curtains. Timber lined, with dim lighting and darkish colours, it is a most restful and relaxing haven, at least at one of the ten tables upstairs. Main courses are simple tasty grills, lamb chops, steaks and salmon, or *le pot au feu Faitout*. For those with seafood inclinations, starters include oysters, fish soup, *rillettes de saumon*, *salade de calamars*, warmed oysters *à la fondue de poireaux* or snails. Desserts are a sorbet and ice-cream lover's delight, with cassis, passion fruit and peach sorbets or armagnac, rum and pistachio ice-cream. The *formule Faitout* consists of four courses: starter of the day (for example, fresh salmon marinated in anis or *salade de gésiers confits*). the *plat du jour* (grilled fillets of *rouget*), cheese and dessert. Simple good value in comfortable surroundings.

La Moulerie
73 rue au Blé, 50100 Cherbourg
Tel: (02) 33 01 11 90
Menus from 100F

When this was recommended to me by a local, I was warned that it was absolutely impossible to get into on a Friday night without a reservation. This was almost true, but the friendly management will do their utmost to fit you in. And you can understand why this bright, cheerful restaurant, with its seagull lampshades and wipe-down blue and white checked tablecloths, is so popular. Huge steaming bowls of mussels are served with vast plates of chips (and excellent they are too), from *moules marinières normandes* with *crème fraîche*, flambéed with Calvados, to the house special, cooked in white wine, onion, bacon, celery and cream. Specialities include mussels with sauerkraut, and scallops. The children's menu (42F) takes care of it all with a small portion of mussels or hamburger, chips, dessert and a drink. Best with a beer (Schoenberg pression) or *cidre bouché Normandie brut* (25F per bottle).

Le 32

32 rue Maréchal Foch, 50100 Cherbourg
Tel: (02) 33 94 30 39
Menu express 49F

What this very central restaurant lacks in atmosphere, despite a tiled floor and beamed ceiling, it certainly makes up for in sheer good value. The *menu express* (and it really is) offers two courses and a glass of wine (or beer or water). The smoked salmon quiche was light, fluffy and delicious, with salad or country terrine as alternatives. Main course choices included salmon in sorrel sauce, carpaccio of beef or a grilled steak. Unbeatable value.

You will probably not be too interested in the brief wine list when you order the 95F menu, which includes a *kir* to start, and then unlimited house wine in carafes. Start with a scallop terrine or warm goat's cheese salad, follow with grilled duck breast in green pepper sauce, a sirloin or rump steak, or monkfish in a basil sauce. Try the Normandy apple pancakes for dessert; more apples in the form of a *tarte Tatin* or a *crème brûlée*.

The Yacht Club

Port Chantereyne, 50100 Cherbourg
Tel: (02) 33 53 02 83
Closed on Sunday
Menus from 70F

There's always a bit of a buzz in and around the Yacht Club, as Cherbourg is an international yachting port with a large marina. Distinctive sailing atmosphere as you pass the noticeboards with charts, detailed weather forecasts and much used shower rooms, up to the first floor bar and restaurant. There is usually a strong contingent of English-speaking yachtsmen around the bar. No Michelin stars here, just well-prepared food, friendly service and fair prices. The 70F menu offers a fish soup, *moules marinières* or *salade aux lardons* to start, then a *confit* of duck, salmon in sorrel sauce, a steak or grilled fish as the main course, followed by dessert, say a *crème brûlée*. No stars at all for the wine list; have a beer or a bottle of cider.

Dieppe

Dieppe is one of prettiest of the Channel ports having escaped the devastating bombing that destroyed many of the others. It is also one of France's oldest resorts and is famously known as the *plage de Paris* (beach of Paris). Market day is Saturday and stalls are found all along the Grande-Rue behind the Eglise St-Jacques.

How to get there
Car ferries run by Stena take 4 hours from Newhaven.

Where to buy wine
Poivre et Sel
101 Grande-Rue
76200 Dieppe
Tel: (02) 35 82 08 76
Closed Monday morning
An attractive speciality food and wine shop, where you can buy a bottle or two of wine with some gourmet foods. Fine wines include a Lalande de Pomerol 89 from Château des Annereaux (72F), a Margaux 89 from Château Lascombes (151F) and the superb Château Batailley Pauillac 92 at 104F. Or perhaps a chilled bottle of champagne to drink on the beach?

63

Dieppe

What to see
Château de Dieppe
rue de Chastes, 76200 Dieppe
10–12am and 2–5pm daily; closed on Tuesday from 30
September–31 May
High up on the cliffs at the western end of town, the 15th-
century castle now houses a wide-ranging collection
which covers the history of the town from its days as a
Roman seawater spa, through its heyday as the chief port
of Renaissance France, to its importance as an ivory-carv-
ing centre and a bathing resort. There are also a number of
paintings by Pissarro, Dufy, Monet and Braque who
worked around Dieppe.

Parc des Moustiers
Varengeville-sur-Mer
10–12am and 2–6pm daily
The house here was designed by Sir Edwin Lutyens in
1898 and pride of place is given to a Burne-Jones tapestry.
The Parc is famous for its rhododendrons and azaleas in
May and June, for roses and hydrangeas in July and Au-
gust, and for the autumn foliage of its exotic trees from
China, Japan and the Americas.

Côte d'Albâtre (Alabaster Coast)
From Dieppe west to Etretat (65 miles/104km)
The cliffs along here are actually chalk and very like their
opposite numbers on the English south coast, and the re-
sort towns of Varengeville-sur-Mer, St-Valery-en-Caux,
Fécamp and Etretat, have grown out of fishing villages.

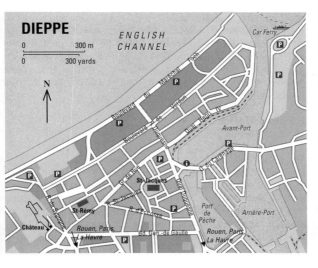

LC Vins
1 Grande-Rue
76200 Dieppe
Tel: (02) 35 84 32 41
Closed Sunday afternoon
A small, central shop selling a good Sancerre 94 Clos Paradis
from Fouassier et Fils, and a Coteaux du Layon 92 from
Château des Rochettes in Concourson-sur-Layon.

M Pommier
22 place Nationale
76200 Dieppe
Tel: 35 84 14 62
Closed Sunday afternoon
An upmarket coffee, tea, wine and spirits emporium selling
several fine wines including champagne from Joseph Perrier

'as supplied to their late majesties Queen Victoria and King Edward VII' (at 110F), a Savennières Roche-aux-Moines 92 Clos de la Bergerie from Nicolas Joly's famed Château de la Roche-aux-Moines (110F), a Pouilly-Fumé 93 Tinelum Vieilles Vignes from Caves de Pouilly-sur-Loire (74F), a Bourgogne Aligoté 92 from Louis Jadot (53F) and a Mercurey 90 from Louis Latour (80F).

L'Epicier Olivier
18 rue St-Jacques
76200 Dieppe
Tel: (02) 35 84 22 55
Closed Sunday afternoon and Monday
This gourmet deli has a huge selection of cheeses and other delights – *pâtés*, coffees and wines. Although there is a Nicolas sign in the window, only part of their range is stocked. Browse through the wines, and look out for the special offers. On my visit Ruinart was on offer at 119F and Roederer at 118F.

Prisunic
5 arcades de la Bourse
76200 Dieppe
Tel: (02) 35 82 51 60
Closed Sunday
In the basement of this central department store, the wine section is convenient if you want to pick up a bottle or two. Best buy in the inexpensive wines was a Bordeaux 93 from Château La Vieille Eglise (C Hollier, *négociant-éleveur* at St-André-de-Cubzac, Gironde), a soft wine (21F or in half-bottles at 14F).

Mammouth
off the N27 (in the direction of Le Havre and Rouen)
Closed Sunday
A bright, sparkling new complex, so it's very pleasant to shop here. The wines stocked here are the same as at other major Mammouth stores. For more detail see page 42.

Le Sommelier
27 rue des Maillots, 76200 Dieppe
Tel: (02) 35 06 05 20
Closed Sunday afternoon and Monday
There are no cut-price wines here (a Jacob's Creek Chardonnay 93 is 50F), but there are certainly some interesting ones: a champagne from Bouche Père et Fils of Pierry, who make some very respectable cuvées, is only 79F, and there are Alsace wines from Wantz, an old house in Barr.

Where to stay in town

Hôtel de l'Europe
63 boulevard de Verdun, 76200 Dieppe
Tel: (02) 32 90 19 19
Double 340F
Many of Dieppe's hotels are on the beachfront, and most are way past their due date for refurbishment. A welcome exception is the Hôtel de l'Europe, which has fresh, bright rooms which are large and comfortable, and all with splendid views of the ocean. Bathrooms are new and sparkling. This is more like a motel than hotel. The 24-hour reception desk is the only sign of life – even a cup of tea or coffee is unobtainable, though cold soft drinks are available from a machine. Breakfast is served in a canteen style room. Trolleys are available for your luggage, with parking on the street just outside.

Au Grand Duquesne
15 rue Saint Jacques
76200 Dieppe
Tel: (02) 35 84 21 51
Double 250F
This restaurant with rooms is a lively, friendly and welcoming place to stay. Very pleasant, fairly priced rooms are particularly good value; a room with shared shower is only 160F. Central, so parking *payant* on the street during the day.

Where to stay out of town
Auberge Clos Normand
22 rue Henri IV
76370 Martin-Eglise (4 miles/7km southeast of Dieppe)
Tel: (02) 35 04 40 34
Closed Monday, Tuesday; mid-November to mid-December
and early April
Double 370–460F

This peaceful brick *auberge* is attached to the restaurant (see
Where to eat), overlooking a gurgling stream and a garden with
mature trees. Rooms vary, so check them first. The restaurant is
very good, so there is no need to look for anywhere else to eat.
How to get there: On the D1 out of Dieppe (direction Neufchâtel-en-Bray and Arques), passing Leclerc supermarket on your
right, then into Martin-Eglise.

Where to eat in town

Le Saint Jacques
12 rue de l'Oranger
76200 Dieppe
Tel: (02) 35 84 52 04
Closed Wednesday and Thursday lunchtime
Menus from 65F

Just opposite the church, sit by the window here and enjoy the
pretty view. Lunchtime parking is easy; there is no parking
charge between 12.30 and 1.30pm, so if you park at say 12.15,
your ticket will add an hour to your time limit, a very civilized
idea. The 65F menu offered a densely flavoured *terrine maison
aux cèpes* on a mixed salad of lamb's lettuce and finely shred-
ded cabbage to start, an escalope of salmon or *filet de cabillaud*
for the main course, and a *tarte normande* that took forever to
arrive, but was worth the wait: a featherweight apple tart, dense
apple flavour with the lightest of pastry and cream. Very pleasant staff and owners, excellent value.

Au Grand Duquesne

15 rue Saint Jacques
76200 Dieppe
Tel: (02) 35 84 21 51
Menus from 72F. Rooms available from 160F.

Packed at lunchtime with local business people, the restaurant is lively but has a mellow atmosphere. Exceptional choice of dishes available on the 72F menu. Start with a seafood *feuilleté* (mussels and shrimps), mussels, snails or a smoked salmon pancake; for main course there was salt cod with garlic, skate with capers, trout, seafood pasta or salmon with sauerkraut or grilled lamb chops. A huge choice of desserts included a *crêpe dieppois*, which consisted of a densely flavoured *crêpe* with pear compote, a whole pear on top, on a strawberry *coulis*. Expensive drinks, though, with a glass of champagne at 45F and water at 25F.

Café des Tourelles

rue Comm Fayole, 76200 Dieppe
Closed Sunday evening and Monday
Menus from 59F

For authentic local atmosphere and an honest 59F menu: simple *gésiers*, *charcuterie* or seafood salad to start, for main course a steak with roquefort sauce, *filet de cabillaud* with a *sauce crevettes*, or *boudin blanc* (if you haven't eaten this yet, you must try it), and cheese or dessert. Or you could splash out on the 69F menu which includes *moules*, *gigot d'agneau* and *pintade forestière*.

La Musardière

61 quai Henri IV, 76200 Dieppe
Tel: (02) 35 82 94 14
Closed Monday
Menus from 89F

Stroll along the waterfront to get to this small restaurant – you can't miss the pink and white entrance. Good value and extensive choice on the 89F menu. To start, fish soup, snails, oysters, mussels or a seafood plate, followed by *marmite de poisson au curry*, *escalope de saumon à l'oseille* or *entrecôte*, a good choice of cheeses, and a *crêpe* with a red berry *coulis* (or other dessert).

All this was served quickly by cheerful, informal but attentive staff. Pink tablecloths, carpet on the wall, lots of artificial flowers and swirly carpet on the floor. Half a bottle of water costs 20F, and the wine is also expensive.

Le Parisien
7 quai Henri IV, 76200 Dieppe
Tel: (02) 35 84 18 08
Menus from 45F
Day trippers' heaven it may be, with English menus on boards outside and right on the quay, but the bright and cheerful Parisien serves food fast. But this is fast food with a difference: *moules marinières* or *crudités* to start, fish and chips, omelette or mussels with chips as main course, and cheese or dessert. Fair prices on the drinks: 10F for a beer, 7F for a coffee. Good budget value.

Where to eat out of town

Auberge Clos Normand
22 rue Henri IV
76370 Martin-Eglise (4 miles/7km southeast of Dieppe)
Tel: (02) 35 04 40 34
Closed Monday, Tuesday; mid-November to mid-December and early April
Menus from 160F
Arrive early for an *apéritif* in the shady gardens by the stream, and a warm and friendly welcome. This is a good-looking half-timbered building, and the restaurant is steeped in atmosphere, with quarry-tiled floors, a dark, heavily beamed ceiling and copper and brass pots hanging on the tapestry fabric-covered

walls. The low lit dining room is intimate and homely, the tables laid with white linen and fresh flowers. Chef and owner Régis Hauchecorne can be seen working in his open blue and white tiled kitchen, cooking with precision and a deft touch. Servings are vast, so order accordingly; excellent fish dishes, and a sublime *soufflé Grand Marnier*, fit for two. On no account miss the coffee ritual.

How to get there: On the D1 out of Dieppe (direction Neufchâtel-en-Bray and Arques), pass Leclerc supermarket on your right, then turn into Martin-Eglise.

Dunkerque

Dunkerque cannot compare to Calais, just down the road, in its range or quality of wine outlets, and anyone serious about their wine shopping would have to choose Calais as their destination. However, you may be in Dunkerque for other reasons, in which case there are a couple of reasonable stores.

How to get there

Sally Line sail to Dunkerque from Ramsgate.

Where to buy wine

Chais de la Transat

25 rue du Gouvernement

Quartier de la Citadelle, 59140 Dunkerque

Tel: (03) 28 63 78 25

Closed Sunday and Monday

This is one of the nicest parts of Dunkerque, away from the traffic and urban congestion, an interesting quarter in which to take a stroll. This wine warehouse is a branch of the original cellars in Le Havre and full details are given on page 77.

Dunkerque

What to see

Musée Portuaire
9 quai de la Citadelle
59140 Dunkerque
10–12am and 2–5pm daily; closed on Tuesday from 30
September–31 May
Tel: 28 63 33 39
This museum, in an old tobacco warehouse, describes how
the harbour has been an important element in the technical,
social and economic development of the town over the
centuries.

Musée d'Art Contemporain

avenue des Bains
59140 Dunkerque
10–12am and 2–5pm daily; closed on Tuesday from 30
September–31 May
Tel: 28 59 21 65
Designed by architect Jean Willerval, this museum and
sculpture garden cover the most important art movements
since 1950 and include works by César, Manessier, Arman,
Schlosser and Sam Francis.

Cora
59210 Coudekerque-Branche (2.5 miles/4km south)
Exit 31 from A16 in the direction of Belge
Open Monday to Saturday 9am–9pm
Not as easy to locate as other out-of-town Coras, and not quite
as new. The wine department is furthest from the entrance into
the supermarket. The stock, however, is the same as at other
branches and full details are given on page 31.

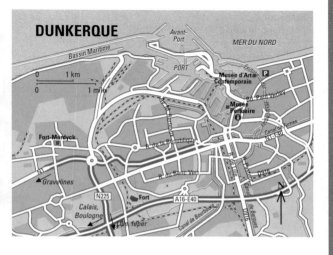

Where to stay

Mercure
2 bordure du Lac d'Armbouts-Cappel
59380 Bergues (5.5 miles/9km south of Dunkerque)
Tel: (03) 28 60 70 60
Double 450F

Slightly out of town, this Mercure is by far the best quality hotel in the area. Although the building looks rather box-like, the hotel is elegant and comfortable. Public rooms look out onto a small peaceful lake.

The hotel is sometimes heavily booked for days on end, even out of season, so make a reservation in advance. Parking is easy and the staff are charming.

How to get there: Exit Bergues from the southbound N225.

Campanile
au bordure du Lac d'Armbouts-Cappel
59380 Bergues (5.5 miles/9km south of Dunkerque)
Tel: (03) 28 64 64 70
Double 280F
A reliable, mid-range hotel chain that provides good value.
How to get there: Exit Bergues from the southbound N225.

L'Hirondelle
46–48 avenue Faidherbe
Malo-les-Bains, 59240 Dunkerque
Tel: (03) 28 63 17 65
Double 306F
One block away from the beach, this hotel is situated in a pleasant part of town. Bland building, nondescript breakfast room, but recently refurbished rooms are quite comfortable with good beds and bathrooms. Check the location of your room to avoid being next to the lift or having no view at the rear.

Welcome Hotel
37 rue Raymond-Poincaré, 59240 Dunkerque
Tel: (03) 28 59 20 70
Double 380F
In the heart of the old town, with parking on the street, this is a lively place with a bar and brasserie. Bathrooms are in good condition, and rooms adequate.

Where to eat in town

Au Bon Coin
49 avenue Kléber
Malo-les-Bains, 59240 Dunkerque
Tel: (03) 28 69 12 63
Closed Christmas to early January
Despite the garish orange, green and blue sign outside, and painting inside, this is a comfortable old-fashioned place with

wooden chairs and white linen tablecloths. A super value 75F menu offers *terrine de foie*, half a dozen snails or *soupe de poissons* to start, simply prepared *entrecôte* steak or *truite meunière* as a main course, and *tarte maison* or *crème caramel* for dessert. Half a bottle of Côtes du Rhone at 25F sums up their philosophy: reasonable prices and straightforward cooking.

Where to eat out of town
Au Cornet d'Or
26 rue Espagnole
59380 Bergues (5.5 miles/9km south of Dunkerque)
Tel: (03) 28 68 66 27
Closed Sunday evening and Monday
An excellent 150F menu is on offer here during the week.

La Meunerie
174 rue des Pierres
59229 Téteghem (3.7 miles/6km southeast of Dunkerque)
Tel: (03) 28 26 14 30
Closed Sunday evening and Monday
Rather expensive, with a 250F menu, but good food.

Le Havre

Bombed out in the last world war, not much remains of the romantic port city where Jean-Paul Sartre spent several years, during which time he wrote his famous existentialist novel, *La Nausée*. In an example of large scale post-war town-planning, the city was rebuilt according to the designs of an otherwise talented architect, Auguste Perret, leaving a legacy of soulless concrete. Architects and town planners will find Le Havre of interest, especially Oscar Niemeyer's cultural centre, and art lovers will enjoy the delights of the Musée des Beaux-Arts André Malraux, but otherwise travellers tend to pass through

Le Havre

What to see
Musée des Beaux-Arts André Malraux
on the waterfront
Open 10–12am and 2–6pm daily except Tuesdays
Tel: (02) 35 42 33 97
This magnificent steel and glass construction houses works by Raoul Dufy who was born in Le Havre in 1877, Honfleur-born Eugène Boudin, and Claude Monet who worked here. There are also paintings by Renoir, Jongkind, Manet and Sisley here.

Château d'Orcher
Gonfreville
Park open 9–5 daily except Thursday; château open 2–5 daily or by appointment
Tel: (02) 35 96 00 21
Dating back in part to the 11th century, the château today is mostly 18th century. The most spectacular element of a visit here is the view from the Terrasse d'Orcher, across the mouth of the river to Honfleur and Le Havre.

the city en route to Rouen. The new Pont de Normandie is such an exquisite piece of engineering and design that it might even be worthwhile landing in Le Havre on your way to Normandy just to experience a drive across this stunning bridge.

How to get there
P&O sail from Portsmouth to Le Havre (daytime, 6 hours; night crossings 7–9 hours). Irish Ferries from Rosslare and Cork (around 18 hours).

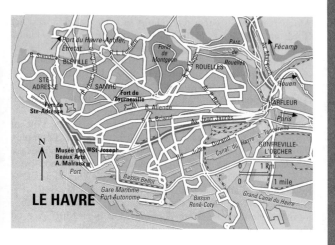

Where to buy wine
Chais de la Transat
avenue Lucien Corbeaux
76600 Le Havre
Tel: (02) 35 53 66 65
Closed Sunday

Le Havre was the home port of the inter-war trans-Atlantic luxury liners of France. During that era, a superb wine cellar was stocked to supply the ships of the French line. After the final sailing of its most famous liner, the France, in 1947, the wine cellars became the basis of today's wine business.

The warehouse premises are clean and brightly lit, with parking under cover. The range of wines is broad, from 12F-a-bottle table wine to a 520F Château Margaux 89, a 1942 Bas-Armagnac St-Gayrand at 802F and a Château d'Yquem 82. The labels on the non-vintage house bordeaux are more romantic and exotic than the wine, but at 20F worth tasting. Monique

Aldebert produces consistent quality at Château Suau, and her Bordeaux rosé 94 is particularly successful (27F). Domaine Sarda-Malet is a well regarded vineyard producing Côtes du Roussillon; the Blanc 93 has lovely aromas, is well made, and should not be missed at only 23F. The château-bottled Bordeaux 94 from Château Bel Air La Gravette is a dry red (with a fair amount of tannin), that would go well with spicy food, for example. Good colour, and no complaints at 24F.

There is only one Sancerre in stock, and it is a gem: Vincent Pinard's Cuvée Flores 94 has a wonderful bouquet – a complex round wine well worth trying, although it is 56F. All the Alsace wines are from Sparr of Sigolsheim, one of the most well known producers in the region. Taste the Gewürztraminer 93 Réserve (42F) and the Tokay-Pinot Gris 93 at 47F. Both *vendanges tardives*, the Riesling Altenbourg 90 and Gewürztraminer Mambourg 90 are delicious, but over 120F. A good place to browse.

The Wine and Beer Company
quai Frissard
76600 Le Havre
Open Monday to Saturday 9am–9.30pm, Sunday 12–5. Closed Christmas to New Year
Although very easy to find and run by friendly people, these premises were pretty rough when they first moved in, and bitterly cold in the winter. The stock is the same as in Cherbourg and Calais. The wines are cleverly presented so that you think most of the stock must be not only quite good quality, but also highly competitive. This seems to be achieved by showing a French franc price and a UK sterling price, where the English price is quite clearly cheaper than the French price: pay in sterling (cash or cheque drawn on your home bank account) *et voilà, le bargain*.

The fact is that not everything here is priced as keenly as it might be, nor is it of consistently high quality. Take for example the South African wines: apart from those from Allesverloren and La Motte (just under £7) and Meerlust (the Merlot 88, just under £9), it is a pretty humdrum, ordinary range, all right for everyday drinking but only if the pricing were much lower.

Whilst there is some relationship between the price of say, Australian wines in Australia and in the shop in France (taking into account additional transport, etc), there appears to be little connection between the prices of South African wines in South Africa and the prices here, which are much higher. In general, you can expect prices in France to be about £1.20 to £1.50 per bottle less than in the UK. Indeed, some French based UK wine merchants will guarantee that difference for you. Check that you are getting a discount approaching this level here.

Of the champagnes, my personal choice would be the half-bottles of Joseph Perrier (£7), a one time royal favourite, and the Pol Roger White Foil Extra Dry, at £13 the best buy in the store (£18 in the UK, although there are a couple of wine merchants charging over £22). There is a good range of basic Australian sparkling wine: Great Western (£3), Killawarra (£3.70), Seaview (£4), Carrington (£4), Angas Brut (£4.50), Seppelt Première Cuvée (£5). And some excellent ones: Yalumba Pinot Noir Chardonnay Cuvée One (£7), a delicious Salinger Brut 90 (£8.80) and an equally fine Green Point Brut 91 (£9). There is a fine selection of Australians, but not at a particularly large discount on UK prices: Penfold's Kalimna Bin 28 Shiraz 91 is a big, intense, rich wine (£6), but it is only 80p more in the UK. Reasonable quality vineyards appear in the Chilean section: Santa Rita (I highly recommend the Santa Rita Reserva Sauvignon Blanc 94, complex and balanced, although at £4 it is only £1 cheaper than in the UK), Cousino Macul, and Los Vascos, which, despite being part owned by Lafite-Rothschild, remains a mid-range producer.

Hidden amidst the bottles of bordeaux with classy names that, I am sure, are not trying to pretend to be châteaux whose names they resemble, are a Haut-Médoc 90 from the reputable Château Ramage La Batisse, a good year for this château, but certainly not ready to drink yet (£8.70, about £9.60 in the UK).

Another wine that will need laying down, at least for a couple of years, is a Côtes de Castillon 92 from Château de Belcier (£5.50), which appears on the wine list, but which I could not find on the shelves when I visited the shop. A 1988 Château Musar features at £7, but check this price against that charged by Majestic, London Wine down at Chelsea Wharf, or indeed at Waitrose.

Where to eat

Le Bistrot des Halles

7 place des Halles Centrales
76600 Le Havre
Tel: (02) 35 22 50 52
Closed Sunday
Menus from 75F

Wine lovers will adore this characterful bistro, with its pale wooden floor, high ceilings and burgundy banquettes lining walls hung with old enamel advertising signs. Tightly packed tables are laid with paper tablecloths on white linen.

A dozen wines are served by the glass, from an inexpensive Beaujolais 94 at 13F to a Savigny les Beaune 90 at 25F, with a Fronsac, Burgundy, Anjou-Villages and Petit Chablis in between. The wine list for bottles is chalked up on a blackboard, and indeed some are for sale to take away in cardboard cartons of six bottles.

The 75F *formule* includes a glass of house Beaujolais and changes daily. I ate very good rare roast beef, and an inspired apple tart. Special of the day was a mussel flan with saffron sauce. The *à la carte* menu certainly tempted with a *carpaccio au basilic*, a beef *tartare* (prepared *à la minute*) and an *entrecôte béarnaise*. In addition, a *cassolette d'escargot au persil plat*, *fondue de tomate* and scallops with an endive fondue were available. If only one had room left for a chocolate and pistachio soufflé or *crêpes suzettes*, both to be ordered at the beginning of the meal.

St-Malo

St-Malo is the most elegant and chic of the Channel ports (unfortunately with prices to match), at least in the part known as the Intra Muros, the old walled city. Whilst many of the buildings are not that old – most of the city was destroyed by bombardment in 1945 – the spirit of the old city, lovingly rebuilt stone by stone, is still there. No yobs or cheap beer here, rather demure *salons de thé* patronized by *la bourgeoisie*, and small trendy bars filled with numbers of *la jeunesse*, not *dorée*, but not yoof either.

For food shopping, wander down the rue de l'Orme and look into Jean Yves Bordier's La Maison du Beurre (since 1927), as well as the *poissonerie* on the opposite side of the street next to Le Clos du Tastevin. Market days are Tuesday and Friday in the old town.

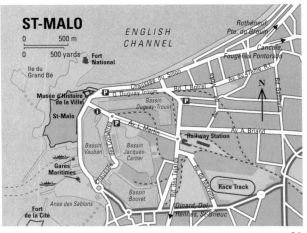

St-Malo

What to see

Musée d'Histoire de la Ville
place Châteaubriand
Open 10–12am and 2–6pm daily, except Tuesdays
In the great keep of St-Malo castle, between Porte St-Thomas and Porte St-Vincent, the museum tells the history of the town through the lives of its great sailors and explorers who travelled and colonized throughout the world.

Ramparts

The 12th-century ramparts have been added to and rebuilt periodically since but are still intact, and the best way to appreciate this historic town is to take a walk around the full extent of the walls. There are views not only of the town and harbour, but of the sea and stretches of the beautiful Emerald coast as well.

How to get there

The nine-hour crossing with Brittany Ferries from Portsmouth is ideal taken overnight. There are no sailings from early January until March, then there is only one crossing per day; from the end of May to the end of September there are two crossings per day. Unfortunately no competition on this route means high fares. It is the most conveniently located port for touring Brittany (bar Roscoff) and for driving down to Nantes and the western Loire Valley. You can also reach St-Malo direct from Cork and Rosslare with Brittany Ferries and with Irish Ferries. It is a long crossing (around 19 hours) but you could look on this as a mini-cruise and enjoy the trip.

Where to buy wine
La Maison du Vin
12 rue Georges Clémenceau
St-Servan, 35400 St-Malo
Tel: (02) 99 82 69 54
Open every day 10–7
This is another branch of the delightful chain written up on
page 55.

Le Tastevin
9 rue Val
35400 St-Malo
Tel: (02) 99 82 46 56
Closed from Sunday lunchtime to Tuesday morning
This is a small, elegant shop with a tiled floor, wooden shelves,
decorated with half-barrels, and rocks and stones from different
wine growing regions, the most unusual from Cahors. The cen-
trepiece is a *pressoir* that belonged to the proprietor's grandfa-
ther. You cannot fail to be entranced by the enthusiasm and old
school French charm of the Gitanes smoking Monsieur
Robineau.

The wines are thoughtfully chosen, and the stock changes
constantly. Of the red wines, the Anjou-Villages 93 from Do-
maines des Rochelles (in Saint-Jean-des-Mauvrets) is one of
the best Anjou-Villages you can buy (43F), with a wonderful
colour, red fruit, slightly tannic and perfectly balanced. Monsieur Lebreton also produces a Coteaux de l'Aubance, a sweet
Loire wine worth tasting. Another Anjou-Villages 93 comes
from Domaine de Haute Perche (39F), from Christian Papin,
whose name is well known in the region. There are several
Coteaux du Layon (a sweet Loire wine) available, but keep an
eye open for value. For example, a Coteaux du Layon 90 from
the excellent Domaine Cady in Saint-Aubin-de-Luigne costs
172F, but, not on sale (yet) in the shop is his 94, which, although not comparable to the 90, is nonetheless very good, and

should be half the cost of the 90. Two other Coteaux du Layon come from reputable winemakers, a 93 from Joël Ménard's Domaine des Sablonettes (75F) and an 89 from Domaine des Baumard (90F), whose Quarts de Chaume 89 is also on sale here (170F).

Forget cheap champagne, and buy as much of the Ruinart 90 as you can afford (185F), a brilliant vintage from a superb house (one of the great originals founded in 1729), and difficult to find. You certainly won't find any of this splendid wine around in a couple of years' time.

Le Moulin à Vins
80 boulevard des Talards
35400 St-Malo
Tel: (02) 99 81 62 80
Open Monday to Saturday 9–12.30am and 3–7.30pm; Sunday 9–12.30
Easy parking

For best value mid-range wines for less than 30F head straight for Le Moulin à Vins, a retail shop beneath the first floor offices of Gaillard, who are primarily wine bottlers and trade merchants. Seek out the manager, Jacques Torcher, who will guide you through his *vins de pays* and inexpensive *appellations controlées* with precise language (in French), accurate descriptions, and an enthusiasm rarely encountered in English retailing. Of all the wine merchants in the ports, Monsieur Torcher has offered the soundest and most consistent advice and suggestions.

Château du Tariquet in Gascogne makes superb Armagnac, the least expensive sold here starting at a mere 265F for one with no particular age. They also produce an intoxicating 46 per cent *eau de vie* Folle Blanche (153F). So it comes as no surprise that a Vin de Pays des Côtes de Gascogne that they have recently started making, even though selling at only 20F, shows the same commitment to quality. What a superb white wine this Domaine du Tariquet is at the price: good fruit, hints of crisp

84

green apples, a little acidity, well balanced. You would do well to buy a case as a private house wine. A Côtes du Rhône 93 Les Cosses from Domaine du Moulin Blanc is another fresh wine, with a slightly grassy nose, easy drinking and good value at 30F.

For a chilled light red wine from the Loire, try the Cheverny 93 from Domaine Maison Père et Fils at Sambin (30F), a very pleasant and soft wine, with nice fruit. Try a Vin de Pays du Jardin de la France 94, a Chardonnay from Domaine du Breuil in Beaulieu-sur-Layon (the same people as Château du Breuil). Do not be misled by its status as a *vin de pays*, this is because the Chardonnay grape is not recognized as an official grape in Anjou; the wine certainly has some character and a lot of finesse (30F).

Other Loire wines include a Sancerre 94 from Henri Bourgeois (56F), and his splendid La Bourgeoise 93 at 80F. At the same price as at the vineyard, you will find a Savennières 93 from Luc Bizard's Château d'Épiré (59F), but to understand the quality he is really capable of achieving, given a good year, try his Savennières demi-sec 90, now 75F for a half-bottle. I bought this wine several years ago, when it was first released, at less than half this price, which shows what can happen when a wine is eventually recognized as being very fine. If you would like a wine investment tip connected with this château, buy the 95 (Savennières demi-sec) as soon as it is released. You read it here first.

Gaillac is an *appellation* from the southwest of France, not yet well known, but whose quality is improving by leaps and bounds. Try the Gaillac 94 from Domaine de Mazou (30F) by Boyals et Fils, a smooth, most enjoyable wine.

A Bordeaux 93 from Château le Mayne, although a gold medal winner in Aquitaine in 1994, was the only wine we tasted in this price range that was disappointing (28F).

In cheaper wines, you can buy *appellation contrôlée* wines transported to, and bottled in, St-Malo by Gaillard, saving about 3F a bottle, starting at about 14F. *Vins de pays* are even less expensive, starting at 9F: a Vin de Pays des Collines de la Maure (Domaine de Launac) at 10F, a Vin de Pays Côtes du Tarn at 12F; and in *appellation contrôlée* wines (bottled in St-Malo), Côtes du Lubéron at 14F, Bergerac at 15F, and bordeaux from 17F. Wines bottled in their own region start at about 17F.

At the back of the shop is an intimate cellar with fine wines, mainly bordeaux. Come armed with a price list from your own wine merchant or from one of the many merchants specializing in bordeaux in the UK. This shop is no exception to the rule that fine bordeaux are generally less expensive in the UK, as a result of the considerable drop in value of sterling over the last few years. That said, there are some stunning wines on sale. Look also at the selection of Calvados here, ranging from Valdigny at 99F to the 30-year-old Clos Minotte at 420F.

There is good value here, but what really makes this shop so successful is Monsieur Torcher, who knows his wines and has a real understanding of customer service.

Les Réserves du Sourcouf

4 rue Toulouse
35400 St-Malo
Tel: (02) 99 40 15 19
Closed on Tuesday out of season, otherwise open until 8pm
This is a shop with great character, wooden floors, huge timber beams, rough stone walls and splendid cellars, via some sloping stairs definitely not for the even slightly inebriated. 330 wines are stocked and there is definitely no price list.

There are some good winemakers here, some less than good vintages lurking amongst the range, and not all the prices are as low as you might be looking for. Reputable winemakers include Robert Klingenfus and Dopff & Irion from Alsace, Claverie at Château Haut-Veyrac (St-Emilion), Perromat at Château Beauregard (Graves) and Briday (Rully). There is even a hotel (Château de Pizay, Morgon).

This shop is very old, very St-Malo, and definitely worth a visit, even if you don't buy anything.

Cora

This Cora is the newest and most salubrious supermarket in St-Malo. The wine section here is extensive and good value. For full details see page 31.

How to get there: Drive out on the road to Rennes (N137), and just as you think you've gone too far, you'll see a BP petrol station on your right, with the Cora store just beyond it, blue and red (on white) Cora flags flying above a pale green steel and timber structure.

Where to stay

There are three very different areas in which to stay: within the city walls, which is densely built, its narrow streets filled with people, restaurants and shops; on the beachfront, where there is plenty of space, there are marvellous views and (comparatively) few people; or south of the city in the suburb of St-Servan. Hotels are very expensive during the summer season, and they try to extend these rates for as long as possible. Know, however, that out of season you should be able to get a double room in any decent hotel for a reduced rate of about 250F.

Within the city walls

Hôtel Jean-Bart
12 rue de Chartres
35400 St-Malo
Tel: (02) 99 40 33 88
Double 300–350F with a harbour view
Closed mid-November to March
A few yards from the hustle and bustle of St-Malo's tourist centre is this small hotel that overlooks the city walls across a quiet street. It is easier finding it on foot than negotiating the maze of one way streets in a car, but it is well worth persevering. Just remember that it faces the eastern wall of the city, overlooking the marina and harbour. The relief is that when you find it, you

can take your time unloading your luggage in front of the hotel without causing a snarl in the traffic, and then have no problem finding an unlimited time parking space nearby on the street.

The welcome from Madame Vasse is warm and sincere. Her interest in, and care for, her guests is reflected throughout the hotel and throughout your stay. The lift is tiny, just room for two (slim) passengers minus luggage which will be sent up after you.

Rooms are as bright and cheerful as your welcome. On each floor two rooms face east over the ramparts with views of the harbour, and two rooms face west overlooking rooftops and narrow streets. Take the harbour facing rooms in the summer, as they will be cooler in the evening, but the west facing rooms might be warmer in winter, even though there is central heating. The rooms are rather small, and, although they don't pass the more stringent cleanliness tests (don't look under the bed or run your finger over difficult to reach surfaces), they do at least look sparkling, and are certainly comfortable. The small refrigerator, rare in this class of hotel, is an absolute boon. Soft drink prices, however, belong in a much more expensive hotel.

Breakfast is simple: orange juice (alas, not freshly squeezed), baguette and croissants, tea or coffee. Ask for cold milk if for some unknown reason, like many other foreigners, you do not appreciate the flavour of hot milk in your tea.

A warm reception, cheerful rooms, a quiet night in a comfortable bed, an owner who wants to please, and easy parking outside, what more could you ask for? Don't be put off by the '*Ici on aime les chiens*' sign, you'll get used to them in restaurants too.

Quic en Groigne

8 rue d'Estrées, 35400 St-Malo
Tel: (02) 99 40 86 81
Double 390–450F
An irresistible name – this hotel is in the heart of the city, 100 yards (91m) from the western ramparts, from which you can

enjoy wonderful views of the sun setting. It is in an attractive stone building (except that the UPVC window salesmen have arrived here too) on a quiet street. Quiet because it is so narrow that nothing big and noisy can drive down it. Leave the wine buyer's favourite estate car at home and bring the family run-about if you want to park at all.

Go up a wooden stairway to small rooms with small bath-rooms and even tinier showers. Front rooms look into a rather cheerless old peoples' home, so draw the curtains and enjoy Canal Plus, France's non-stop movie (and once a week late late porn) channel. Other luxuries include hairdryer, trouser press, tissues and soft loo paper.

There's a small sitting room off the lobby, which makes a so-ciable change for a small hotel, and a bright conservatory (used for breakfast) overlooking the stone-walled courtyard at the back: a good place to take out maps and the guidebook and do your planning. Breakfast is not much, though. There seems to be some degree of vagueness about room rates. There is a garage available.

By the beach

If you are looking for fresh air and a great sweep of beach with views over the channel, only a few minutes easy drive from the city, then this is a good location. But the hotels are even more expensive than in the city.

La Villefromoy

7 boulevard Hébert
35400 St-Malo
Tel: (02) 99 40 92 20
Closed mid-November to mid-March

Tried and tested, this is a comfortable hotel, and just one block from the beach. Beachside rooms have sea views (700F), even if not full frontal, whereas a few (less costly) look out onto the garden (550F) or a nondescript thoroughfare (450F) at the back.

La Korrigane
39 rue Le Pomellec
St-Servan
35400 St-Malo
Tel: (02) 99 81 65 85
Double 550–800F, breakfast 55–120F
Closed January
La Korrigane is a small, very romantic 19th-century townhouse
a couple of miles south of St-Malo with only ten rooms (one of
which is a single), all splendidly furnished with antiques.

In summer you can have your breakfast in the garden. There
is no restaurant, but in a way this works out well, because you
can then try the **Saint-Placide** (see below).

Where to eat

St-Malo has dozens of restaurants and cafés lining the narrow
streets of the old walled town, and along its waterfronts. Most
have pleasant terraces with awnings over the street where you
can eat out in the warmer months and watch the world go by at
the same time.

This is the kind of place where one hesitates to recommend
any one particular restaurant. It is much more fun to stroll
around and look at the menus and at what is being served to
customers, and to get a sense of the atmosphere. A large group
of coach tourists will alter the atmosphere as dramatically as a
total lack of customers. I went to one restaurant highly recommended by a very popular guide book, to find only two tables
occupied. One by a couple of American tourists, and the other
by the proprietor and staff looking depressed. The food may
have been good, but I felt like eating in a more convivial atmosphere that evening.

The seafood is of superb quality and plentiful, fresh off the
boat. Enjoy it anywhere, in a find of your own. Menus range
from 70F upwards. To get you started, the following are a few
of my favourites.

Le Chalut
8 rue de la Corne-du-Cerf
35400 St-Malo
Tel: (02) 99 56 71 58
Closed Sunday evening and Monday; mid-January to mid-February
Menus from 90F

On a freezing winter's night, mid-week out of season, customers without reservations were being turned away from this restaurant, so make sure you reserve your table in advance. Décor is marine, in aquas and pale blue, quarry-tiled floors, pine panelling washed in green, with canvas, nets and buoys, and an aquarium that is, in effect, a crayfish larder.

The 90F menu offered oysters, smoked salmon and *soupe aux buchots* to start It was not late, but the soup was finished. Could I have anything else that was hot for a starter on this cold evening, and I'd be happy to pay a supplement for any difference between the cost of the soup (on the *à la carte* menu) and the alternative? Only if I moved up to the 175F menu. A nearby table was served piping hot soup half an hour later. My query was dismissed with a 'they reserved the soup'. So be warned, reserve, arrive early, and definitely no substitutions (or reserve the soup).

The chef really is talented, even if he does not always get his quantities right. An *amuse-bouche* was the lightest smoked mackerel mousse on toast, topped by a prawn. *Le lieu jaune* was perfectly grilled, just on the underdone side of cooked, served with fluffy parsnip, densely flavoured fried potatoes and caramelized onion sauce. My *crème brûlée* was perfect too, creamy with a delicate *brûlée*.

There is a decent wine list, albeit with a mark-up more noticeable than usual, with the name of the vineyard owner alongside the château or domaine. There are many Luneaus and Papins in Muscadet, but the Muscadet sur lie 94 here is from Monsieur Luneau-Papin and his Clos des Pierres Blanches (63F a half-bottle). A Savennières 93 from Soulez' Château de

Chamboureau is an unfortunate 193F, even if the wine is rather fine, and an equally well made Sancerre 94 from Alphonse Mellot's Domaine la Moussière 163F (49F at the vineyard before trade discount).

Excellent cooking, stern service, and shame about the '*supplément lait 2F*'.

La Chasse Marée
4 rue du Grout St-Georges
35400 St-Malo
Tel: (02) 99 40 85 10
Menus from 87F
This was a recommendation from another restaurateur, and the cooking was up to it. A simple, comfortable restaurant, with beams, white walls, a wooden bar, soft lighting and a gentle, warm atmosphere. From the 87F menu (not after 9pm) I started with a *poêlée de calamars* with salad, exceptionally succulent and tender, then *filets de rouget grillés* with a tomato *coulis*, very beautifully presented with rice and courgettes, finishing with a *tarte à l'orange*, creamy, lush, sharp and very well balanced.

Whilst the wine list is weighted in favour of bourgognes and bordeaux, some of the vintages were odd. Best value would probably be a St-Emilion grand cru 89 from Clos Labarde (158F). Best to choose a simple Saumur blanc 94 from Château de Villeneuve (85F) or a fragrant Ménétou-Salon 93 from Domaine de Chatenoy (105F).

Le Corps de Garde
montée Notre Dame
35400 St-Malo
Closed out of season
This bar-cum-crêperie on the western walls of the city has an incomparable view over the coastline, magical from the wooden tables on the terrace at sunset. Montée Notre Dame is off rue de la Crosse, which is at the end of rue du Boyer.

Borgnefesse
10 rue du Puits-aux-Braies
35400 St-Malo
Tel: (02) 99 40 05 05
Closed Saturday, Sunday and Monday lunchtime
Marvellous port atmosphere in this ancient tavern, right in the
heart of the old town, perfect for a light lunch of two courses
(59F).

A la Duchesse Anne
5 place Guy La Chambre
35400 St-Malo
Tel: (02) 99 40 85 33
Closed Sunday evening, Wednesday; December and January
This was *the* establishment restaurant in St-Malo for many
years, and it is easy to find by the main entrance gate at Porte
St-Vincent. You may need to make a reservation, but before
you do, look in to see if you like the atmosphere. Your food bill,
excluding wine, will be well over 200F.

Saint-Placide
6 place Poncel
St-Servan
35400 St-Malo
Tel: (02) 99 81 70 73
Closed Tuesday evening and Wednesday out of season
If you are staying at La Korrigane, or are simply out this way,
eat here. The 79F lunch – all week (except Sunday) – and the
110F menu in the evening are great value.

Entre Deux Verres
1 rue Broussais
35400 St-Malo
Tel: (02) 99 40 01 46
Tucked away uphill from the plastic-chair-and-umbrella scene
is this little wine bistro, with ten tables and closing early at 10.

It is primarily a place to taste and drink wine. Wooden parquet flooring, formica and wooden tables, timber bar displaying impressive box ends from Petrus 74 to Château Les Ormes de Pez and St-Estèphe-Médoc 83 and a loo with the walls papered with *étiquettes* (wine labels) from great châteaux. The painted glass panels on the wall, gold scrolls on a pale blue background, are unusual.

The list of about eleven wines by the glass, from 11F to 26F for small glasses (13cl) or 17F to 39F for large glasses (18cl), changes every week. Blackboard map and listing shows where the wine is from. When I visited, five white wines were on offer, including a superb Crozes-Hermitage 93 from Domaine des Entrefaux, a wonderful wine from a difficult year, fragrant, complex and round. There were also five reds, including an unusual Bandol rouge 92 from Domaine du Cagueloup, another winemaker worth noting, and a Corsican rosé.

A limited menu with simple dishes, from charcuterie (Bayonne ham, *terrine*, *andouille* and *saucisson* for 37F), to meats you grill yourself on a *pierre chaude* (very), such as *noix de veau* or fillet of pork (60F), with accompanying salads. If you have been indulging in fish and seafood, this might make a change. Your food bill will probably be 130F a head without wine. Convivial and warm atmosphere, full of pleasurable conversation and enjoyment.

Where to drink

Apart from Entre Deux Verres, there are innumerable other atmospheric bars. Here are just a couple to get you started: the **Marie Galante** and **Jazzy**, both quite cool and stylish in their own individual ways, conveniently located en route to the Chasse Marée (see **Where to eat** above), and looking into each other across the place des Frères Lamennais.

Back in St-Malo, if you want a break from wine, the best pub with a wide selection of European beers, including some rather esoteric ones, can be found at the **Hôtel de l'Univers** (place Châteaubriand). You know that you are in France, because each beer is described with tasting notes exactly like those used with wine. The smoky wooden-floored bar has great atmosphere anyway, one common to great European ports, even if it is slightly more Amsterdam than Rotterdam. Terrific outdoor terrace for sipping an *apéritif* or coffee, talking and viewing the world at leisure.

When I was there, sheltering under the canvas canopy from a torrential downpour, two musicians were seated drinking cider from pretty, traditional cups, singing old Breton folksongs to the accompaniment of a small harp.

Roscoff

Roscoff is a small Breton fishing port that has been suddenly thrust into the twentieth century by the cauliflower growers of Brittany who wanted to get their produce to the UK, so they bought a ship and Brittany Ferries was born. The town of Roscoff itself is unspectacular, but it now has a range of small hotels and restaurants which cater to ferry users. Nearby Morlaix, offers better scope for eating, drinking and shopping. Market day in Morlaix is Saturday.

How to get there
Brittany Ferries from Plymouth (7 hours). There are also direct links with Ireland: Brittany Ferries to Cork; Irish Ferries from Rosslare (15 hours). There are often special offers on these routes, especially between September and June.

Where to buy wine
Les Caves de Roscoff
Port de Bloscon
29680 Roscoff
Tel: (02) 98 61 24 10
Open daily 10-6 (later if a ship is leaving late)
Good English spoken

There is also the **Géant Bretagnia Hypermarché** at the top of the hill in Morlaix where most ferry users go to stock up before returning home.

Where to stay

Le Manoir du Lan Kerellec
22560 Trébeurden
Tel: (02) 96 23 50 09
Along the pink granite coast to the east, this three-star hotel has been converted from a Breton manorhouse which overlooks the sea.

Where to eat

If you didn't get up in time to have breakfast on the ferry, there are a couple of delightful cafés just below the viaduct in Morlaix, which open early and can give you your first French coffee or *chocolat* and a *croissant*, in perfect surroundings: one a *fin-de-siècle* survival, the other a delicate *salon de thé*.

For a good value lunch, make your way up the steep hill to the *hypermarché* where you may be going to buy your wine, and try the cafeteria. The word might conjure up images of greasy sausages and thick custard, but nothing could be further from the food now being presented not only in French hypermarkets but in countrywide chains such as *Flunch*. There is usually a good selection of hot *plats du jour*, a wide variety of salads, half-bottles of wine, and crowds of locals eating their lunch. Help yourself from a counter, so there is no complicated ordering in French.

If you are worried about getting back to Roscoff in time for a late ferry, the most highly rated restaurant in town is **Le Temps de Vivre**, place Eglise, 29680 Roscoff (tel: 02 98 61 27 28), which has menus from 110F.

The Loire Valley

The Loire Valley stretches from the port of St-Nazaire on the Atlantic, eastwards past Angers, through Saumur and Tours, slightly north to Orléans, and then curves south past Sancerre at Pouilly-sur-Loire and beyond to its source in central France. It's closer to the ports and Paris than you might think: Angers is three hours from Caen by road, one and a half hours from Paris on the TGV; Tours is only one hour from Paris on the TGV.

The Loire is like a climatic border between the grey north and bright south of France, sunny yet mild. Landscapes are varied, with vineyards on slopes, forests, rivers and many tributaries, fishermen and boats, river walls against flooding, bridges, châteaux and mediaeval villages. For details of châteaux, see **What to see** sections.

From west to east, the wine producing areas are firstly, the **Pays Nantais**, the wine producing area around Nantes. This is fairly flat country and the least scenic part of the Loire Valley. Vast quantities of wine are produced in this region, a cheap dry white called Gros Plant (not an *appellation contrôlée*), and the better known Muscadet de Sèvre-et-Maine (named for the grape and the two rivers which run through the area).

Secondly, there is **Anjou**, the area around Angers, encompassing many *appellations*, the best known being Anjou and Saumur. Anjou has several related *appellations* such as Anjou-Villages. Here there are some small *appellations*, such as Savennières (which has even tinier *appellations* within it, such as the 17-acre (7ha) Savennières Coulée-de-Serrant), Coteaux de l'Aubance, Coteaux du Layon, Bonnezeaux and Quarts de Chaume.

Then comes **Touraine**, which is the wine growing country around Tours and includes, amongst others, the *appellations* of Chinon, Bourgueil and Vouvray.

Finally, **Sancerre** and **Pouilly-Fumé** are the dry, flinty wines from the east.

Pays Nantais

The western end of the Loire valley is the area in which Muscadet is produced. The area stretches from the Atlantic coast of Brittany (to the west of Nantes) to midway between Nantes and Angers. A lesser wine in quality, and therefore also in price, is Gros Plant, produced in quantity in the same region.

How to get there

At the heart of the Muscadet de Sèvre-et-Maine *appellation* is the small town of Vallet, approximately 12.5 miles (20km) southeast of Nantes on the N249. One way to approach this area is via the scenic route along the south bank of the Loire. But if you head west from Angers as far as Liré, then south on the D763 from Ancenis to Vallet, the journey is not as scenic but it is quick.

Where to buy

Maison de Muscadet
4 rue d'Ancenis
44330 Vallet
The Maison de Muscadet represents about 35 *viticulteurs* who produce Muscadet and Gros Plant. They select only three Muscadets and two Gros Plants for tasting each year.

All wines are the same price, with Muscadet under 30F and Gros Plant under 25F. Huge discounts for cases of 12.

Roland Petiteau-Gaubert
Domaine de la Tourlaudière
44330 Vallet
Tel: (02) 40 36 24 86
There are many Petiteaus, many of them make wine, and they live within a few miles of each other. To distinguish one from the other they agreed to add their wives' maiden names to their

own name. The ramifications of this agreement for the next generation could be interesting.

The 94 Gros Plant would be regarded as a typical Gros Plant, slightly green but with a pleasant nose, excellent value at 15F. The 94 Muscadet sur lie is well balanced, and a good buy at 20F.

How to get there: Take the D106 (direction Bonne Fontaine) due west from Vallet. Turn right into the main street of the village of Bonne Fontaine, and follow it to la Tourlaudière.

Philippe Laure

Les Rosiers
44330 Vallet
Tel: (02) 40 33 91 83

It is not easy to make a good Gros Plant. Philippe Laure has. His 17F Gros Plant 94 is very fresh and pleasant, a picnic wine. The Muscadet sur lie 94 is a typical Muscadet, quite fruity but dry. Good value at 20F.

How to get there: From the main square in Vallet, take the D37 (direction les Corbeillières) east and then southeast out of town, past the information office on your right. The turning to Les Rosiers will be on your left.

Louis Métaireau

La Févrie
44690 Maisdon-sur-Sèvre
Tel: (02) 40 54 81 92

Louis Métaireau is known for his commitment to quality. This winemaker is included so that you can taste a Muscadet sur lie of the highest quality. That is, of course, if you are prepared to pay some of the highest prices.

At the top end of his range is his Cuvée One 94, with lovely subtle aromas, at 55F. You might prefer the less expensive Cuvée 10.5 94, which is a light summer wine, refreshing and less alcoholic. The Métaireaus spend a lot of time explaining their wines and Muscadet in general (Louis Métaireau's daughter speaks English). If you do like the wines, please remember that in some vineyards such as this one, the unit of purchase is regarded as a carton of twelve bottles.

How to get there: Driving from Clisson on the D59, cross the junction with the D7 (left to Maisdon-sur-Sèvre, right to Monnières), continue past La Goulatière and La Rebougère, then turn left to the sign for the hamlet of La Févrie.

Once in the hamlet, you will pass the house of Claude Branger on the right (and you could drop in here to taste his Domaine la Haute Févrie Cuvée Excellence sur lie 94, at 24F well worth the extra few francs).

A few yards on, as you arrive at a T-junction, you will see the entrance to Maison Louis Métaireau at approximately 11 o'-clock, slightly to the left then right. The office is up the stairs.

Where to stay and eat

Don Quichotte
35 route de Clisson
44330 Vallet
Tel: (02) 40 33 99 67
Double 295F
Restaurant closed Sunday evening
Menus from 85F

The rooms of the Don Quichotte are in a motel-style block at the rear, surrounded on two sides by vineyards. What the rooms lack in character, they make up for with the things that someone who has been driving all day needs: easy parking outside your room, a sparkling bathroom, a comfortable bed, and a pleasant dining room.

Traffic noise from the Vallet–Clisson road subsides in the evening, and, although within earshot of the N249 from Cholet to Nantes, this is not particularly intrusive. The restaurant is in the older, adjoining main house.

How to get there: Don Quichotte is easy to find on the main Vallet to Clisson road (D763); it is just on your left as you are driving out of Vallet.

Auberge de la Cascade

28 route Gervaux
44190 Clisson
Tel: (02) 40 54 02 41
Double 195F
Restaurant closed Sunday evening, Monday; menus from 65F

On a hot summer's day, there could be few more magical spots than this little patch by the Sèvre river, covered in waterlilies.

The auberge is plain and unassuming. The restaurant is on the first floor, a large room with a restful view over the trees. Although there is a 65F lunch menu (I had an excellent *frisée* salad with bacon, *croutons* and pine nuts, followed by a simple grilled pork chop, and cheese), the 95F menu is more interesting. Start with parma ham from the Vendée, or a salad of gizzards (duck or goose) with a raspberry dressing, follow with duck cooked in Muscadet or salmon steak cooked in butter with anchovies, finish with cheese and dessert.

Where better to drink Muscadet de Sèvre-et-Maine sur lie other than on the banks of the Sèvre itself? There is a choice of five regional wines ranging from 65F, four available in half-bottles. A perfect spot for lunch. Simple rooms available.

How to get there: As you drive in from Vallet, from the north on the D763, take the right fork down a hill towards the bridge that takes you across the river into old Clisson. Before you start driving down the hill, take another sharp right onto the route Gervaux, a very minor road despite its name.

La Bonne Auberge

1 rue Olivier-de-Clisson
44190 Clisson
Tel: (02) 40 54 01 90
Closed Sunday evening and Monday; late February and part of August

The most well known restaurant in this area; affordable if you have the 98F weekday lunch menu. Lovely terrace for summer dining.

Pays Nantais

What to See

Musée des Beaux-Arts
10 rue G. Clemenceau, 44000 Nantes
Monday, Wednesday, Thursday, Saturday, 10–6; Friday 10–9,
Sunday 11–6; closed Tuesday; free on Sunday
One of the best fine art museums in France, the Nantes collection includes major international and French works from the
13th century to the present day.

Château des Ducs de Bretagne
place Marc Elder, 44000 Nantes
Castle: September–June daily, except Tuesday and public holidays, 10–12 and 2–6; July and August daily 10–7. Museum:
daily except holidays 10–12, 2–6
Anne de Bretagne was born here in 1477 – the central courtyard of the castle is reached by crossing a bridge over the dry
moat and passing between two massive round towers. There is
also a Museum of Regional Folk Art which is exceptional.

Château de Goulaine
44115 Haute Goulaine
15 June to 15 September, daily except Tuesday; Easter–15 June
and 15 September–All Saints' Day, Saturday, Sunday and public holidays only 10–12 and 2–6.
This 15th–17th century château is beautifully furnished and has
an exotic butterfly house in the grounds.

Château d'Ancenis
44150 Ancenis
Mostly in ruins, though two Renaissance towers remain, this
ancient castle dates from the 10th century when the port and
town grew up around it. There are tremendous views over the
Loire from the terraced gardens.

Château Olivier de Clisson
rue du Château, 44190 Clisson
This is an impressive medieval castle overlooking a deep valley at the confluence on the rivers Sèvre and Maine.

Lac de Grand-Lieu
You can reach the shores of this remote lake through the village of Passay. It is a haven for birdlife and a rich fishing site. There is a Maison du Pêcheur and the Observatoire de Passay at 16 rue Yves Brisson, 44118 La Chevrolière, tel: 40 31 36 46.

Bateaux Nantais
quai de la Motte-Rouge, 44000 Nantes, tel: 40 14 51 14
Bateaux Nantais offer lunch and dinner cruises along the Erdre with its châteaux or on the Sèvre through the heart of the vineyards, giving a pleasant complementary view of the slopes.

Windmills
There are ruined and restored windmills throughout this region; at Pouzages, Moulin du Pré and La Minière, there are particularly striking views across the countryside.

Wine fairs and festivals

Vallet
Muscadet wine market held annually in the middle of March
La Haie-Fouassière
Wine fair at the end of September
Mauves and Le Cellier
Annual fair at the end of September
Clisson
Wine fair on Ascension Day
Vertou
Wine festival in June
Nantes
Wine fair in the middle of November

Anjou and Saumur

ANJOU

Angers

Angers is a bustling, charming university town on the Loire with good shopping and plenty of restaurants. It's also easy to get to (it takes only three hours to travel from Caen to Angers, using the motorway from Le Mans) and has a splendid range of vineyards within a few miles.

Where to buy wine in Angers
La Maison du Vin
5bis place Kennedy
49100 Angers
Tel: (02) 41 88 81 13
Open Tuesday–Saturday 9–1, 3–6.30; Sundays from April–September

Overlooking the castle near the river, this is one of the most pleasant *maisons du vin* in the Loire Valley, with helpful literature and maps, and friendly staff. The range of wines is far from comprehensive, but offers a taste of each *appellation* from a selection of winemakers (usually changed annually).

Château de Piégüe in Rochefort-sur-Loire consistently produces Anjou Blanc of the highest quality. Madame Laroche from Domaine aux Moines is one of the proprietors of the 80-acre (33ha) of Savennières Roche-aux-Moines, the *appellation* that borders the more famous 17-acre (7ha) of Savennières Coulée-de-Serrant. Here the Savennières Roche-aux-Moines 90 (a very fine year) sells at 80F. Luc Bizard at Château d'Épiré also produces Savennières: his 94 sells at 66F (less at the château, of course). Keep an eye out for his 95 *demi-sec*.

The Coteaux du Layon 94 from Domaine Gaudard (42F) is still young, but its richness is already evident. Curiously enough, the Coteaux du Layon 85 from Vignobles Touchais at

68F is marginally cheaper here than at Maison Touchais itself. Other Coteaux du Layon come from Domaine des Barres (the 94 at 54F), Vignoble Bidet's La Magdelaine (the 91 at 73F), Domaine des Maurières (the 1990 at 130F) and Château du Breuil (the 88 at 56F), all well known winemakers.

Domaine de Terrebrune's Bonnezeaux 93 at 93F and Pierre Soulez's Quarts de Chaume 93 at 175F are an expensive way to taste these *appellations*, but only 2000 bottles of this Quarts de Chaume were produced in 93, so it's rather exclusive.

The Anjou-Gamay 94 from Vaillant's Domaine des Grandes Vignes is a splendid wine, despite the difficult year. The Anjou-Villages 93 by Pascal Cailleau at Domaine du Sauveroy (32F) is one of the best examples of an Anjou-Villages that you'll find. I have long been a fan of Jean-Luc Mary at Domaine de la Cune, whose Saumur-Champigny 94 is here at 39F. Bouvet Ladubay's Cuvée Saphir is a fine sparkling Saumur (58F).

Where to stay in Angers
Hôtel d'Anjou
1 boulevard Foch, 49100 Angers
Tel: (02) 41 88 24 82
Double room 400F
In the heart of bustling Angers, this hotel is in an elegant building with warm décor, comfortable rooms and private parking. Front rooms overlook the busy six-lane boulevard, with its cinema and inexpensive brasseries.

Pavillon Paul le Quéré
3 boulevard Foch, 49100 Angers
Tel: (02) 41 20 00 20
Restaurant closed on Sunday
Double room 450–1200F
Next to the Hôtel d'Anjou nestles this elegant 19th-century mansion, looking more like a chic ambassadorial residence than a restaurant and townhouse hotel. Turn off busy boulevard Foch (watch out for the bus lane and the pedestrians) through

grand gates (nearest the Hôtel d'Anjou) into the courtyard. This is essentially a restaurant with rooms, so you may find that the porter is also the assistant *sommelier*, the receptionist the *maître-cuisinier* and proprietor. Rooms (accessible by lift) are on the second floor; *appartements* (huge rooms with high ceilings and grand windows) are on the first floor.

The beds are exceptionally comfortable and the bathtubs huge. Have the 60F breakfast in the large front dining room or in bed, enjoying the fine Limoges porcelain, sterling silver, pretty linen and cheerful room service. Even the least expensive room was a pleasure to stay in.

Where to eat in Angers
Le Toussaint
7–9 place du Président Kennedy
49100 Angers
Tel: (02) 41 87 46 20
Closed Sunday evening and all day Monday
Menus from 98F

My favourite restaurant in Angers, Le Toussaint, is easy to find on place Kennedy – it's on the first floor with large windows overlooking the square and castle. This is an elegant high-ceilinged room in subdued colours, very intimate and extremely comfortable. The 98F menu is available in the evenings as well as at lunchtime. Starters may include oysters, duck *rillettes*, *quiche aux poireaux* and crab soup with croutons and gruyère. The dense flavour of the *estouffade de boeuf* is from hours of cooking in Anjou rouge. The *tarte maison* is an inspired *tarte Tatin*, leagues ahead of many.

The prices of some of the drinks are high – a half-bottle of water is 20F. But there are 15 half-bottles of Loire wine available: try a Saumur rouge or blanc 94 from Château de Beauregard. There are also some very interesting (and expensive) wines, such as Madame Joly's Savennières Coulée-de-Serrant 90, a vintage virtually impossible to find these days, and a Bonnezeaux 85 and 88 La Chapelle from Château de Fesles.

Pavillon Paul le Quéré (see page 105)
Closed Sunday evening
Menu 150F

There are two dining rooms here: one in the main room with high ceilings, very formal and grand; the other in a gracefully curving conservatory – spacious, warm in winter and modern.

A beautiful three course meal, *Les coups de coeur de Paul*, including pre-dinner nibbles (*amuse-gueule*) and after dinner *mignardises* costs 150F, or 200F to include cheese and wine. Unfortunately *vin compris* does not mean three different glasses of wine to match the food, but is simply a half-bottle (per person) chosen from a list of four. This is a pity, given the interesting wine list.

Where to buy wine at the vineyards

Open Monday–Saturday 9–12 and 2–5. Closed Sunday and public holidays unless otherwise stated, or you phone ahead.

Savennières

Less than a hundred hectares make up this *appellation*, making it rather exclusive, and almost unobtainable in the UK. Made from Chenin Blanc grown in vineyards on the right (north) bank of the Loire, it can be dry or *demi-sec*, a fact not always noted on the wine labels. Its flinty taste is derived from the preponderance of slate in the soil, the area having once been volcanic (hence the names Roche-aux-Moines and Coulée-de-Serrant – literally Monks' Rock and Serrant Lava Flow). In a good year, Savennières can be flowery and fruity, and a good *demi-sec*, although expensive, can be honeyed and heavenly.

The *appellation* covers only a small area, and the wine has the lowest yield for a dry white in Anjou, resulting in limited quantities. Some winemakers also like to give their wines some bottle age, so you have conditions leading to high prices and a degree of prestige. Certainly not to be missed in a tasting, even if you decide to buy only the Anjou wine produced alongside Savennières.

Château d'Épiré

place de l'Ancienne Eglise
49170 Epire, near Savennières
Tel: (02) 41 77 15 01
Winemaker: Luc Bizard (speaks English)
A splendid 17th-century property with 25 acres (10ha) of vines. Stop at the 12th-century church at the entrance, for it's here that the winemaking takes place (marked *chais*).

The vineyards here are some of the oldest in Savennières. There are two price brackets: the good Anjous and the superb Savennières. The Anjou rouge 95 has a good colour, and great promise (30F). Taste the fine Savennières *demi-sec* 95. This is a rich and complex sweet wine, tasting of quince and honey, with a pretty colour. Well worth 68F if you're looking for a delicious wine that is unusual and virtually impossible to buy elsewhere.
How to get there: Drive from Rochefort-sur-Loire (early closing day is Wednesday) north across the river (and across the Ile Béhuard) into Savennières, turn right, following the road with the railway line running alongside on your right. At Les Forges, the road turns sharply to the left. When you reach Épiré, follow the main road which curves to the left between walls on either side. Before you reach the village church and phonebox, take a right into rue des Platanes which leads to the château entrance.

Château de Chamboureau

49170 Savennières
Tel: (02) 41 77 20 04
Winemakers: Pierre and Yves Soulez
Tastings by appointment only
Follow the signs a couple of kilometres north from Coulée-de-Serrant to visit this famous château, whose origins date back 500 years. The name Soulez is well known amongst the best winemakers in the region. Their finest wine is probably the seductive Quarts de Chaume, L'Amandier. They also produce a remarkably fine Savennières.

Savennières Coulée-de-Serrant

Château de la Roche-aux-Moines
49170 Savennières
Tel: (02) 41 72 22 32
Winemaker: Nicolas Joly

La Coulée-de-Serrant is world renowned, as much for its quality as for its high price of 150F a bottle. The *appellation* consists of 15 acres (7ha) of vines owned entirely by the Joly family. Nicolas Joly is committed to a macrobiological approach, using only organic materials, no chemical pesticides or fertilisers, and with some respect for astrological confluences. The château also produces a less expensive Savennières 94 Bécherelle (65F) and Roche-aux-Moines 92 (80F). Tastings only if you undertake to spend a hefty 250F.

Where to eat near the vineyards
Les Tonnelles
Ile Béhuard
Tel: (02) 41 72 21 50
Open all week except Monday March–October; out of season weekends only

Ile Béhuard is a small island in the middle of the Loire between Rochefort-sur-Loire and Savennières. The village is an utterly peaceful place, lost in time. The church is built on one of the volcanic outcrops that are part of the *terroir* of Savennières. Les Tonnelles is not a place for an inexpensive lunch, with the cheapest menu at 165F; and the one you'll be interested in, with four different glasses of wine included, is 250F. This might be *foie gras* with wild mushrooms and a young Coteaux du Layon, mussel soup with a Savennières, roast duckling with a young Anjou-Villages, cheese with an older Anjou-Villages, followed by dessert. Gérard Bosse is as passionate about wine as he is about food, so you'll be able to try many interesting Loire wines by the glass (18–35F). I tasted a Savennières 79 from

Baumard (in Rochefort) and an 89 from Madame de Jessey's Domaine du Closel. Worth a visit – a charming proprietor, a relaxing and unpretentious restaurant, and an unusual village.

As you cross the river from Rochefort, you'll see the **Restaurant du Grand Pont** on the left, on the river bank. It is open every day at lunch, but the price of a sandwich and beer would buy more elsewhere.

Coteaux de l'Aubance (and Anjou)

These vineyards cluster around the pretty river Aubance, a tributary of the Loire. There are about 198 acres (80ha) of Chenin Blanc, which makes a sweet white wine that is rather soft and gentle.

Domaine Richou

Chauvigné
49610 Mozé-sur-Louet
Tel: (02) 41 78 72 13
Winemaker: M. Richou

This is a traditional country house with white shutters and pots of geraniums outside, but the winemaking takes place in a modern building next door. The tasting room is rustic with beams, gnarled wooden candelabra and furniture, and a quarry-tiled floor. Richou father and his son (who speaks English) can be hard pressed if a large number of clients arrive at once to talk, taste and buy.

The Anjou Blanc sec 94 is dryish and pleasant (27F). For just about half the price, you can bottle your own, with both Anjou Cabernet and Anjou Blanc available in bulk.

Take this opportunity to taste a Coteaux de l'Aubance. This is another rare white wine, grown beside a tributary of the Loire in a vineyard that covers only 198 acres (80ha). The Richous' appley, honeyed Coteaux de l'Aubance 94 Les Trois Demoiselles (77F), well rounded, complex and refreshing, is much more distinctive than their cheaper, plain Coteaux de l'Aubance 94.

110

How to get there: Drive out from Mozé in the direction of Denée for half a mile (1km) until you reach the N161 Angers–Cholet road. Cross this major highway, and continue for another mile (2km) in the direction of Denée. Domaine Richou is on your left.

Coteaux du Layon, Coteaux du Layon-Chaume, Quarts de Chaume and Bonnezeaux

The vineyards of these *appellations* are on the banks of the river Layon, which flows into the Loire. Made of Chenin Blanc grapes, the wine is sweet or semi-sweet, lush, honeyed and an unusual alternative to a more expensive Sauternes. In terms of prestige, the smaller the quantity produced, the more highly regarded the wine. The commune of Chaume produces the superior Coteaux du Layon-Chaume with a slightly higher minimum alcohol content and a lower maximum yield. The finest quality sweet wines come from the two most prestigious *appellations*, Quarts de Chaume and Bonnezeaux, which are now very expensive.

Domaine Ogereau

44 rue de la Belle Angevine
49750 St-Lambert-du-Lattay
Tel: (02) 41 78 30 53
Closed the last two weeks in August
Winemaker: Vincent Ogereau

Vincent Ogereau is a winemaker of much repute, who works from a modest suburban home. His finest and most expensive wine is an outstanding Coteaux du Layon – the St-Lambert Cuvée Prestige 93 at 60F shows his undoubted winemaking skills. It's a very interesting wine, complex, rich, subtle and satisfying. His Anjou blanc sec 94, made of pure Chenin grapes, is very pleasant and dry; the Cabernet d'Anjou 94, and particularly the Anjou-Villages rouge 93, are well worth tasting (all less than 30F). For a few weeks in April and May, wine is available *en vrac* at 18F a litre for red and white Anjou, down to 11F a

111

litre for a red *vin de pays*.

How to get there: Follow the N160 from Angers to Cholet as it passes through the village of St-Lambert-du-Lattay. The road curves slightly round the church (on the left), then continues out towards Cholet. After passing the post office on your left, number 44 is on your right.

Domaine Gaudard

route de St-Aubin
49290 Chaudefonds-sur-Layon
Tel: (02) 41 78 10 68
Open Monday–Saturday 10–12, 2–5 including public holidays
Winemaker: Pierre Aguilas

Pierre Aguilas makes some superb wines. His Coteaux du Layon is renowned and the most recent St-Aubin de Luigné 94 is particularly good value at 37F. It's still young but is already showing richness. Open the bottle well ahead of drinking. The Cabernet d'Anjou 94 is a good rosé with some substance; the Anjou blanc sec 94, made from the Chenin grape, also has some bite. Both well made and very reasonable.

How to get there: Go through Chaudefonds on the D125 towards St-Aubin. Passing the cemetery on the right, you'll come to Domaine Gaudard on the left.

Château de Montguéret

49560 Nueil-sur-Layon
Tel: (02) 41 59 26 26
Winemakers: Dominique and André Lacheteau

A most attractive 19th-century château overlooking 212 acres (86ha) of vineyard and rolling hills. The creeper clad house stands elegantly in impeccably maintained grounds and the winemaking takes place in a nearby modern building. The Anjous are light Loire wines for drinking now. The best of the inexpensive wines is the Anjou blanc 94, with a pretty colour and good fruit (20F), and a good Saumur rouge 94. If there are stocks of Anjou-Villages rouge 90, taste some. Fruity and well made, this wine (29F), from a very good year, would be perfect with any red meat dish.

The sweet, honeyed Coteaux du Layon 90 Petit St-Louis (102F) is a magnificent golden colour; a beautiful wine, supremely versatile, which can be taken as an *apéritif*, or at the beginning of a meal with, for example, *foie gras*, or at the end with dessert. If you're tempted, however, remember that you're entering a price range where there are some formidable *moelleux* or *liquoreux* wines from other *appellations*.

How to get there: Take the D69 from Doué-la-Fontaine south-wards (towards Argenton). About 6 miles (10km) from Doué, turn right onto the D77 to Nueil-sur-Layon. You drive into the town square at the bottom right corner, and head out at the bottom left corner. Taking the D170 to Passavant, drive on to Château de Montguéret on your left, the last building before open rolling countryside.

Maison Touchais

25 avenue du Maréchal Leclerc
49700 Doué-la-Fontaine
Tel: (02) 41 59 12 14
Open Monday–Friday only, during business hours

There's no sign at all at number 25 indicating that Maison Touchais can be found in a warehouse at the back. This is prob-ably intended to discourage the general public, who would be coming here in droves if they discovered the astonishingly low prices.

Maison Touchais is probably most well known for its rosé *vin de table* Cuisse de Bergère (Shepherdess's Thigh) – I sus-pect more for the picture of an alluring country lass with her skirts riding dangerously high than for the wine itself. It may be cheap at 10F50 (and rather appropriately described by one taster as 'leg-over' wine), but live dangerously, and splash out 13F50 on the Cabernet d'Anjou. Even those not normally en-amoured of rosé will have to admit the astonishing value of this AOC wine. The 1994 that I tasted was a pretty colour, had a light fragrance with hints of smokey vanilla and spice – a brilliantly refreshing summer wine (good with a salad and garlic *vinaigrette*) and in an elegant bottle too. Tremendous value, as is their Coteaux du Layon (21F).

Bonnezeaux

This is a rather special *appellation* covering only 320 acres (130ha) of steep slopes south of Thouarcé, although not all of this area is in production. You might think of this sweet white wine as exclusively a dessert wine, but it also makes a fine *apéritif*.

Château de Fesles
49380 Thouarcé
Tel: (02) 41 54 14 32
Proprietor: Gaston Lenôtre
Winemaker: Jacques Boivin

This is a beautiful property built only a few years after 1066. Pause at the gates and enjoy the view of the valley below before heading for the tasting rooms.

The Bonnezeaux at Château de Fesles is aged in oak barrels from Château d'Yquem, one of the most prestigious wines in the world. The Bonnezeaux 93 (64F) is a fragrant and luscious Loire wine, but takes a while to open up. Serve it less chilled than you might normally and leave it in your glass for half an hour. Then enjoy this sweet, but not cloying, wine with hints of vanilla and echoes of Muscat, Tokay and late picked Sémillon. It may taste even better the next day, a sign that the wine will age gracefully over many years. Perfect, of course, with *pâté de fois gras*.

Château de Fesles, unlike many other vineyards, is able to hold some stock from exceptional years, like 89 and 90, so you should be able to buy a Bonnezeaux from those years. Another wine that you might like to taste is their Coteaux du Layon 92 (45F).

How to get there: Château de Fesles is easy to find. Driving from Thouarcé on the D125 towards Martigné, you'll come to a junction with the D114; turn left onto the D114 towards Chavagnes, and you'll see the château on the hill on your left. Half a mile (800m) up the hill you'll come to the entrance gates.

Track down Gérard Depardieu to the village of Tigné where, when he's not busy acting, he is seigneur and winemaker at **Château de Tigné**, and you may have the pleasure of tasting his Anjou-Villages Cuvée Cyrano.

SAUMUR

Saumur
Saumur is one of the most charming towns on the Loire. Its location, midway between Angers and Tours, makes it possible to reach several different and interesting wine areas in an easy half hour's drive, leaving you with more time for a leisurely drive between vineyards, tastings, conversations and meals. It's an elegant town on the banks of the Loire, straddling the river with part of the town built on an island – *mignon* (sweet) is how many French people describe it. At the foot of the 14th-century château is the old town with pretty squares, cafés and narrow cobbled streets taken over by stalls on market day. Closing day in Saumur is Monday and there is a lively Saturday market at place St-Pierre.

Saumur and Saumur-Champigny
Saumur is probably best known for its sparkling wines, although its white and red wines (especially Saumur-Champigny) are a real find. The *tuffeau* soil gives the wines a distinctive taste, the white (from Chenin Blanc grapes) is somewhere between Anjou and Vouvray in style.

Saumur-Champigny is regarded as the best Saumur rouge (with prices to match), and is made from Cabernet Franc grown on slopes just east of Saumur near the Loire. Its deep colour and scent are unmistakable.

115

Where to buy
Maison du Vin de Saumur
25 rue Beaurepaire
49400 Saumur
Tel: (02) 41 51 16 40
Open Monday–Saturday 9–12.30 and 2–6.30, closed Sunday
and public holidays, out of season closed on Monday
Wines on sale here from reputable winemakers (in the 23–27F
price range) include: Philippe and Alain Gourdon's Château de
Beauregard in Le Puy-Notre Dame (Saumur blanc 94); the
Lycée Viticole de Montreuil-Bellay Saumur rouge 94 (not to be
confused with Château de Montreuil-Bellay); Jean-Marie
Reclu in Montreuil; Domaine Armand David (his lovely
Vieilles Vignes 94); and Paul Filliatreau's Château Fouquet.

The Maison du Vin also stocks Saumur-Champigny from
some good winemakers: Château du Hureau, Château de Villeneuve, Domaine St-Vincent, but there are several others not
included, who are worth visiting. Coteaux de Saumur is the
sweet white wine of Saumur, and a good example is on sale
here: Les Rotissants 94 from Alain Rouiller's Domaine de la
Perruche (68F).

Where to buy at the vineyards
Domaine de la Cune
Chaintres, 49400 Dampierre
Tel: (02) 41 52 91 37
Winemakers: Jean and Jean-Luc Mary
Only a short drive from Saumur, hidden away in a beautiful
landscape of gentle rolling hills covered in vines and surround-
ed by woods, is the property of Jean-Luc Mary; an immaculate-
ly kept stone house, pretty with pink and white geraniums,
golden marigolds and purple petunias.

Across the courtyard from the house is the *cave*, taking you
out of the heat through a wooden door into the simple elegance
of a cool, tiled, sparsely furnished room, with white stone walls
and a timber ceiling.

Jean-Luc Mary is one of the new breed of winemakers, with a university degree in oenology – in his case from Bordeaux – one of only four major universities offering the course (the others are Montpellier, Dijon and Reims). Charming, knowledgeable and articulate, he takes the time to talk to you about his wines.

Saumur-Champigny is regarded as the best of Saumur, and the Caudalie selection is even more highly regarded. If you have never tasted a Saumur-Champigny before, then try Jean-Luc Mary's Saumur-Champigny Caudalie and you'll be totally enamoured of this *appellation*. His very fine 94 is 55F.

A different, less complex and slightly cheaper Champigny, is a most enjoyable Cuvée Charl'Anne, named after his children. The commitment of this family to quality is obvious, shining through at every turn, from the vineyards, to the house, to the wine itself.

Château de Villeneuve
49400 Souzay Champigny
Tel: (02) 41 51 14 04
Winemaker: J.P. Chevallier
The welcome at this château is always exceptionally warm. As you come up the driveway, stop just before the house, ring a bell loudly, then drive on to the tasting room and stores in a modern building past the house.

If you think you have tasted this wine in the UK, you may be mistaken. This is definitely not the same wine as Charles de Villeneuve, a wine sold as Ch. de Villeneuve in the UK.

The Saumur blanc 95 (30F), from vines that are, on average, 35 years old, is round and dry. The Saumur blanc Les Cormiers 95, from 100 per cent new wood, is particularly interesting, although it does cost more.

The red Saumur-Champigny Vieilles Vignes 95 will be available in 1997, deeply coloured and fruity, this wine will keep for many years. You might be prepared to pay more for his other Saumur-Champigny 95 Le Grand Clos.

Anjou and Saumur

What to see
Château d'Angers
boulevard de Général de Gaulle
49000 Angers
1 June–15 September 9–7; 16 September–15 April 9.30–12.30 and 2–6; 16 April–31 May 9–12.30 and 2–6.30. Closed 1 January, 1 November, 11 November and 25 December
This massive feudal fortress with its huge walls and 17 towers is home to one of the largest and most magnificent tapestries in the world, the *Tapisserie de l'Apocalypse.*

Galerie David d'Angers
33bis rue Toussaint, 49000 Angers
13 June–18 September daily 9.30–7; 19 September–12 June 10–12 and 2–6. Closed public holidays
In the Abbaye Toussaint, which has a glass roof, this collection of work by artist and sculptor David d'Angers is unique.

Château de Saumur
avenue du Dr Peton, 49400 Saumur
1 April–15 June and 16–30 September 9–12 and 2–6; 16 June–15 September 9–7; 1 October–31 March 10–12 and 2–5; closed Tuesday and 25 December–1 January
Including the Museum of Decorative Arts and the Museum of the Horse, this fairytale 14th-century château sits majestically above the town overlooking the Loire. Climb the Tour du Guet for the best view.

Ecole Nationale d'Equitation
Terrefort BP207, 49411 Saumur. Tel: 41 53 50 50
The Cadre Noir (cavalry) put on remarkable riding displays in July every year; they can be seen training at other times and guided visits are available. Phone for details.

Musée du Champignon

St-Hilaire-St-Florent, 49400 Saumur

15 February–15 November daily 10–7

The tufa stone used for many of the châteaux of this area is riddled with underground galleries which are ideal for storing wine and for growing mushrooms. The constant temperature and the darkness produce three quarters of the national output of *champignons de Paris*.

Abbaye Royale de Fontevraud

49590 Fontevraud l'Abbaye

1 June–mid-September 9-7; rest of the year 9.30–12.30 and 4–6; closed 1 January, 1 and 11 November and 25 December

This superb Abbey was built in the 12th century and is the resting place of royalty – Henry II, Eleanor of Aquitaine (his wife), Richard I Coeur de Lion, and Isabelle of Angoulême (his sister-in-law, the wife of King John).

Musée de la Vigne et du Vin d'Anjou

place des Vignerons

49750 St-Lambert-du-Lattay

This museum tells the story of winemaking from the first planting of the vines, and includes a tasting.

Wine festivals

Angers

Wine fair on the first weekend in January

Saumur

Wine fair on second weekend in February; Salon des Vins de Saumur on the first weekend in May

Chalonnes

Wine fair on the last weekend in February

St-Aubin-de-Luigné

Millésimés wine fair on 14 July

Montsoreau

Wine fair on the first Sunday in August

Château Fouquet/Domaine Filliatreau

Chaintres
49400 Dampierre
Tel: (02) 41 52 90 84
Open Saturday and Sunday, by appointment only

The Saumur rouge 94 from Château Fouquet is particularly good (37F), with a lovely deep red, slightly purple colour, and fairly tannic. For real depth, taste the more expensive Saumur-Champigny 93 Vieilles Vignes from Domaine Filliatreau. Although the welcome here is warm, and the surroundings congenial, you might prefer to taste and buy the wines at La Grande Vignolle, the Filliatreau's rather attractive, if slightly tourist-oriented, restaurant and tasting rooms carved into the *tuffeau* cliff high above the Loire at Turquant (tel: 41 38 16 44).

Château de Brézé

49260 Brézé
Tel: (02) 41 51 62 06
Winemaker: Le Comte de Colbert
Open until 4.30pm weekdays, weekends by appointment only

This elegant château has been in the same family since the 17th century. Although quite simple and modest, it still retains a certain formality and weightiness, rounded and sensual in its shapes. From a distance it looks rather squat, 'like a bouncy castle' was one unkind overheard remark, but all is explained as you discover the depth of its empty moat and the bottom half of the château. Park by the woods just through the gates, and stroll across the shaded grounds: idyllic with humming bees, birdsong and views across the valley.

The *cave* is in one of the old stone grain stores (the other was being used as a stunning venue for a wedding reception during my visit), and is a remarkably pleasant place to do some tasting. Their finest wine is the Coteaux de Saumur, a honeyed, luscious sweet wine made from the oldest vines, perfect with a delicate *pâté* or a light dessert. The best of the last few years, the 90, is still available at 68F. The Saumur blanc 94 is fresh and dry, and the Saumur rouge 93 very typical of this *appellation*. The Saumur Blanc de Blancs 93 is a splendid sparkling Saumur, aromatic, light and refreshing. All under 35F.

The Count also owns the attractive Château St-Ahon in Blanquefort, Bordeaux where he produces a Cru Bourgeois Haut-Médoc, the 93 superb value at 40F (in Bordeaux), 44F here in Brézé.

How to get there: If you are approaching the village of Brézé from the south, do not be misled by what looks like the only château in town and turn off the main road. Keep going into town, and there will be a sign to the château at the rue du Château, a narrow road, on your right. The sign is clearer if you are driving through Brézé from the north (from Saumur), and it's on your left, signposted just after the Mairie.

Château de Targé
49730 Parnay
Tel: (02) 41 38 11 50
Winemaker: Edouard Pisani-Ferry

An elegant small château perched high above the valley with splendid views, and Edouard Pisani-Ferry's welcome is warm and charming. Part of the house is built into the cliff face, or rather carved out of the tufa. Park in the gravelled courtyard, and walk up the steps to the tasting room. The simple elegance of the beamed ceiling, quarry-tiled floor and tapestries hanging on rough stone walls, is most conducive to tasting this fine wine. The Saumur-Champigny is very consistent: currently available is the 94 (38F), a good light summer wine with a lovely colour and fairly tannic. But if there is any left, taste the splendid 90, very round and complex. Minimum order is a case of 12 bottles, which is the normal unit of purchase for wine in France.

How to get there: As you come into Parnay from Saumur, pass a shop and when you see a small war memorial (opposite the Mairie on your left) turn right. From here, carry on up the hill, and the château is well signposted.

Cave des Vignerons de Saumur (Cave Co-opérative)
49260 St-Cyr-en-Bourg
Tel: (02) 41 83 43 23
Open Monday–Saturday 8–12 and 2–6 (7 in the summer)

The Co-opérative is signposted from all parts of the village, albeit with rather small signs. The drive out to St-Cyr is through a light industrial suburb. The warehouse and tasting room of the co-op are also fairly industrial, but this does not put off huge numbers of French customers who drive out here to load their cars with cases of wine. This is a well known winemakers' co-op with a reputation for consistently high quality.

Prices range from 32F for a sparkling Saumur Mousseux Brut to 37F for a Crémant de Loire Brut. The Saumur-Champigny 93, with its deep colour, lovely aroma and well balanced fruit is great value at 30F, deserving of its gold medal in Paris. The Saumur rouge 94 and Saumur blanc 94 are of high quality, and very good value at less than 20F. Prices are even lower if you buy by the litre to bottle yourself. If you are buying wine *en cubitainer*, you should bottle the wine as soon as possible. It may start to deteriorate after 48 hours, even though some suppliers may suggest you can keep it in cubitainers for up to seven days. Such advice may not always be sound. You could compromise and buy bag-in-a-box wine.

Drive-in tours (10F) of the 7.5 miles (12km) of cellars are available from Easter to the end of September, every half hour from 9.30–11 and from 2–4.30. The tour takes one hour including a tasting. There is an English speaking guide from June until the end of August.

Le Puy-Notre-Dame

Southwest of Saumur, in the centre of the wine-growing area, Le Puy-Notre-Dame has an interesting 13th-century church, built in the Angevin style which was introduced to this area by Henry II.

If you have time, try to visit the flourishing Vinothèque which offers tours in English.

Where to buy
Clos de l'Abbaye
49260 Le Puy-Notre-Dame
Tel: (02) 41 52 26 71
Winemakers: Henri and Jean-Luc Aupy

Jean-Luc Aupy is now the winemaker here. He started in the *caves* at the tender age of four by following his father around. He also enjoys relating that before his wife would agree to marry him, he had to prove his worth by making a wine worthy of her. She is now his partner in winemaking. These are up-and-coming winemakers, and you have the opportunity of buying before the rest of the world has even heard about them.

The 95 Saumur rouge tastes very promising, with a good colour and bouquet; the Saumur blanc is dry and substantial, probably best with fish in, say, a buttery sauce, rather than with oysters (both under 25F). His sparkling Saumur brut (34F) is certainly worth tasting; although *brut*, it's round and not too dry or hard. For those interested in bottling their own, both red and white are available at almost half the cost of bottled wine, but remember that 48 hours is the recommended time limit from time of buying to bottling.

How to get there: From Le Puy-Notre-Dame, take the D77 to Montreuil-Bellay. Driving down the hill, you'll see Clos de l'Abbaye on your right.

Château de Beauregard
2–4 rue St-Julien
49260 Le Puy-Notre-Dame
Tel: (02) 41 52 24 46
Winemaker: Philippe Gourdon

This is an elegant château with pleasant tasting rooms. The Saumur blanc 94, made entirely from Chenin Blanc, is pretty in colour, fresh and slightly floral; the rosé, a Cabernet de Saumur 94, is a delicate wine that should be drunk within a year (both around 25F). Their wines are served in several well known restaurants (Tour Eiffel, Pavillon Paul le Quéré in Angers, Les Délices du Château in Saumur) and are sold by the Wine Society in the UK.

How to get there: Take the D77 to Nueil out of Le Puy (turn left at the *boulangerie*). Just as you come out of the built-up area and see vineyards, turn sharp left. You'll see the château on your left; turn into the first gate.

Where to eat in Le Puy-Notre-Dame
Auberge de la Collégiale
rue des Hôtels
49260 Le Puy-Notre-Dame
Facing the church on rue des Hôtels, the slightly gloomy Auberge does its best to remain unnoticed, but if you gather the courage to brave the shut doors and go in, another closed door to the left opens to the restaurant with yellowing floral wallpaper, pink tablecloths and lace curtains.

Start with a plate of mussels, cured Bayonne ham, or a salad with *lardons* (small chunks of bacon). The main courses are hearty and simple, lamb chops with spinach, haricot beans and chips, or chicken casseroled with tarragon, followed by cheese and dessert (80F).

More fun at lunch is sitting at formica covered tables on wooden benches in the café eating the weekday *menu ouvrier* for less than 50F. Start perhaps with a plate of different salamis, ham and *pâté* served with *cornichons*, a simple main course like steak and chips, a few cheeses to choose from, and a no-choice dessert, probably ice cream served in its plastic tub.

Some very basic rooms with a shared bathroom are available upstairs. Number 4 looks out to the church and has a view of distant hills.

Saumur Mousseux (sparkling Saumur)
The champagne method was brought to this region by Jean Ackerman in 1811. The quality and success of the product obviously worried the makers of champagne enough to press the

authorities to ban the use of the term *méthode champenoise*. Now it's known as *méthode traditionelle*.

There are several well known makers of sparkling Saumur based in St-Hilaire-St-Florent, including Langlois-Château (3 rue Léopold Palustre, tel: 41 50 28 14, open all week in summer) who are owned by Bollinger. It is, however, their Saumur blanc, and indeed the rouge Vieilles Vignes, that has a reputation for outstanding quality.

You may have seen on sale in the UK the sparkling Saumur of Ackerman-Laurence (49400 St-Hilaire-St-Florent, tel: 41 50 25 33), whose Cuvée Jean-Baptiste is particularly palatable. Jean Ackerman takes the credit for introducing the *méthode champenoise* outside the Champagne district itself, when he moved here from Champagne in 1811 to found the firm. It is now used all over the world.

Where to buy Saumur Mousseux

Gratien et Meyer
Château de Beaulieu
49401 Saumur
Tel: (02) 41 51 01 54
Open every day including Sunday
Gratien and Meyer looms large over the road from Saumur to Chinon. The address misleads slightly, in that the wine is generally neither tasted nor sold at the château, but in an industrial building further up the driveway. Tours of the cellars, in English, are available, including a tasting, at a cost of 15F, refundable on purchases over 100F. Of some interest are their summer (May–Oct) winetasting classes at their wine school. Write (or fax 41 51 03 55) for full details and for reservations.

Gratien and Meyer also own a champagne house under the name of Gratien, which produces some outstanding champagne (try their unusual Paradis Brut). Here in Saumur, their flagship wine is the outstanding Saumur Cuvée Flammé (57F), but in a more reasonable price range are the Saumur Brut and Crémant de Loire.

125

Bouvet-Ladubay
rue de l'Abbaye
49400 St-Hilaire-St-Florent
Tel: (02) 41 50 11 12
Open on Sundays, and at lunchtime in summer

Bouvet-Ladubay has the prettiest of courtyards surrounded by elegant 19th-century buildings, constructed in the beautiful local stone. Bouvet-Ladubay is part of the Taittinger group and has a good pedigree, starting in these *caves* in 1851. There is a tour of the magnificent *caves* for 5F and wonderful candlelit concerts are occasionally held here. The elegant warehouse is also highly recommended. Wooden stairs lead to a private library of some 5000 labels dating from the 19th century – if you are particularly interested, you can make an appointment.

Bouvet-Ladubay's most admired sparkling wine, Trésor Brut, is made in limited quantities, aged in oak barrels, and the bottles are still turned by hand. As costly as champagne at 81F, this very fine and distinguished wine is made from Pinot de la Loire (80 per cent) and Chardonnay (20 per cent) under stringently controlled conditions. The Bouvet Brut costs 44F, Saphir Brut 51F. Total production is two million bottles from grapes which, although supplied by a large number of growers, are rigorously selected.

Where to stay in Saumur
Central Hôtel
23 rue Daille
49400 Saumur
Tel: (02) 41 51 05 78
Double room 250–300F
Parking 30F per day

What the hotel building lacks in character and personality it makes up for in comfort with immaculately clean, cool and restful rooms. Although in the heart of town, rooms are reasonably quiet, except for those overlooking the delivery area of the supermarket opposite. Room 30 may have small windows and

126

plumbing noises, but it's my favourite, spacious and tranquil. The breakfast room off the marble lobby is a bit cheerless and not a good place to sip tea whilst poring over maps discussing the day's itinerary. Nor is breakfast itself particularly memorable, but this hotel is good value, which is why so many business people stay here.

Hôtel Anne d'Anjou

32–33 quai Mayaud
49400 Saumur
Tel: (02) 41 67 30 30
Double room 410–550F, single 270F
Breakfast 48F, parking 50F per day
Closed 23 December–4 January

If you are looking for a building with character and style, the Anne d'Anjou is an 18th-century hotel on the banks of the Loire, looking out over the river at the front, and across a garden to the château at the back. A perfect hotel in the summer with its courtyard garden and terrace. Across the courtyard in a converted barn is the restaurant, Les Ménestrels, although, alas, menus start at 160F.

Most rooms have splendid views though they vary in size, and a couple of mansard rooms have little view (only skylights). The *chambres de style* are larger and more expensive – mine was certainly palatial with two toilets and two handbasins but otherwise a shade under-equipped for the price, and I did have some difficulty in discerning *le style*. Probably the best value in the hotel is room 214, which is exceptionally pleasant for a single room (a rarity in most hotels these days) with a view of the château.

Breakfast is a self-service buffet in the bar area. Tea drinkers will note that the water for the tea is not boiling.

The hotel feels rather like an apartment building with a polite and pleasant reception desk. The bar is tucked away behind the office and is not particularly sociable. There is a small lounge off the courtyard with an (unused) fireplace.

Best Western Loire Hotel
rue du Vieux Pont
49400 Saumur
Tel: (02) 41 67 22 42
Double room 490F (370F in winter)
Breakfast 48F

For a room with a postcard view of the château, cross the Pont Cessard to an island in the middle of the Loire, where the well-equipped rooms at this modern hotel look back to Saumur. A window table in the restaurant provides the ultimate view.

Where to eat in Saumur
Le Gambetta
12 rue Gambetta, 49400 Saumur
Tel: (02) 41 67 66 66
Menus from 75F

Not far from the centre, but out of the way, the Gambetta is often overlooked. I found it because Madame Dussert at the Central Hôtel insisted that I eat here. It's a pretty restaurant with high ceilings, wooden floor, wicker chairs and pastel fabric walls.

Wines from many of the best local winemakers are on the wine list: Saumur-Champigny 93 and 94 from Château de Chaintres, Château de Targé, Domaine de Filliatreau and Château de Villeneuve, most available in half-bottles (53–61F). Saumur rouge 92 comes from Château de Montreuil-Bellay, Langlois-Château and Saumur blanc 94 from Château de Villeneuve. You would also enjoy a Pouilly-Fumé 92 from de Ladoucette at Château du Nozet or a Sancerre 93 from Marnier-Lapostolle's Château de Sancerre.

The 75F menu offered, to start, poached eggs with haddock or a *gratin de cuisses de grenouilles tièdes* (a light and fluffy quiche) with *salade champêtre*. The *blanquette* of veal was served with brown rice and healthy vegetables. There were at least a dozen cheeses to choose from, followed by dessert. Absolutely charming service, deft cooking and great value.

La Croquière

42 rue Maréchal Leclerc
49400 Saumur
Tel: (02) 41 51 31 45
Closed Sunday evening and Monday
This restaurant is a good choice for a simple wholesome meal in unpretentious surroundings. It's well patronised by locals enjoying eating out with their families, not to mention, of course, the ubiquitous dogs. Come at lunch or early in the evening (before 8pm) for the best value menu at 80F.

A couple of doors away is **L'Escargot**, where you can enjoy a weekday lunch of an *entrée* and the *plat du jour* with a quarter litre of wine for 59F.

Les Chandelles

71 rue St-Nicolas
49400 Saumur
Tel: (02) 41 67 20 40
Closed Thursday evening and Wednesday (except in summer); and all of March. Menus from 88F
Les Chandelles is in a convenient location on a lively street. In the summer it's pleasant to sit at a table on the pavement. The 88F menu may offer a *salade de moules au safran et coeur de laitue* to start, followed by grilled beef *à la croque*, and then cheese or dessert. A no-choice 100F menu includes a welcome *kir*, and offers fairly rich traditional cooking.

Hôtel Cristal

10–12 place de la République
49400 Saumur
This is the liveliest spot in town, as close to left-bank Paris as you'll get in a small provincial city. The café is jammed with Saumur's young *monde*, smoke, music and conversation. However, late night spots are prone to the dictates of fast changing fashion, so what was 'in' might be very much 'out' a year later. A good late night spot for a drink on the pavement.

Where to stay outside Saumur

Hôtel Le Bussy
49730 Montsoreau
Tel: (02) 41 51 70 18
Closed during winter
Double room 320–350F

The hotel is perched high above the Loire on a quiet road just behind the castle of Montsoreau. Rooms are timber beamed and simply but comfortably furnished. Those with the finest views of the castle and the Loire are on the first floor. Room 12 offers two double beds, a bath and a small dining table by a window with a view. The lobby and breakfast area are warm and welcoming with exposed stone walls, beams and a flag-stone floor. The reception desk is down the hill at the Restaurant Diane de Méridor. Across the street there is secure private parking, beyond which is the hotel's private garden which looks onto the castle grounds and river.

Hôtel Restaurant Diane de Méridor
49730 Montsoreau
Tel: (02) 41 51 70 18
Closed in winter
Double room 150F

By the busy riverside road from Saumur to Chinon, this is a restaurant with rooms (three) and the reception desk for the quieter and more elegant Hôtel Le Bussy up the hill. If you don't mind sharing the toilets used by the restaurant's many customers, can live with late 60s décor and want a cheap room with a view of fishermen setting out in the early morning, then room 2 should be suitable. Room 4 at the rear, which looks straight into another building across the narrow street, will probably be cooler in the summer, and offers two double beds and more space. Breakfast, 38F per person, is not as generous as you might expect from a restaurant with rooms. A basic budget hotel, but some charges for extras are five star.

Hôtel La Croix Blanche

place Plantagenets, 49590 Fontevraud
Tel: (02) 41 51 71 1
Double room 300F
Closed November and January

At the crossroads of wars, civilisations, religions and trade, Fontevraud is one of the most fascinating towns in the region (see page 119). La Croix Blanche is a comfortable hotel built around a sunny courtyard, with potted flowers, white garden chairs and shaded tables. There is good parking at the rear.

The restaurant is uncluttered and modern. A vegetarian menu (97F) is a most welcome addition to the 100F menu, which offers, for example, to start a *salade de boudin* with apples or a *terrine de lapin*. Main courses include, depending on season, of course, such delights as guinea fowl with mushrooms or *sauté de biche*, followed by cheese and dessert.

Where to eat in Fontevraud

Café-Bar La Croix Blanche

place Plantagenets
49590 Fontevraud
Tel: (02) 41 51 71 11
Closed November and January

A good spot for a lunchtime *apéritif* is the traditional café-bar at the front of the Hôtel La Croix Blanche, with wicker chairs and tables on the pavement. Cyclists, motorists, tourists and locals stop here for a coffee, beer or a sandwich. If you're missing a good cup of tea, there's an excellent selection at the *salon de thé* next door to the Hôtel.

La Licorne

allée Ste-Catherine
49590 Fontevraud
Tel: (02) 41 51 72 49

For a full lunch, try La Licorne. It offers a good value, no-choice 110F three course *menu.*

131

Touraine

CHINON

The town of Chinon is a remarkably charming and pretty town, overlooking the River Vienne and backed by its historic castle. The vineyards in this *appellation* are on the left bank of the Loire and on both banks of the Vienne, a beautiful part of the Loire Valley between Tours and Saumur.

The wine, mainly a splendid ruby red made from Cabernet Franc, is fast growing in stature, and ranges from light and fruity (from vineyards on the slightly sandy soil near the Vienne) to quite intense in flavour (from vineyards on the *tuffeau*). This wine can generally be drunk after a year, but the best wines from the best vintages (such as 89, 90 and 95) will keep, and indeed improve, over many years.

Where to buy wine
Vignoble de la Poêlerie
37220 Panzoult
(7.5 miles/12km east of Chinon)
Tel: (02) 47 58 53 16
Winemakers: Guy and François Caillé
Open all week including Sunday
If you own a caravan and enjoy a chilled glass of wine in the sun on a summer's day, this is the ultimate site for you. La Poêlerie is a working farm and vineyard with 15 camping and caravan sites. The camping ground is bordered by a field of wheat on one side, with a shady grove at the far end. Very rural and as peaceful as a working farm can be.

A simple summer wine, the Caillé's Chinon rosé 95 is perfect for drinking chilled on a hot day – it's crisp, clean and refreshing, a fragrant wine with a gorgeous colour, a treat for rosé lovers. This is a wine to drink with friends on a picnic – dangle it in the river to keep it cool.

The Chinon Cuvée Vignoble de la Poêlerie 95 is a light quaffing wine and available at almost half the price *en vrac* for home bottling. The Chinon Cuvée Vieilles Vignes 93 is long and well balanced. All at under 30F a bottle.

How to get there: As you drive into Panzoult from Cravant-les-Coteaux, turn right (towards the River Vienne), through a hamlet called Le Marais, then take a right following the signs marked *Camping*.

Domaine de la Perrière

Cravant-les-Coteaux
37500 Chinon
Tel: (02) 47 93 15 99
Winemakers: Jean and Christophe Baudry

You can taste the wines of Domaine de la Perrière in two places: the main business premises are on the D21 out of Chinon towards Cravant-les-Coteaux. Just before you reach the village of Cravant, you'll see a sign for Bernard Baudry (who has a separate business), followed by one for Jean and Christophe Baudry of Domaine de la Perrière. Overlooking the courtyard and buildings on your left is a stone house set up high against a steep wooded hillside. Park across the road behind the lavender bushes.

The tasting room, part of the *caves*, is an old dwelling with a huge wooden table and fireplace. If there is nobody here, go on to the Domaine itself. Drive into Cravant, turn right onto the D44, then left onto the D8 at the River Vienne. The entrance to the Domaine is clearly marked by two fir trees on your left. The long driveway leads to a courtyard and simple white shuttered house.

The Chinon rouge 94 (30F) is a well balanced wine, has a lovely colour, and would make a delicious lunchtime wine, especially with something like a lamb dish. You might also enjoy the Chinon rosé 94, quite dry and very pleasant drinking (25F). Give the Chinon Cuvée Vieilles Vignes 93 more time in the bottle (40F). Good value.

133

Couly-Dutheil
12 rue Diderot
37500 Chinon
Tel: (02) 47 93 05 94

Couly-Dutheil is one of the leading names in Chinon, as much a result of marketing as of skilled winemaking. The marketing helps support prices higher than most; they let it be known that their wines are served in the restaurants of France's best known chefs such as Boyer in Reims, Roger Vergé in Mougins and Jean Bardet in Tours.

The main office, tasting room and warehouse is less than a minute's drive from the Hôtel Diderot (see below). Least expensive of their wines at 33F is Chinon les Gravières 94, a light, soft wine that can be drunk young with white meat and fish. The Chinon 94 Domaine René Couly (36F) is slightly rounder, and a wine that can also be drunk young. One of their finest wines is the Chinon Clos de l'Echo, from the vineyard within the city walls that once belonged to the Rabelais family, whose best vintage is the 89 followed by the 90.

During the summer, Couly-Dutheil operate a tasting room and sales counter on the hill leading out of Chinon opposite the castle walls. At the bottom of the same hill, you'll find the shop, **Au Vieux Marché** (tel: 47 93 04 10), overlooking the Vienne on the road to Bourgueil. This is open at weekends, although loading your car involves crossing a rather busy road.

Where to eat near the vineyards
Bar-Tabac La Sybille
37220 Panzoult
7.5 miles (12km) east of Chinon
Restaurant open weekdays only; closed two weeks in August

This simple establishment has a small bar with five tables (and a glowing fire in winter) and a restaurant with seven tables. It offers a basic four course *menu ouvrier* including wine for 55F. The wine is not Chinon, for that you'll need to buy a half-bottle for 30F.

134

Where to stay in Chinon
Hôtel Diderot
4 rue Buffon
37500 Chinon
Tel: (02) 47 93 18 87
Closed over Christmas
Double room 280–380F

This hotel is an oasis of calm a few minutes' walk from the centre of town. The Diderot is an elegant shuttered townhouse overlooking a walled and gated courtyard. No view of the river, but then no view of tourist buses either.

Rooms vary enormously in style: room 5 is spacious and has lots of character with wood floors, double bed with a huge headboard, and two large windows overlooking the courtyard. Room 3 is another large room looking out to the courtyard but with extra beds, an armchair and a desk. Some of the rooms at the rear look out across a narrow street to a garden wall, but I was happy in number 8, a pleasant and quiet room.

A simple breakfast is served in the dining room whose crackling fire offers welcome warmth in winter and on chilly autumn and spring mornings. Good parking in the courtyard, and charmingly run by Cypriot owner Theo Kazamias and his staff.

Where to eat in Chinon
L'Océanic
13 rue Rabelais
37500 Chinon
Tel: (02) 47 93 44 55
Closed Sunday evening, Monday, all of January, one week in June and one week in September or October
Menu 98F

The small Océanic has twelve tables that are always filled with a contented clientele. The interior is plain and restful, with pale walls and fresh flowers on every table.

The 98F menu consists of an *amuse-gueule*, and perhaps a

135

tartare of ocean trout, oysters or a *chausson de pétoncles* with garlic sauce to start. Main courses are all fish, including perhaps a *fricassée* of calamari or a *savarin* of pike in a langoustine sauce. Three breads – walnut, poppy seed and country – are served with cheese, followed by dessert, maybe *nougat* in a *crème anglaise*.

In addition to a rather daring brush with foreign winemakers – proudly announcing a Vin d'Australie from David Wynn at Eden Ridge 92 – the wine list offers a good selection of Loire wines, many available in half-bottles. There is a choice of 30 Chinons from 70F. Many of the wines come from local vineyards which you'll be able to visit, such as Domaine de la Perrière, Couly-Dutheil, Château de Ligré and Château de la Grille. A Saumur blanc from Château de Villeneuve would be perfect with fish. Luc Bizard's elegant Savennières *demi-sec* 89 from Château d'Epire would be beautiful with dessert.

Service is solicitous but discreet, the staff professional but personal.

Au Plaisir Gourmand

2 rue Parmentier
37500 Chinon
Tel: (02) 47 93 20 48
Closed Sunday evening and Monday; also mid-January to mid-February
Menu 175F (no smoking)
Impossible to get into without a reservation during the season, Jean-Claude Rigollet's highly-praised restaurant is in a gorgeous mediaeval building near the river, entered through a courtyard. Décor is plush mediaeval, with tapestries on the bare stone walls (and on the chairs), sombre paintings of food, and heavy linen and silver on the tables.

The 175F menu, *La Cuisine du Terroir*, offers a four course meal with regional specialities, such as *sandre de Loire*, a river fish. Deft and inspired cooking is evident from lightly grilled, slightly spicy, tender langoustine served on a salad of artichoke

136

hearts, avocado, lamb's lettuce, *frisée* and baby beans.

The wine list has a superb range of Chinons dating back to 1947, many from the splendid years of 89 and 90, and includes wine from Monsieur Rigollet's own vineyard. Couly-Dutheil's Les Gravières 94 is one of the more modestly priced wines here at 90F.

A warm welcome from Monsieur Rigollet himself was replaced by rather stern and smile-free service, and I missed the pampering you would normally expect in a restaurant of this calibre.

Where to stay out of town
Manoir de Montour

37420 Montour (near Beaumont-en-Véron)

Tel: (02) 47 58 43 76

Double room 350F (including breakfast)

Elegant and imposing, this stone house is also fading and slightly worn. The garden, too, is pretty but a bit scruffy, and is a wonderful place to sit outside in the summer in the shade of a tree, reading and listening to birdsong. This is not an immaculately run hotel; it's a slightly bohemian home, which some of you will love.

The living room décor is distressed blue wash on timber frames, stone floor and fireplace, a lovely wooden table, *chaises longues*, the room dominated by a huge bunch of dried flowers and leaves in front of a vast mirror.

Up some wooden stairs, there are three rooms, the most dramatic being *La Chambre Louis XIII*, whose face glowers from a portrait that hangs in the room. The floor is tiled, the ceiling heavily beamed, the furniture partly 17th century with a four-poster bed and a stunning table.

How to get there: Take the D749 west out of Chinon (in the direction of Avoine or Bourgueil). At Coulaine, about 3 miles (5km) from Chinon, take a left off the main road towards Savigny-en-Véron. The first village you drive into is Montour and you can't miss the Manoir.

137

TOURAINE-AZAY-LE-RIDEAU

This is a tiny *appellation,* within Touraine, with approximately 124 acres (50ha) of vines, producing only white and rosé wines. Its vineyards surround the charming town of Azay-le-Rideau, whose magical château is an essential destination (see **What to see**, page 148).

Where to buy

During the summer months, you can taste and buy wine from local producers at a small **Maison du Vin** just off the town square in Azay-le-Rideau.

The largest producer, owned by Deutz of Champagne, is **Château de l'Aulée** (route de Tours, tel: 02 47 45 40 58) which offers tastings and cellar tours.

Robert Denis
11 rue de la Rabière
La Chapelle-St-Blaise
37190 Azay-le-Rideau
Tel: (02) 47 45 46 57
Winemaker: Robert Denis

A modest man, Robert Denis produces some of the best examples of this small *appellation.* 1990 was one of the finest vintages in the last 25 years, so if you can, taste the Touraine-Azay-le-Rideau blanc 90, a gently dry wine with the prettiest straw colour, and the blanc moelleux 90.

The 93 blanc sec is a lovely summer wine, certainly of interest to those of you visiting Azay-le-Rideau (28F). His rosé sec 93 is soft and inviting (35F).

How to get there: Leave the centre of Azay-le-Rideau heading south across the River Indre. La Chapelle-St-Blaise is on the south bank. As you drive up the main road, just after the restaurant **L'Automate Gourmande** (see below), take a left fork up a narrow road which goes up the hill.

Where to stay near Touraine-Azay-le-Rideau
La Prieuré Ste-Anne
10 rue Chaude
37510 Savonnières
Tel: (02) 47 50 03 26
Double room 310F (including breakfast)
Open mid-March to October
This 15th-century building has taken 30 years to restore, and it has been a labour of love by the Caré family.

There is a suite of two rooms which offers by far the best value of the private bed and breakfast establishments, and this is often booked weeks ahead. Access to the suite is by an external staircase from the walled courtyard. The walls are bare stone, and the room is austere, elegant and subtly lit with a large antique weaving loom and a double bed. The adjoining room is also beamed, shuttered and stone floored, with twin beds, a child's bed, a good table and a desk. You pass through a hall, past a 17th-century staircase with an original *colombage* wall, to the bathroom, which is modern and completely out of keeping.

Breakfast is served downstairs at a table seating ten, in a room with stone walls covered by tapestries, beams, beautiful wooden furniture and a huge open fireplace used on cold nights and mornings. Madame Caré is proud of her house, and genuinely pleased to be sharing the pleasure of the restoration with her guests.

Château le Gerfaut
37190 Azay-le-Rideau
Tel: (02) 47 45 40 16
Open April to October
Double room 490F (including breakfast)
Home of the Marquis de Chenerilles and run by the very charming Madame Salles. There are six bedrooms but if you are staying for a week, the best value accommodation is an

apartment for a family or three couples (2500F per week, extra 300F in July and August, available all year). There are three double bedrooms, one of which has two double beds, parquet floors, a desk and splendid views to the front of the house.

Where to eat in Azay-le-Rideau
L'Aigle d'Or
10 rue Adélaide-Riche
37190 Azay-le-Rideau
Tel: (02) 47 45 24 58
Menus from 90F
Closed Sunday evening, Tuesday evening (low season), Wednesday; also most of December and February
Best value lunch in Azay-le-Rideau for 90F, with a respectable Loire wine list.

Grand Monarque
3 place de la République
37190 Azay-le-Rideau
Tel: (02) 47 45 40 08
Closed Monday lunchtime, Thursday (out of season); mid-December to the end of January
Menus from 90F
For summer outdoor eating and for sipping an *apéritif*, the characterful Grand Monarque has a shady courtyard, with lunches from 90F.

L'Automate Gourmande
1 rue Parc
La Chapelle-St-Blaise
37190 Azay-le-Rideau
Tel: (02) 47 45 39 07
Menus from 90F
For regional cooking, head south from Azay-le-Rideau, across the river to this restaurant which offers a four-course weekday lunch for 90F.

TOURS

Surrounded by such stunning countryside, with beautiful châteaux, excellent vineyards, and traditional *auberges* and restaurants on the Loire, Tours may hold little attraction for some travellers, because, interesting though it can be, it is nevertheless a busy provincial city. But having said that, Tours is magnificently sited with both the rivers Loire and Cher running through its heart, and the wide boulevards and light stone buildings give the city a particularly airy feel.

If you do stop in Tours, ignore reports from travel writers and holidaymakers that it's impossible to find your way around the city and that parking is a nightmare. A likely cause for this view is that most drivers will have been driving for a few hours from the coast, will be tired and in need of a break just as they are approaching Tours, and their navigator is fast asleep. At this point drivers expect signposting that is better than anywhere else, and it isn't. All you'll need is an alert passenger to navigate, a map of the city, to know which hotel you want and head straight there.

To orientate yourself, you need to know the location of four landmarks: the river, the cathedral, the old town (place Plumereau) and the railway station. The river runs through the north of Tours from east to west. The rue Nationale is the major street that runs from south to north through the centre of Tours, crossing the river at Pont Wilson. The cathedral (St-Gatien), the château and the Musée des Beaux-Arts are east of rue Nationale and just south of the river. To the west (and just south of the river) is place Plumereau, at the heart of the pedestrian precinct of the old town. This often confuses travellers who expect a cathedral to be at the heart of the mediaeval town.

The tourist information office is in Jean Nouvel's striking new building on boulevard Heurteloup opposite the railway station: you can't miss this sleek building whose awning protrudes over part of the street.

Where to buy in town

There are a large number of very good vineyards only a short drive from Tours where the wine will be much less expensive than in town. But if you are waiting for a train, or staying at the nearby Hôtel Moderne, you might enjoy a brief visit to André Vaillant's **Vinothèque de Tours** (16 rue Michelet, tel: 02 47 64 75 27). This small shop caters to a clientele that appreciates his fine wines. The champagne section will give you an idea of what his customers buy: Billecart-Salmon, Bollinger, Taittinger, Roederer, Krug and Dom Pérignon.

Chinon from the splendid vineyard of Olga Raffault in Savigny features strongly. Best examples, and not easy to find any longer, are a Chinon 90 and an 89 Les Picasses, as well as several vintages of Selection Vinothèque from the same winemaker; 1990, 1992 and 1994 at under 45F. A Vouvray 90 from Huet, a *moelleux* Le Haut Lieu at 100F is a superb wine, a great year from one of Vouvray's best winemakers.

The selection of Sancerres and Pouilly-Fumés is limited but well chosen, especially the Sancerre rouge 93 from Vacheron and the blanc 94. The 350 fine wines and spirits include an interesting *eau-de-vie* Poire William by Etienne Brana, St-Jean Pied de Port in the 200F plus bracket.

Where to stay in Tours
Hôtel Moderne
1 et 3 rue Victor-Laloux
37000 Tours
Tel: (02) 47 05 32 81
Open all year
Double room 200F (with shared bathroom), otherwise 290F
This is where to stay in Tours if you're looking for somewhere cheap, easy to find, easy to park, as central as you could wish, yet in a side street that makes it remarkably quiet. The hotel is adequately comfortable, unpretentious and welcoming. Best value are the garret rooms (up several flights of stairs; beware

there's no lift) with shared toilet, but own showers and basins. Room 26 has a double bed and overlooks the courtyard. Rooms on the middle floor have their own (noisy vacuum) loos, and walls could be thicker; largest is room 8 with its own fridge, essential for serious wine tasters.

The parking spaces immediately outside the Hôtel Moderne are both free and without time limit. There are also a few paying spaces in the next street, with no time limit. For more secure parking, there is a garage at 6 boulevard Heurteloup, next to the Mairie. The cost is not excessive for a day or so and your car is parked for you. The garage is closed from 8.30pm to 7am, and on Sundays and public holidays.

Hôtel Mirabeau

89bis boulevard Heurteloup
37000 Tours
Tel: (02) 47 05 24 60
Open all year
Double room 290F

Don't be put off by the Mirabeau's location on busy boulevard Heurteloup: it makes it easy to find, there's plenty of free parking right outside the hotel and front rooms are double-glazed. The décor and lighting are a little austere, but if you're looking for space, large rooms and high ceilings, this is the place. Ground floor rooms and a lift are a real bonus if you have a lot of luggage. A lock-up garage costs 35F per night.

Jean Bardet (Relais et Châteaux)

57 rue Groison
37100 Tours
Tel: (02) 47 41 41 11
Open all year
Double rooms 750–1900F

One of the finest (and most expensive) restaurants in France is here in Tours. Attached to it is a small luxury hotel, one most of us can only dream of. It's situated north of the river in Tours, so there's no need to drive into town; just turn off the main road, up a crunchy gravel driveway, be shown your room, someone will bring up your luggage, leaving you free to flop into a vast bubble bath with an ice-cold drink from the fridge. A perfect way to start a holiday.

The 19th-century mansion is set in a large romantic garden (known as a *parc* in French), with its tree-lined avenues, ponds, greenhouse and beautiful contemporary sculpture, overlooked by the restaurant and most of the rooms. Of course, the rooms are comfortable, and the marble bathrooms have deep bathtubs. Savour the beautifully presented breakfast (albeit at 120F) in the conservatory or in summer on your balcony.

Where to eat in Tours
Le Singe Vert
5 rue Marceau
37000 Tours
Tel: (02) 47 61 50 10
Closed Sunday
Lunch from 65F, evening menus from 94F

This is the best value restaurant in Tours, and also my favourite. Its tiled floor, bare wooden tables and chairs, large mirrors and old enamelled advertisements (from chocolate to cognac) lining the walls, may, in a moment of vinous confusion, look like a *Café Rouge* or *Dôme*, but that's where the similarities end.

After a day of tasting Vouvray, I sat down and ordered a beer. The enthusiastic patron looked at me wistfully, "*Pas de vin? Quel dommage!*". And quite right he was too, with virtually every wine from the good Loire list, such as Saumur from Filliatreau, Chinon from Jean-Claude Baudry's Domaine de la Perrière and Vouvray from Domaine des Perruches, available by the glass.

On a cold and wet winter evening, this place was packed with locals, a lively crowd in jeans and checked shirts. After a vast and delicious *salade du pêcheur* (*filet julienne flambée*, salmon, prawns and strips of smoked salmon on tartly dressed salad leaves), my lamb chops arrived virtually *bleu*. On their return from the kitchen more thoroughly grilled, another huge chop had been added to my plate. I couldn't possibly manage the dessert on the 94F menu. How many other restaurateurs would have the generosity to deduct the cost of my beer from the bill as a result? No wonder customers flock back to this oasis.

The lunchtime menu is 72F, offering, for example, *terrine de lapin* or a *salade aux foies de volailles* to start, a main course of *andouillette à la moutarde*, *rognons blancs en persillade* or tripe for the brave, followed by dessert. Two courses would be more than enough for some at only 65F. Terrific value.

Tourangelle
23 rue de Commerce
37000 Tours
Tel: (02) 47 05 71 21
Closed Sunday evening and Monday
Menus from 90F
For a more formal and elegant atmosphere, try the Tourangelle around the corner from Le Singe Vert. The 90F lunchtime menu (Tuesday to Saturday) is good value. Start perhaps with a *salade de magret de canard avec copeaux de foie gras*, followed by a *filet mignon de porc* with a paprika sauce, and perhaps a *crème brulée* with vanilla and *lait de chèvre* for dessert.

Le Canotier
6 rue des Fusillés
37000 Tours
Tel: (02) 47 61 85 81
Closed Sunday, Monday lunchtime and public holidays
Around one more corner you'll come to Sophie Bardet's modern minimalist *Le Canotier*. Yes, indeed, another member of this awesome culinary clan: Sophie is Jean Bardet's daughter. She serves a 90F two course menu with a glass of wine in the evenings as well as at lunchtime.

145

Jean Bardet

57 rue Groison

37100 Tours

Tel: (02) 47 41 41 11

Closed Sunday evening and Monday in winter; Monday lunchtime in summer

Vegetarian menu 250F; Sunday menu 450F including wine; main menu 750F

If you really want to splash out and celebrate, visit Jean Bardet, one of the most renowned chefs in France. This is probably the most expensive restaurant in the Loire. Vegetarians will be thrilled to find a vegetarian menu in such a fine restaurant, with all the vegetables grown and freshly picked from the garden and greenhouse. You'll need to save up for the other main menus but you'll get a perfect meal with impeccable service – a sublime experience.

Bardet makes magic in the kitchen, creating dishes so light, so delicious, with so many extraordinary flavours, that you might be tempted to come back one day and do a cooking course with him.

The wine list is a Loire paradise. Whilst there are some serious bordeaux here, it's the range of Montlouis and Vouvrays that is really interesting. The list of Vouvrays goes as far back as 1919 with wines from the best winemakers in the region. Even the list of Chinons is impressive (29 in all), but most useful is the huge range of half-bottles from the Loire.

The staff are friendly and very helpful, offering advice on the best wines to have (and that includes the least expensive wines) and explanations about the food.

There are no prejudices in this house: just as vegetarians have a place, so do smokers, who can relax without comment in the clubby cigar room and enjoy themselves with a glass of old Armagnac, Cognac or Calvados.

Where to drink in Tours

The small zinc bar at **Le Singe Vert** (see page 144).

VOUVRAY

Although Vouvray is probably best known in the UK for its sparkling wine, this *appellation* produces the full gamut of white wines (from dry to *liquoreux*) as well as two degrees of sparkling wine, *pétillant* and *mousseux*. The wine is made from the Chenin Blanc grape, which thrives in local soil conditions. The price range for Vouvray is very broad.

Where to buy wine

For the best value in Vouvray, drive through Vouvray itself to the village of **Vernou-sur-Brenne**. As you enter the village turn right for rue Neuve, which is well signposted (turning left will bring you to the Hostellerie les Perce-Neige, see below). The sign at 51 rue Neuve, 'C. Métivier', is in fact for **Eliane Métivier** and her son Vincent (tel: 02 47 52 01 95). The location may be suburban, but her wine is inspired. When her *moelleux* 95 is released, try it, buy it and put it in your cellar. Its lineage is one of superb *moelleux*, rich, lush yet elegant. In the meantime, enjoy her light Vouvray sec 93 and fruity sparkling Vouvray. Terrific value at less than 30F.

Several of our recommended vineyards in Vouvray happen to create an easy **circular tour**.

Drive along the Loire to **Vouvray**. At the lights turn left, driving along the D47 to the edge of the town. On your right you'll see **Château Gaudrelle**, 87 route de Monnaie (tel: 02 47 52 67 50, winemaker Alexandre Monmousseau). You might not appreciate the less than welcoming sign 'Please ring the bell. We sell not less than six bottles' but you'll certainly appreciate the Vouvray sec 93 and 94.

Crossing over to La Vallée Coquette, you might drive past two rather scruffy yards belonging to two rather good wine-makers, **Marc et Laurent Maillet** (tel: 47 52 76 46) at number 101, and **Daniel Jarry** (tel: 02 47 52 78 75) at number 99, after which there is a sign indicating the Auberge La Cave Martin,

Touraine

What to see

Château de Chinon
November–March 9–12 and 2–5; March–September 9–6 (7 in July and August, 5 in October)
There has been a castle here since the 11th century; Henry II and Richard Coeur de Lion both died here, King John married Isabelle d'Angoulême here, Joan of Arc stayed in the château – there is a museum devoted to her life in the Clocktower.

Musée Animé du Vin et de la Tonnellerie
12 rue Voltaire, 37500 Chinon
April–September 10–6
An outstanding collection of artefacts used in the 19th century for the cultivation and harvesting of grapes, winemaking and barrel making. There are animated models and winetastings.

Château d'Azay-le-Rideau
37190 Azay-le-Rideau
March–June, September–October 9.30–6; July and August 9–7; November–February 9.30–12.30 and 2–5.30. Closed 1 May, 1 and 11 November, 25 December
This beautiful 16th-century château is built on piles over water and the reflections make the *son et lumière* (sound and light) performances in the summer particularly memorable.

Cathédrale St-Gatien
37000 Tours
Summer 8.30–12 and 2–8; winter 8.30–12 and 2–7.30
Many of the superb stained glass windows date from the 13th century, and one of the chapels has the tomb of Charles VIII's children. The lovely Renaissance carving in the adjoining choir school dates from 1440.

Musée des Vins de Touraine
16 rue Nationale, 37000 Tours
Daily except Tuesday 9–12 and 2–5 (6 in April–September)
In the 13th-century wine cellars of the Abbey of St-Julien, the displays explain the relationship between wine and mythology, religion, family and social rituals, and health, as well as describing vine culture and winemaking.

Château de Langeais
37130 Langeais
April–September 9–6.30; July and August 9–7; October 9–12 and 2–6.30; November–March 9–12 and 2–5
Closed Christmas Day
This 15th-century fortress château is reached by way of a drawbridge which operates daily at 10 and 4. The furnishings are outstanding, particularly a collection of Flemish and Aubusson tapestries.

Château de Villandry
37510 Villandry
Daily 9–dusk
The recreated Renaissance gardens of this 16th-century château have an international reputation with terraces on three levels – the kitchen gardens, the ornamental gardens and at the highest level the water gardens. The château was one of the last great Renaissance castles to be built along the banks of the Loire.

Château de Cheverny
41700 Cheverny
Daily 9.30–12 and 2.15–5 (5.30 in March; 6.30 in April and May; 6.45 June–September)
Non-guided visits allow you to wander at will through this late Renaissance château, completed in 1634. Kennels house a pack of some 70 hounds and the trophy room has over 2,000 stag antlers.

Château de Chambord
October–March 9.30–12.15 and 2–5.15 (6.15 April–September, 7.15 July, August); closed some public holidays
'The epitome of all that human artifice can create,' so the Emperor Charles V described the Château of Chambord.

Château de Chenonceaux
Daily 9–dusk
Diane de Poitiers created the beautiful formal gardens and the galleried bridge over the river Cher. There is a waxworks museum here, a tearoom and restaurant, and you can taste and buy the excellent red, white and rosé wines produced on the estate.

Wine festivals and fairs
Amboise
Easter wine fair; wine fair on 15 August
Vouvray
Wine festival on last Saturday in January; wine fair 15 August
Bourgueil
Wine festival on the first weekend in February; Easter wine fair
Tours-Fondettes
Wine fair on second Saturday in February
Azay-le-Rideau
Wine fair on the last Saturday in February
Chinon
Wine fair on the second Saturday in March
Onzain
Wine fair on the second Saturday after Easter
Panzoult
Touraine wine fair on 1 May
Meusnes
Easter wine fair
Thésée
Touraine wine fair on the first Saturday in July
Montlouis
Wine fair on 15 August

110 yards (100m) to the right (see **Where to eat** below). Continue to number 64 for **Domaine de la Fontainerie** (winemaker Catherine Dhoye-Déruet, tel: 47 52 67 92) for a Vouvray sec 93 at 33F.

The **Cave des Producteurs** (tel: 02 47 52 75 03) is at number 38. Their wine may not be renowned, but the staff are friendly, cheerful and helpful. Worth dropping into for a tasting. There are plenty of French customers here. The Vouvray sec 94 (28F), sparkling Vouvray, *pétillant* or *méthode traditionelle* at 32F, and from the great years of 89 and 90, an 89 *demi-sec* and *moelleux* 90 Réserve Producteurs.

Jean-Pierre Laisement (tel: 02 47 52 74 47) is at numbers 15 and 22. His flowery Vouvray sec 94 (winner of a bronze medal in Mâcon in 95) and demi-sec 93 (bronze medallist in Angers in 95) epitomize wines that are perfectly matched to food. This year's Vouvray *mousseux brut* is particularly pleasing (all at around 30F). The more expensive sweet (*moelleux*) Vouvray 90 is stunning with *foie gras* or dessert .

J.C. Aubert at number 10 (tel: 02 47 52 71 03) is another winemaker producing quality Vouvray, particularly a Vouvray sec 93 and a demi-sec 94, both at 30F. Of his *moelleux*, go for the 90 Réserve Tris at 70F.

Where to stay
Hostellerie les Perce-Neige
32710 Vernou-sur-Brenne (near Vouvray)
Closed mid-January to early February and one week in October
Double room 280F
On the main road through Vernou, this hotel has always appealed to me, with its gravel drive, rambling and rather dishevelled gardens, the main building white-shuttered and creeper clad, but until its recent change of ownership the service was simply not up to it. The new owners are working hard and on this basis it's worth investigating.

You'll have to choose between a view and romance, as rooms overlooking the garden only have twin beds. In summer, have an *apéritif* outside on the terrace before eating in the restaurant. It's worthwhile taking *demi-pension* terms for at least one night (440F for two), a substantial saving on the total cost of a room plus breakfast and dinner.

Typical of the 98F menu was a starter of pheasant pâté with pistachios and an onion *confiture*, *boudin blanc* stuffed with apples as the main course, cheese and dessert.

There is a nice wine list, but there is little need to order from it, given that the house wine is an excellent inexpensive Chinon from Pierre Ferrand's Château de Ligré.

Where to eat in and near Vouvray
Auberge La Cave Martin
66 La Vallée Coquette
37210 Vouvray
Tel: (02) 47 52 62 18
Closed Sunday evening, Monday and all of January
Carved into the rock, this restaurant certainly has a charm of its own, with a log fire burning in cooler weather. There are only ten tables with yellow and faded red tablecloths.

A simple 62F lunchtime menu (Tuesday to Saturday) offers, for example, a salad, a *bavette poêlée à l'échalotte*, and dessert, as well as a quarter carafe of wine – not a bad AOC Chinon from Pierre Ferrand. Alternatively, if you haven't already done so at the vineyards themselves, you might want to try a Vouvray from Laisement, Château Gaudrelle or Château Moncontour, all about 90F.

Le Vouvrillon
Tel: (02) 47 52 78 80
In the centre of Vouvray itself, come here for a 60F *menu ouvrier*. It can become very crowded with local workers, although in summer you can spill out onto the shady terrace. This offers a basic but satisfying four-course lunch, with wine by the jug, although this is definitely not good local wine. For that you'll need to buy a bottle of Vouvray sec (from Le Lièvre) for 76F.

Sancerre

Sancerre lies some distance from Tours to the east. When route planning, think of Sancerre as separate to the rest of the Loire Valley in terms of distance from the Channel ports.

Sancerre is best known for its lively, fragrant white wines, made from the Sauvignon grape. They are pale in colour, with a memorable and delightful aroma. Sancerre is a wine for drinking and enjoying now, or at least within a year or two of bottling, not for keeping in your cellar. This area produces some of the most expensive wines in the Loire. It's not an area for good wines between 15 and 30F a bottle; it's never inexpensive, usually costing over 40F a bottle. About a fifth of the grapes grown are Pinot Noir, used for the lesser known reds and rosés. You'll find the winemakers here frequently talk about *terroir*, the soil in which the vines are grown. There are essentially three different ground conditions in Sancerre that each produce different styles of wine, which you'll be able to distinguish when you drink the wines alongside each other.

Where to buy wine
Domaine Vacheron
rue du Puits-Poulton, 18300 Sancerre
Tel: (02) 48 54 09 93
Suppliers to Fortnum and Mason, Berry Bros, Adnams, Waitrose and Majestic, Vacheron still treat you as their most important client of the day, a welcome as sincere as it's warm and indeed helpful. Madame Vacheron showed me around the beautiful old cellars and the immaculate winemaking equipment. After tasting there's little doubt that you'll want to buy a case, but there's no pressure at all to do so. After all, the wine sells itself; one client who went away with only one bottle now orders thousands of bottles a year for his company.

An impeccable Sancerre rouge 93, matured in new oak, is a slightly spicy, typical Sancerre with hints of woody vanilla. Well balanced, well made, and well worth 50F. The similarly

153

priced Sancerre blanc 94 is equally well made; the 93 won an IWC silver medal under Fortnum's label at £10 in the UK.

There's no need for you to go out to the vineyards to taste the wines from both Mellots. Their shops in Sancerre are convenient and charge exactly the same prices as at the vineyards:

Joseph Mellot
place Nouvelle
18300 Sancerre
Tel: (02) 48 54 21 50

Mellot are another centuries old winemaking family of father and son teams since 1513. The vineyard is half a mile (1km) out of town on the road to Ménétréol, but there is a shop in the main square in town.

The Sancerre blanc 94 La Châtellenie is a beautiful, elegant and fragrant wine (gold medal in Mâcon), whilst the Sancerre rosé 94 Le Rabault (bronze medals in both Mâcon and Paris) is also fragrant and fresh, good value at 47F. Taste the Sancerre rouge 94 or the more expensive red-berry scented Le Connétable 93. The complex, delightful Pouilly-Fumé 94, Cuvée du Troncsec (gold medal in Angers in 1995 and an International Wine Challenge commendation) is available here for 47F (in the UK it is £6.80 plus carriage – surprisingly little saving).

Alphonse Mellot
Domaine la Moussière
3 rue Porte César, 18300 Sancerre
Tel: (02) 48 54 07 41

Alphonse Mellot's office is on one corner of Nouvelle Place, his restaurant *La Moussière* on the other. The shop is two doors up from the office, on the other side of rue Porte César. This family have been *vignerons* since the 16th century, and are obviously part of the establishment in Sancerre. The Sancerre blanc 94 is fresh but nonetheless quite sophisticated, the Sancerre rouge 94 has well balanced fruit and the Sancerre rosé 94 is pretty and delicate. Excellent wines at under 50F.

154

Bernard Reverdy et Fils
Chaudoux
18300 Verdigny
Tel: (02) 48 79 33 08
There are four other Reverdys making wine in Verdigny (so read the signs in town carefully): the *fils* of Bernard is Noël, and a Bernard-Noël also makes wine. Bernard Reverdy et Fils have been making wine for many generations, as shown by the fascinating family tree painted on tiles in the tasting room.

Their Sancerre rosé 94 is fragrant and complex, an astounding wine, refreshing and a gorgeous colour. The Sancerre blanc 94 is fruity and very typical. Taste the Sancerre rouge 94. Well worth buying at under 45F.

Domaine Daulny
Chaudenay
18300 Verdigny
Tel: (02) 48 79 33 96
You may have seen this wine in the UK (imported by Haynes, Hanson and Clark of Stow-on-the-Wold, as well as Lay and Wheeler of Colchester), since most of his exports go to the UK and Switzerland. The Sancerre rouge 94 is typical of the *terroir*, and of the Pinot Noir grape with its red-berry fragrance. Taste his very pleasant Sancerre blanc 94. Both around 40F.

Where to stay
Hôtel Panoramic
Rempart des Augustins
18300 Sancerre
Tel: (02) 48 54 22 44
Open all year; restaurant closed Wednesday from November to March and the whole of January
Double room 320F
The hotel is in a modern building with little character but it has terrific views over the vineyards. Everything works and rooms are fairly comfortable, if dull. Popular with business people (try

155

to listen in to UK wine buyers talking loudly about the strategic plans of their supermarket employers), and for conferences in the winter, with plenty of tourists during the summer.

The bar, lobby and lounge are in international airport style alongside a slightly regimented breakfast room – eat here to enjoy the stunning view. Go for a room with a view, but avoid those by the lift. Slightly cheaper rooms overlook the street. Parking is easy and there are useful trolleys for any precious cargo you might have with you.

Where to eat
La Tour
31 place de la Halle
18300 Sancerre
Tel: (02) 48 54 00 81
Menus from 99F

A remarkably peaceful, comfortable and elegant restaurant. A gorgeous 15th-century room downstairs, heavily beamed, the lighting low, background classical music, and a huge open fireplace. For a room with a view, a bright glassy studio upstairs is opened in the summer, modern and entirely different to the room downstairs.

A brilliant wine list features virtually every village in the region: Bué, Chavignol, Crézancy, Ménétréol, Montigny, St-Gemme, St-Satur, Sury-en-Vaux, Sancerre, Thauvenay and Verdigny. And from each, all the best winemakers: for example, from Sancerre itself wines from Fouassier, Jolivet, Marnier-Lapostolle (Château de Sancerre 94, superb but expensive here), Alphonse Mellot (La Moussière 94), Joseph Mellot and Vacheron. There are also Pouilly-Fumés from excellent winemakers: Michel Redde, Masson-Blondelet, J.C. Châtelain, Serge Dagueneau, Jolivet, and de Ladoucette (by Château du Nozet). Wine of the Year must be Bernard Reverdy's stunning Sancerre rosé 94. Go and visit his vineyard where you can buy this wine if there is any left from the small quantity made.

Oh yes, there's food as well at this, the best, restaurant in Sancerre. The 99F *menu voyageur* (also available in the evening) offered a duck terrine with pistachios or *mousse de fromage de chèvre frais* with a tomato *coulis* to start, followed by *confit de joue de porc piqué d'ail* or *effilochée de cabillaud*, and dessert – I had a *clafoutis aux cerises aigres*. The service by a youngish staff was formal and rather stuffy when I ate there, until owner Daniel Fournier emerged from the kitchen, at which point it became very relaxed and friendly. Dress smartly to feel at home here.

Two winemakers have also opened their own restaurants on the main square: on one corner of the square is Alphonse Mellot's **Restaurant La Moussière**; on the other side of the square is **Auberge Joseph Mellot**, which serves a simple 85F meal of terrine, a smoked ham omelette, and *crottin de Chavignol*, the goat's cheese for which this area is so well known, to accompany a selection of Joseph Mellot wines. It's a pity that the wine prices in the restaurant are almost double the shop price (a couple of steps away on the same floor), but you can buy most of the wines by the glass (20F) or in half-bottles (45–50F).

Pouilly-sur-Loire

Pouilly-Fumé is a delicate wine, also made from the Sauvignon grape, grown around Pouilly-sur-Loire. It is also known as Pouilly Blanc Fumé and Blanc Fumé de Pouilly and should not be confused with Pouilly-Fuissé, a white burgundy from vineyards near Mâcon. It's a pale wine, quite lively, often described in France as *nerveux,* but still firm in its flavour. One of its best known characteristics is its 'flinty' aftertaste, put down to the *terroir*. Most are at their best if left for a year or so before drinking.

In this area another white wine, which you are unlikely to come across outside France, Pouilly-sur-Loire, is made from the Chasselas grape. This is considerably less expensive and is for everyday drinking.

157

Where to buy wine
Michel Redde et Fils
La Moynerie, 58150 Pouilly-sur-Loire
Tel: (03) 86 39 14 72
Michel Redde is one of the most renowned winemakers in the region, and his tasting room is busy and convivial. The vineyard is easy to find on the RN7. His Pouilly-Fumé La Moynerie is very typical, fragrant, flinty, fine (54F). Half-bottles are available (difficult to find in the UK). To understand how complex a Pouilly-Fumé can be, try the 89 Cuvée Majorum (126F).

Domaine Masson-Blondelet
1 rue de Paris, 58150 Pouilly-sur-Loire
Tel: (03) 86 39 00 34
Try a brilliant Pouilly-Fumé Les Angelots 94 from vines growing on ground known as *caillottes;* a flowery wine, drink it now (46F). Taste the well-balanced Pouilly-Fumé Villa Paulus 94 (from different ground, known as *terres blanches*) alongside Les Angelots to discern the differences. To get the best from it drink within a year. Half-bottles available.

Domaine Tinel-Blondelet
La Croix Canat, 58150 Pouilly-sur-Loire
Tel: (03) 86 39 13 83
Try an outstanding Pouilly-Fumé L'Arrêt Buffatte 94 – a classic that is substantial, balanced and fruity (49F). There's also a very pleasant Sancerre blanc 94 (45F).

Domaine Châtelain
Les Berthiers, 58150 St-Andelain
Tel: (03) 86 39 17 46
As you enter Les Berthiers coming from RN7, Domaine Châtelain is on your right. Jean-Claude Châtelain makes a superb Pouilly-Fumé, much of which is exported. You can taste the Sauvignon in his Pouilly-Fumé 94 – long and satisfying.

158

Domaine Patrick Coulbois
Les Berthiers
58150 St-Andelain
Tel: (03) 86 39 15 69
At the other end of Les Berthiers, nearer St-Andelain, Patrick
Coulbois has made a brilliant Pouilly-Fumé 94 which is flinty,
peachy and alive. It's incredible value at 40F, so buy as much as
you can fit into your boot.

Caves de Pouilly-sur-Loire
(Les Moulins à Vent)
58150 Pouilly-sur-Loire
Tel: (03) 86 39 10 99
Open on Sundays during the summer
This is the place to buy a Pouilly-sur-Loire 94 (known locally
as *chasselas*), an interesting, slightly peachy wine for only 26F.

The Pouilly-Fumé 94 Vieilles Vignes is much more expensive, and you might prefer to spend the 49F on one from an individual winemaker.

The Coteaux de Giennois is rarely seen outside the region,
but even at 19F this one was a bit of a disappointment.

Where to stay
Hôtel de l'Ecu de France
64 rue Waldeck Rousseau
58150 Pouilly-sur-Loire
Tel: (03) 86 39 10 97
Closed last two weeks in June and over Christmas
Double room 210F
Pouilly-sur-Loire is just a short and scenic drive from Sancerre,
which has a wider choice of restaurants. However, if you do
choose to stay in Pouilly, you'll find the 210F rooms at the
L'Ecu de France are quite acceptable, provided that you can
live with a slightly delapidated shower cubicle in the bathroom.
Rooms overlook the narrow main street or the courtyard to the
rear, where you can park your car.

159

Where to eat

Restaurant de l'Ecu de France (see page 159)

Huge portions of home cooking here for 60F at lunchtime: *charcuterie* or *crudités* to start, grilled *andouillette* or (briefly) fried steak, chips and *ratatouille*, finishing with cheese or dessert. Quite formal in the no-smoking dining room, with its red and white striped walls and pink tablecloths. Smokers will enjoy adjourning to the wooden tables in the café for a good cup of coffee. A few local wines are available.

On the road between Sancerre and Pouilly, stop off in Ménétréol for a drink at **Bar-Restaurant Les Chamons**, overlooking the canal. They serve a no-choice four-course lunch *menu* that might include herring fillets to start, *entrecôte*, cheese and dessert for 55F.

Sancerre

What to see

La Verrerie

Aubigny-sur-Nère

Louis XIV gave this château to Louise de Keroualle, Duchess of Portsmouth and mistress of Charles II; the adjoining Parc de la Duchesse de Portsmouth was laid out in the 17th century, and is one of the loveliest gardens in France.

Wine festivals and fairs

Sancerre

Easter wine fair; wine fair on the last weekend in August

Pouilly-sur-Loire

Wine fair on 15 August

Quincy

Wine fair on the last weekend in August

Alsace and Champagne

Alsace

Alsace is one of the most delightful wine producing regions in France. Beautiful countryside with the backdrop of the Vosges mountains, charming mediaeval architecture in the old villages and interesting food and wine. Whilst it is known as one of the more expensive areas of France (it is an easy drive for the high earning denizens of Strasbourg, Brussels and Luxembourg), it can offer good value, especially when eating out at lunchtime.

Getting there
It is a long day's drive from Calais to reach the north of the wine growing region of Alsace, getting on for 500 miles (800km). But there are good quality roads all the way through France though the best of these are autoroutes where you will have to pay tolls.

About Alsace wines
The classification of wines is different in Alsace from other regions of France, a complicated system that is not always of real use to the consumer. It is probably more useful to know the main **grape varieties** used in Alsace winemaking:

Sylvaner (makes a light, fresh wine)
Pinot Blanc (makes a dry white wine, *nerveux*, *souple*)
Klevener (dry, traces of butter and spice)
Riesling (usually has delicate aromas and good fruit)
Tokay-Pinot Gris (Tokay d'Alsace) (rich and dry)
Muscat (tends to be dry and have a good bouquet)
Gewürztraminer (*corse bien charpenté*, good bouquet, fills the mouth)
Pinot Noir (makes dry rosé)

161

In addition, the **Crémant d'Alsace** is a delicate sparkling wine with a fine *mousse*. *Vendanges tardives* wines are picked late and are very concentrated.

The wine regions

The wine region of Alsace roughly follows a north to south swathe from Marlenheim (west of Strasbourg) to Thann (north-west of Mulhouse). Here we have divided the area into three sections: the Northern Vineyards, the Heart of the Vineyards and the Southern Vineyards.

THE NORTHERN VINEYARDS

Traenheim and Molsheim

Whilst Molsheim is probably the best place to start your trip through the vineyards of Alsace, if you are coming into Alsace on the motorway from Champagne or Luxembourg, you might find the short detour into Traenheim worthwhile before driving on to Molsheim.

Where to buy wine in Traenheim

Frédéric Mochel
56 rue Principale
67310 Traenheim
Tel: (03) 88 50 38 67
Closed Sunday
Credit cards including AmEx

Mochel owns 20 acres (8ha) of vineyards, half of which grow on the renowned Altenberg de Bergbieten. He is a meticulous winemaker, and you can see the result in his Riesling grand cru Altenberg de Bergbieten Cuvée Henriette 93, which is very typical, lively, full of fruit, round and long. Hints of smokiness were rather interesting. Well made, and essential buying, even

162

at 64F. His Gewürztraminer Altenberg 93 is a refined and well balanced wine, almost creamy in texture, with a very pleasant nose (55F). Here is an opportunity to taste wine made from Klevener: a Klevener de Traenheim 94, round, concentrated, and with good length at 33F. I particularly liked his Muscat Altenberg 94, full of fruit, elegant, balanced, complex and long, 66F. Least expensive of his wines is a superb Sylvaner 94, ripe, long and rather fine at 24F.

Where to buy wine in Molsheim

The location of all the winemakers recommended in Molsheim is clearly indicated by signs in the town. Best to start in town at René Boehler, on the place de la Liberté (a couple of blocks away from the main square in town, the place de l'Hôtel de Ville), out of which runs the rue de Saverne. Just after Bernard Weber (at number 49 on the right) you will find rue Ettoré-Bugatti to the left. If you are in the place de l'Hôtel de Ville, you should try a beer and a pretzel in the vaulted dining room of Mutzig, a magnificent 16th-century building.

René Boehler

4 place de la Liberté
67120 Molsheim
Tel: (03) 88 38 53 16
For superb value at the 20F level, it is hard to beat Boehler's Sylvaner 94, and his refined and satisfying Pinot Blanc 94. I also enjoyed his Riesling 94, fruity and ever so slightly minty. A subtle, smoky Gewürztraminer vendanges tardives 92 is not overly weighty and is particularly enjoyable (98F for 50cl).

Bernard Weber

49 route de Saverne
67120 Molsheim
Tel: (03) 88 38 52 67
Open Monday–Saturday
A heavy wooden gate stands between you and the large family

Alsace

What to see

Musée d'Unterlinden
place d'Unterlinden, Colmar
The greatest treasure in this 13th-century former convent is the nine-panelled Issenheim altarpiece by Matthias Grünewald, one of the most moving of religious paintings.

La Petite Venise
Colmar
So-called because of its many canals, this beautifully preserved district of Colmar is perfect for strolling, shopping, and relaxed eating and drinking.

Mont Ste-Odile
Dedicated to the patron saint of Alsace, this 2,500ft (762m) mountain is capped by a convent and the tiny 12th-century Chapelle de Ste-Odile. There are views from here over the plain of Alsace to the Black Forest in Germany.

Munster
12 miles (19km) southwest of Colmar
Munster is a cheesemaking centre founded by monks in the 15th century. There is a Route du Fromage (cheese road) which you can follow with a map from the tourist office on the central place du Marché.

Haut-Koenigsbourg
High above the plain of Alsace (2477ft/755m), this much restored fortified castle now has a distinctly mediaeval flavour with two rings of walls and a drawbridge.

dog who announces your arrival. Walk across the cobbled courtyard to the stylish, heavily beamed tasting room with an ambience enhanced by low lighting.

Least costly of Bernard Weber's wines at 25F is his delicious Sylvaner 94, a perfect quaffing wine. His Riesling grand cru Bruderthal 93 is fresh and long (50F). Savour the intense aroma of his Gewürztraminer grand cru Bruderthal vendanges tardives 89, a gloriously full wine, 140F. My personal choice for value would be the Muscat grand cru Bruderthal 93, an elegant, delicate Muscat at 45F, whilst, if you have the necessary funds, you could go for the Muscat grand cru Bruderthal vendanges tardives 89 at 150F.

His most outstanding wine is the Riesling grand cru Bruderthal sélection de grains nobles 92 at 250F for 50cl.

Gérard Neumeyer
29 rue Ettoré-Bugatti
67120 Molsheim
Tel: (03) 88 38 12 45
Open Monday–Saturday 9–6;
Sunday 9–12

Neumeyer honours the man after whom the street is named with his equally well crafted winemaking. The house is ordinarily suburban; his wines are everything but.

Recommended wines under 30F are his very pleasant, round Pinot Blanc 94, and well made Sylvaner 94, which is a wine to be drunk with a meal, rather than by itself.

There is a bit of a leap in price with his Riesling grand cru Bruderthal 94, which is very substantial and rich, a wine which will keep (61F). I loved his Tokay-Pinot Gris Bruderthal 94, rich, full, with perfect acidity and an exquisite coffee finish (89F).

If you are looking for a superb *vendanges tardives* and are happy to spend 120F, taste and buy the Riesling 90, rich, honeyed, with hints of vanilla and beautifully made.

165

Where to stay near Traenheim
Neufeldhof
67280 Oberhaslach
Tel: (03) 88 50 91 48
Double 270F including breakfast

This is a large, comfortable country house, friendly, homely and generous. Don't miss a great value evening meal around a communal table for 75F.

This is the perfect stopping place for horse lovers (you can ride from here) and the heated pool is just what you need after the long drive from the coast.

How to get there: From Traenheim, drive southeast to Balbronn, then take the scenic route via the D75 into the mountains towards Oberhaslach.

Andlau

Andlau is a beautiful Alsace town of which its inhabitants are justifiably proud. Have a look at the church with its 13th-century frieze. All the winemakers are within an easy stroll and are clearly signposted from the main square.

Where to buy
Rémy Gresser
2 rue de l'Ecole
67140 Andlau
Tel: (03) 88 08 95 88

Known for his philosophy of working with nature, rather than fighting against it, Gresser also works with his own natural talent, which is evident when you taste his range of wines. His Sylvaner 94 is light and refreshing (23F), and his Riesling 94 (34F) concentrated and very well balanced.

Also recommended are an intense Muscat Brandhof 94 at 34F and a delicious Andlau Gewürztraminer 93 at 60F. For a truly superb Riesling, taste his intense Riesling grand cru

Kastelberg 91, more expensive at 70F. His Tokay-Pinot Gris Brandhof Vieilles Vignes 90 is exceptional (85F).

Domaine Marc Kreydenweiss

12 rue Deharbe, 67140 Andlau
Tel: (03) 88 08 95 83

Passionate about the environment and a proponent of biody-namic methods of growing grapes, Kreydenweiss is a superb winemaker. Kastelberg is grown on land that gives its wines a distinctive mineral flavour.

Unfortunately there are no wines under 40F, but they are nevertheless very good value. Try his Andlau Riesling 94 at 55F and Kritt Gewürztraminer 94 at 67F. And the wonderfully fresh, concentrated, and balanced Riesling grand cru Wiebels-berg vendanges tardives 90, whose taste will linger in your mouth, 150F. The peaceful tasting room is opposite the church.

Moritz

6 rue du Gal-Koenig, 67140 Andlau
Tel: (03) 88 08 01 43
By appointment Monday–Saturday

Both Moritzes are from winemaking families. They produce some superb Rieslings, and tasting their whole range is fasci-nating: the Riesling grand cru Kastelberg, the Riesling Re-hbuel, the grand cru Moenchberg and the grand cru Wiebelsberg. Although their least expensive wines (not the Rieslings) are under 30F, the best must be their Gewürztramin-er vendanges tardives 90, a beautiful colour, concentrated yet nevertheless fresh, an elegant wine at 95F.

André Dürrmann

11 rue des Forgerons
67140 Andlau
Tel: (03) 88 08 26 42

A man for all seasons, André Dürrmann is a winemaker, tour operator, part-time fireman and president of the local *syndicat*

viticole. You'll enjoy both his Gewürztraminer 93 at 40F and
his very interesting Riesling grand cru Kastelberg 93 at 56F.

Check out his two apartments to rent, one at 1600F per week,
the other at 1900F per week, both sleeping five. He also has
some mountain bikes to rent at 80F per day.

Domaine Ostertag
87 rue de Finkwiller
67680 Epfig
Tel: (03) 88 85 51 34
André Ostertag's singleminded commitment to quality results
in some of the finest wines in Alsace. His honeyed Riesling
d'Epfig sélection de grains nobles 90 is heavenly, rich and complex – save up for this most stunning wine (192F a half-bottle).
I have found one, sole, half-bottle of this wine in the UK at
Morris & Verdin (tel: 0171 357 8866, an excellent wine merchant, well worth contacting), at the very reasonable price of
£27.50, a mere £1.75 more than at the vineyard.

Ostertag's Sylvaner Vieilles Vignes 94 at 36F is also available in the UK for £6.90, so the saving in France is about £1.75
to £2, depending on the exchange rate. This confirms the general rule that you should be able to save about £1.50 on any bottle
in France, and that therefore the largest percentage savings are
on the least expensive wines.

Other winemakers producing high quality wine are **Seltz and
Klipfel** in nearby Barr.

Where to stay near Andlau
La Romance
17 route de Neuve-Eglise
67220 Dieffenbach-au-Val
Tel: (03) 88 85 67 09·
Double 300–330F with breakfast
An attractive pink chalet-style house in a suburb of this small
village, with steep roofs, shutters and a beautiful carved wood-
168

en balcony. Great views, suburban décor, clean and comfortable rooms.

Maison Fleurie

19 route de Neuve-Eglise
67220 Dieffenbach-au-Val
Tel: (03) 88 85 60 48
Double 230F including breakfast
Closed January

Across the street, and just before the Romance, Maison Fleurie, owned by Doris Engel-Geiger, offers three rooms, again with rather suburban décor, in a three storey chalet-style home with views from its hillside location. It is very Alsace with its pretty flowerboxes outside every window. There is jam made from organic fruit at breakfast. Well kept and friendly.

How to get there: Drive from Sélestat on the D424 to Ville, then take the D697 from St-Maurice.

Chez Ruhlmann

34 rue Mal Foch
67650 Dambach-la-Ville
Tel: (03) 88 92 41 86
Double 230F including breakfast
Open from Easter to mid-October

On the main road through the pretty village of Dambach, in the heart of the vineyards, this bed and breakfast is definitely for wine lovers. The wine growing estate was established 300 years ago, and it is a pleasure to be staying in rooms above the cellars, winemaking and bottling rooms.

Pine clad rooms with shared loo have slightly gloomy lighting, but are spacious and clean. Breakfast is served in a large room that doubles as a tasting room. There are gorgeous early morning walks to be made through the vineyards a few yards away at the back. Afterwards take some time to sit down and taste the Ruhlmann wines, enjoy listening to the winemaker (in French), and buy a few bottles to take home.

169

Alsace

Wine fairs and festivals

Wuenmeim
Festival of New Wine last weekend in September

Guebwiller
Ascension wine fair

Rorschwihr
Crémant night on the first Saturday of July

Soultzmatt
Grand cru Zinnkoepflé wine festival on the first Saturday of August

Rouffach
Ascension weekend eco-biological festival

Pfaffenheim
Wine cellar festival on the second weekend of July

Gueberschwihr
Friendship festival with wine cellars open to the public on the penultimate weekend of August

Voegtlingshoffen
Wine festival on the last weekend of June

Eguisheim
Winegrowers' festival on the fourth weekend of August; presentation of new wines on the second Sunday in March

Turckheim
Wine fair in late July

Colmar
Alsace regional wine fair in the week of the 15th August

Ammerschwihr
Wine fair in April

Kientzheim
Wine fair on the last weekend of July

Ribeauvillé
Wine festival on the penultimate weekend of July
Scherwiller
Art, craft and Riesling festival, third weekend in August
Dambach-la-Ville
Wine fair on the 14th and 15th August
Andlau
Wine fair on the first weekend of August
Mittelbergheim
Wine fair on the last weekend of July
Barr
Wine fair around the 14th July. Harvest festival on the first
Sunday in October
Heiligenstein
Klevener festival in mid-August. Klevener is a grape variety peculiar to Heiligenstein
Obernai
Wine fair on the weekend nearest the 15th August; harvest
festival on the third Sunday in October
Molsheim
Regional wine fair on 1st May
Wangen
Wine festival on the Sunday following the 3rd July

Hôtel le Vignoble
1 rue d'Eglise
67650 Dambach-la-Ville
Tel: (03) 88 92 43 75
Double rooms from 275F; closed November to February
You might also like to check out the Hôtel le Vignoble, which
is, as you might expect from the address, right by the church.

Hôtel Kastelberg

10 rue du Général Koenig
67140 Andlau
Tel: (03) 88 08 97 83
Double 340F
Open mid-March to mid-November; Christmas
A large, modern, chalet-style building, with flower-filled balconies overlooking the valley. Comfortable rooms.

Zinck Hotel

13 rue de la Marne
67140 Andlau
Tel: (03) 88 08 27 30
Closed mid-December and February
Double 295–600F
Lots of high style in this converted mill with a striking Corbusier-inspired staircase and the rooms, all differently decorated, will be a delight to fashion victims, and perhaps too much for others. Rooms cost more on Saturday nights.

The least expensive rooms are fairly small and ordinary, but the others are decorated in vivid colours: one in very bright yellow and blue, one with a four poster bed and beautiful painted antique cupboard in peach and green, and the grooviest of all has a canopied bed, in lime green, red and deep pink. There is bound to be a room to suit your mood, so check out a couple before you choose. Certainly has a lot of character.

Hôtel Arnold

98 route du Vin
67140 Itterswiller
Tel: (03) 88 85 50 58
Double 440–545F
An absolutely typical Alsace hotel, brimming with flowers. Very comfortable and immaculately kept rooms, most with superb views over the vineyards. The restaurant and *winstub* (winebar) are across the road, with traditional cooking from

130F. Rates are reduced between mid-November and mid-August. A solid establishment, much patronized by visitors from Strasbourg and across the Rhine. Itterswiller is a delightful town to stroll through and to use as a base.

Where to eat in Andlau

Le Relais de la Poste
1 rue des Forgerons
67140 Andlau
Tel: (03) 88 08 95 91
Open March to November
Closed Monday and Tuesday
Menus from 95F

Just the *winstub* in which to enjoy the most interesting Alsace specialities. Lovely outdoor terrace full of flowers overlooking the square, and a soothing, low lit, panelled dining room with comfortable banquette seating.

The family also own the Maison Boechel vineyard in nearby Mittelbergheim.

Au Boeuf Rouge
6 rue Dr-Stoltz
67140 Andlau
Tel: (03) 88 08 96 26
Closed Wednesday evening, Thursday
Also closed January and end-June to early July
Menus from 122F

For more formal dining, cross the square. There is a blazing fire here in colder weather.

The 122F menu offered a typical Alsace meal of a salad of *poitrine de canard fumée*, followed by more duck in the form of *confit* on *choucroute*, and a dessert of apples and cherries with a (real) vanilla sauce.

A very good value Riesling 93 at 66F was recommended for the meal.

173

HEART OF THE VINEYARDS

Bergheim

Where to buy
Marcel Deiss
15 route du Vin
68750 Bergheim
Tel: (03) 89 73 63 37
Open Monday–Saturday (Monday–Friday out of season), including public holidays, but phone ahead
Jean-Michel Deiss is one of the most gifted winemakers in Alsace, a perfectionist, growing vines on 50 acres (20ha), and making wines which are intensely aromatic and extraordinarily concentrated. His wife Clarisse Deiss looks after the tastings.

Taste his Alsace grand cru Riesling Schoenenbourg 92, a wonderful lemony vanilla smell, a fresh and fruity wine at 120F. Considerably less expensive are his Pinot Blanc 93 (45F), a Muscat 93 (55F) and a Tokay-Pinot Gris 93 (67F). The late harvest wines – *vendanges tardives* – include a superb Tokay-Pinot Gris Bergheim 90 at 130F and a Gewürztraminer 89 at 150F.
How to get there: Marcel Deiss is a pinky beige building with wooden shutters on your right as you drive into Bergheim from Ribeauvillé, just before the road bends left at the sign to Rorschwihr and St-Hippolyte.

Spielmann
route de Thannenkirsch
68750 Bergheim
Tel: (03) 89 73 35 95
Open Monday–Friday, weekends and holidays by appointment
Sylvie Spielmann brings a background of studies in oenology at Montpellier and exposure to winemaking in the New World to bear on her own winemaking. The result is interesting wines from only 24F, certainly worth a visit.
174

Her Riesling grand cru Kanzlerberg 92 is light and refined at 51F. The Gewürztraminer grand cru Altenberg de Bergheim 92 is flowery, slightly peppery and well balanced (51F), and her Pinot d'Alsace Réserve 92 a rather lively wine with a pleasant nose (32F). The Gewürztraminer 90 sélection de grains nobles Altenberg de Bergheim is superb, but unfortunately 190F.

How to get there: Take the road to Thannenkirsch and Haut-Koenigsbourg, past the hotel, and on to the vineyards. The Spielmann construction supplies yard is on the same property.

Gustave Lorentz

35 Grand'Rue
or 91 rue des Vignerons
68750 Bergheim
Tel: (03) 89 73 22 22

Most of the grand cru vineyards of this winemaker are located on the famous (and sunny) Altenberg de Bergheim: taste the Tokay-Pinot Gris grand cru Altenberg 91 at 68F, and their other grand cru, Kanzlerberg, in the form of a Riesling 91 at 67F. Of the less expensive wines, the fragrant Alsace Riesling 93 Cuvée Particulière (45F) is worth buying (and worth cellaring for a few years).

Where to eat in Bergheim
Winstub du Sommelier

51 Grand'Rue
68750 Bergheim
Tel: (03) 89 73 69 99
Menus from 170F
Closed Sundays; Monday from November to June; and all of February

With a name like this, how can you resist eating here? The name is not invented either – owner and chef Jean-Marie Stoeckel was voted Best Sommelier in France in his younger days. Superb cellar, of course, and hearty rich food like duck *confit* with sauerkraut, and tempting tarts.

Admire the old bar and the pretty green wrought iron sign outside of a gentleman with a jug of wine and a glass standing in a field of vines and tulips.

How to get there: It is opposite the brightly coloured **Auberge des Lavandières**, along the main street from the 14th century gate tower.

Rorschwihr

Another fascinating mediaeval town.

Where to buy wine
Rolly Gassmann
1 and 2 rue d'Eglise
68590 Rorschwihr
Tel: (03) 89 73 63 28

What welcoming and friendly people the Gassmanns are. Their wines start at 26F for the Sylvaner 94 up to 450F for the heavenly Gewürztraminer sélection grains nobles 89. Compare the Riesling 94 at 43F with the Riesling Pflaenzerreben 89 at 65F. Also taste the Gewürztraminer 93 (65F) and the Muscat 94 (50F).

Where to eat
La Vignette
rue d'Eglise
68590 Rorschwihr

A few yards away from Rolly Gassmann, you can't miss La Vignette, a mustard painted building with brown shutters, just opposite the church.

From the café terrace, you can see the war memorial which sums up the history of Alsace: every surname is of German origin, every Christian name French.

Sit on the terrace and enjoy some Alsace specialities such as *quiche lorraine* (onion tart), *choucroute alsacienne* or a *tarte flambée* (*flammenkuchen*) with Munster cheese.

176

Auberge Saint-Martin

80 rue de la Liberté
68240 Kientzheim
Tel: (03) 88 82 04 78
Menus from 129F
Closed Wednesday, Tuesday lunchtime out of season, Christmas period; end June–early July
A regional restaurant, with a great Alsace wine list, regional specialities, and a brilliant *tarte flambée*. The 129F menu includes onion tart, *choucroute*, Munster cheese and the tart.

Relais de Kientzheim

74 rue de la Liberté
68240 Kientzheim
Closed on Tuesday, and Monday evening during the winter
Whilst the Auberge gets the rave reviews, three doors down is the bright blue, half-timbered Relais de Kientzheim, which gets the price right. Their 58F menu offers *tourte vigneronne*, *émincé de boeuf nouilles* and a *tarte aux pommes*.

Where to stay near Rorschwihr

Aux Ducs de Lorraine

16 route du Vin, 68590 St-Hippolyte
Tel: (03) 89 73 00 09
Open March–November and Christmas
Double 400–700F
A magnificent half-timbered building and beautifully crafted wooden balconies with distant views over vineyards towards Château Haut-Koenigsbourg. The older rooms (700F) are elegant and immensely comfortable, although only with (large) twin beds. The less expensive rooms in the more modern extension, which also have balconies and lovely views, are more package-hotel with orange chairs. Rather grand dining room with heavy parquet floors. A solid, traditional hotel with high standards.

Ribeauvillé

Where to buy
André Kientzler
50 route de Bergheim
68150 Ribeauvillé
Tel: (03) 89 73 67 10

Drive through town, past Trimbach, towards Haut-Koenigs-bourg. The estate building is a chalet on a hilltop overlooking the vineyards.

Some stunning wines, especially Riesling (and of these, the Geisberg grand cru 93 at 90F is particularly good). His Riesling starts at 36F for the 94, with the Réserve 92 at 46F. Try the splendid Muscat Kirchberg grand cru 93 at 60F.

Most of the *vendanges tardives* and *sélection de grains no-bles* wines are limited to sales of a maximum of six bottles, not that everyone could afford even six bottles at 300F for the di-vine Gewürztraminer sélection de grains nobles 88 or the Ries-ling Geisberg grand cru sélection de grains nobles 88.

Trimbach
15 route de Bergheim
68150 Ribeauvillé
Tel: (03) 89 73 60 30

Trimbach makes some of the finest Rieslings, with very pure aromas. The extraordinary Riesling Clos Sainte-Hune vendan-ges tardives 89 shows what can happen when wine from a su-perb vineyard, a brilliant year, and outstanding winemaking skills come together at the same time. It has all the finest quali-ties of Alsace Riesling, mineral, fruit, dry, round, all of which balance beautifully after about ten years in the bottle.

Beyond the reach of many at 269F, as may be the superb, complex Gewürztraminer vendanges tardives 90 at 178F, the standard Rieslings and Gewürztraminers are more accessible from 51F. Particularly elegant is the Gewürztraminer Cuvée des Seigneurs de Ribeaupierre 90 (99F).

How to get there: At the road sign out of Ribeauvillé for D1bis to Bergheim, you will see green steel gates leading to a cream half-timbered building with green shutters. Turn in here – the Trimbach sign is only visible on the side of the building after you have passed the gates.

Riquewihr

This mediaeval and Renaissance city is packed with beautifully preserved houses and courtyards, castles and towers.

Where to buy
Roger Jung

23 rue de la 1re-Armée
68340 Riquewihr
Tel: (03) 89 47 92 17

Taste Roger Jung's particularly nice fruity Riesling 93 Le Kronenbourg for 42F, and Gewürztraminer 93 Le Rosenbourg.

At the more expensive end of the range, the Gewürztraminer 89 vendanges tardives (105F) and Riesling 89 grand cru Schoenenbourg sélections de grains nobles (320F) are particularly outstanding.

Hugel

3 rue de la 1re-Armée
and 25 rue du Général de Gaulle
68340 Riquewihr
Tel: (03) 89 47 92 15

This old house dates from 1639, and offers wine lovers the rare opportunity of buying from a large range of old vintages of *vendanges tardives* and *sélections de grains nobles*.

Their *vendanges tardives* from Schoenenbourg are exquisitely elegant wines, and the *sélections de grains nobles* have an extraordinarily pure aroma. One of the finest wines of 89 is probably Hugel's Gewürztraminer sélection de grains nobles Special 89.

Dopff & Irion

Au Château de Riquewihr, shop at 26 rue du Général de Gaulle
68340 Riquewihr
Tel: (03) 89 47 92 51
Open every day from April to mid-November
One of the most famous houses in Alsace, Dopff & Irion is part
of the establishment of Riquewihr. Stunning cellars dating back
to the 16th century, when the château was built by the Duke of
Wurtemberg. Tours are available by appointment. Magnificent
large timber-ceilinged and low-lit tasting room.

Whilst the Riesling Les Murailles 93 at 60F and the Riesling
grand cru Schoenenbourg 89 at 80F are wines of the highest
quality, there is less expensive Riesling from 36F.

Dopff au Moulin

2 avenue Jacques-Preiss, 68340 Riquewihr
Tel: (03) 89 47 92 23
Open Monday–Friday, and weekends from Easter–November
The topiary in front of this elegant mansion (opposite the *bar à
vins* **Le Moulin à Crémant**) is superb. Philatelists will adore
the old envelopes displayed in the entrance hall, received from
clients in the most exotic, if not slightly shady, parts of the
world: Medellin in Colombia, Havana, Angola, Congo, Viet-
nam in 1952, Iraq in 1951, not to mention their own office in
Brussels, postmarked 1943.

Taste the Gewürztraminer de Riquewihr 93 (63F) and a lively Riesling 93 (60F). Tastings are held in a room with old casks
and a magnificent old chest.

Becker

4 route d'Ostheim, 68340 Zellenberg (near Riquewihr)
Tel: (03) 89 47 90 16
Open Monday–Friday and Saturday morning; Monday–Sunday
Easter–September
Zellenberg is a charming small hilltop village, complete with
storks' nests, and the Becker family have been making wine
180

here since 1610. Recommended wines include an outstanding Pinot Blanc 93, almost toasty, a full wine, with a lingering flavour at 33F; a well made Riesling grand cru Schoenenbourg 93 at 56F; and a beautiful Gewürztraminer 90 grand cru Froehn vendanges tardives (141F). Wines for everday drinking from 25F for the Sylvaner 94.

Paul Blanck
32 Grand'Rue
68240 Kientzheim
Tel: (03) 89 78 23 56
Open Monday–Saturday
Try the delicious fruity Riesling Schlossberg 93 (68F) and the Muscat 93.
How to get there: As you drive into Kientzheim, Paul Blanck is on the main street (you can turn off to the co-op either here or the block before).

Cave Vinicole de Kientzheim-Kayserberg
68240 Kientzheim
Tel: (03) 89 47 13 19
Open Monday–Friday; weekends and holidays from Easter to mid-November
Comfortable tasting room, a good place to try several wines. Taste the slightly spicy Tokay-Pinot Gris Réserve 93 at 43F, the Riesling Schlossberg grand cru 90 at 50F and the Muscat Réserve 92 at 35F.

Where to stay near Riquewihr
Hôtel au Riesling
68340 Zellenberg
Tel: (03) 89 47 85 85
Closed January
Double 350–450F
This is a comfortable mid-range hotel. The more expensive rooms with baths have balconies looking down onto the vine-

yards of Zellenberg. Rooms at one end of the building share a large balcony with views towards the Rhine and up to Haut-Koenigsbourg.

There are splendid views from the pretty beamed restaurant as well. With 36 rooms and the spacious dining rooms, the hotel does appeal to tour groups during the season.

La Maison Bleue

16 rue St-Nicholas
68340 Riquewihr
Tel: (03) 89 27 53 59
Double 310F including breakfast
Minimum stay three nights
Painted a vivid blue, this pretty shuttered and half-timbered house offers studios with their own kitchenette, with croissants and bread for breakfast delivered to your room.

La Maison Bleue is not officially regarded as a hotel, so there are no street signs indicating its location. English is spoken – if you can find it.

Le Sarment d'Or

4 rue du Cerf
68340 Riquewihr
Tel: (03) 89 47 92 85
Double 290–380F
Closed January to mid-February, and end of June
Restaurant closed Sunday evening and Monday
Near the top end of the main street in Riquewihr, you will see a red and green *winstub* on the corner with rue de Cerf; Le Sarment d'Or is a rather quaint and charming 17th-century building, with a cosy stone-walled restaurant (with a blazing log fire in cold weather) downstairs.

Rooms do vary, so check them carefully before you choose. One small room at 180F with tiny windows and a tiny shower is for the very slim. A warm and welcoming hotel, but no parking outside.

La Couronne

5 rue de la Couronne
68340 Riquewihr
Tel: (03) 89 49 03 03
Double 310–370F

If you are in need of secure parking, rare in this mediaeval town with its narrow streets, this is the place to stay. The hotel is in a restored 16th-century building of some character, with a welcoming bar downstairs. The *winstub* downstairs might be rather lively on a summer evening.

Hôtel La Tour

1 rue de la Mairie
68150 Ribeauvillé
Tel: (03) 89 73 72 73
Double 375F
Open mid-March to December

In the heart of the mediaeval quarter of town, simple but comfortable rooms in an old mansion. There is no restaurant.

Les Alisiers

5 rue Faudé
68650 Lapoutroie
Tel: (03) 89 47 52 82
Double 275F
Closed Monday; January, first week in July and the week before Christmas

Lapoutroie is slightly off the wine route, west of Kayserberg, but well worth the detour and scenic drive into the mountains.

Despite the address, the hotel is not in the town itself, but is a mountain top eyrie some 1.8 miles (3km) away, overlooking the valley and the town below. The winding drive up the mountain is delightful by day, but although it is well signposted, try to get there before dusk. There are stunning views over the valley and the Vosges mountains. The place has real character and a friendly chalet atmosphere.

   Rooms can be rather small, as is the case with many mountain hostelries, but linen sheets, comfortable beds and the views from the terrace and public rooms should make up for this. The restaurant downstairs is no-smoking, as is the salon. Good value 95F menu.

Hôtel du Faudé
28 rue du Général Dufieux
68650 Lapoutroie
Tel: (03) 89 47 50 35
Closed March and November
Double room 360F
Another option in Lapoutroie itself is the Hôtel du Faudé on the slightly noisy main street. It is more expensive than Les Alisiers, but it has a pleasant terrace and garden, and its swimming pool is a real bonus.

Whilst in Lapoutroie, don't miss **Fromagerie Jacques Haxaire** (18 rue du Général Dufieux, tel: 89 47 50 76), also on the main street, for a range of superb Munster cheeses.

Where to eat near Riquewihr
Aux Ducs de Lorraine
16 route du Vin
68590 St-Hippolyte
Tel: (03) 89 73 00 09
Menus from 100F
Open March–November and Christmas.
Closed Sunday evening and Monday (except in summer)
There is an excellent local wine list on offer in this pretty, traditional *auberge*, with its rather grand dining room in a magnificent timbered building. Flowers are everywhere, and there are views of the vineyards, the Vosges mountains and Château Haut-Koenigsbourg.
   The 100F menu offers a *quiche lorraine* or *médaillons de*
184

crème de foie d'oie to start, *filet mignon de porc* or *coq au Riesling-Spaetzle* as a main course, and Munster cheese or a tart to finish. You might prefer to order local specialities *à la carte* in the way of local trout, *choucroute* and veal dishes. Simply good cooking.

The owners are also proprietors of the Alsace-Munsch vineyard in St-Hippolyte.

L'Auberge de l'Ill
rue Collonges
68970 Illhaeusern
Tel: (03) 89 71 89 00
Closed Monday (open at lunchtime May–October), Tuesday; February to mid-March
Menus from 500F
It may be extremely expensive, but gourmets won't want to miss a meal prepared by Marc Haeberlin, one of the most lauded chefs in France.

The Auberge also happens to have one of the most beautiful locations possible, in a series of rambling buildings overlooking pretty riverside gardens on the banks of the River Ill.

Cheval Blanc
122 Grand'Rue
68150 Ribeauvillé
Tel: (03) 89 73 61 38
Closed Monday and Friday lunchtime
Menus from 50F.
Rooms upstairs at 270F (closed December and January)
Althought the most appealing room is the bar, it is not available to you at lunchtime as it is reserved for workers only. Instead, you will have to eat in the tarted up dining room.

At the top right hand of the menu you will notice a discrete one line *menu du jour* for 50F. The food is as hearty as you could wish, with vast quantities brought to the table in serving bowls and dishes. The *menu du jour* consisted of vegetable broth to start, a beetroot and sausage salad, followed by roast chicken and rice, and finally a *tarte* or cheese. Good home cooking that is terrific value.

Haut-Ribeaupierre
1 route de Bergheim, 68150 Ribeauvillé
Tel: (03) 89 73 62 64
Menus from 110F
Closed Wednesday
This is a pretty half-timbered restaurant with three different dining rooms: *winstub*, turn-of-the-century, or conservatory. Imaginative cooking with interesting flavours.

Les Vosges
2 Grand'Rue, 68150 Ribeauvillé
Tel: (03) 89 73 61 39
Menus from 145F
Closed Sunday evening, Monday; February
One of the best restaurants in town and a good Alsace wine list. Friendly welcome and service.

Auberge au Zahnacker
8 rue du Général de Gaulle, 68150 Ribeauvillé
Tel: (03) 89 73 60 77
Another good restaurant in Ribeauvillé which serves traditional fare in vast quantities.

Zum Pfifferhüs
14 Grand'Rue
68150 Ribeauvillé
Tel: (03) 89 73 62 28
Closed Wednesday, Thursday; Christmas–New Year, March, and first week in July
An appealing, traditional *winstub*, with a good selection of local wines and regional cooking. There is no smoking in the restaurant.

Les Alisiers
5 rue Faudé
68650 Lapoutroie
Tel: (03) 89 47 52 82
Menus from 79F
Closed Monday evening and Tuesday; January
There are fantastic views from this mountain top restaurant,
with its modern dining room (no smoking). The atmosphere is
warm and the staff charming.

The 79F menu offers *crudités* (very fresh and in copious
quantities), *collet fumé* with a warm potato salad, and a *tarte au
fromage blanc*.

You might enjoy the 98F menu more, with its typical Alsace
dishes of onion tart, *choucroute* (enough to feed an entire family) and a *sorbet citron au marc de Gewürztraminer*. There is
also a useful children's menu for 49F.

Very comfortable and welcoming. Rooms upstairs if it has
all been too much, or it has gone dark and you don't feel like
negotiating the winding mountain road which brought you up
to this eyrie.

Le Sarment d'Or
4 rue du Cerf
68340 Riquewihr
Tel: (03) 89 47 92 85
Menus from 110F
Closed Sunday evening and Monday; January to mid-February
and end June
A very intimate and comfortable restaurant with a blazing log
fire in cold weather to warm the bare stone walls of this quaint
17th-century building.

The 110F menu may offer a veal and chicken terrine to start,
dos de lapereau rôti with garlic and herbs as a main course, and
a dessert.

Straightforward cooking served in an elegant room, the tables laid with cream linen and appealing cutlery.

La Table du Gourmet

5 rue de la 1re-Armée
68340 Riquewihr
Tel: (03) 89 47 98 77

Closed mid-January to early March; Wednesday lunchtime out of season and Tuesday

This restaurant was undergoing complete renovation when I last visited. It has always had a good reputation for well-presented and typical Alsace cuisine, and it is certainly worth visiting.

Le Bistrot

17 rue du Général de Gaulle
68340 Riquewihr

For a quick quiche or onion tart at 35F and an 18F glass of wine, drop in here.

THE SOUTHERN VINEYARDS

Where to buy

Zind-Humbrecht

route de Colmar
68230 Turckheim
Tel: (03) 89 27 02 05

Monday–Friday only, by appointment

This is one of the most distinguished houses in Alsace. It has magnificent cellars of modern concrete and old vats, and beautiful views of the vineyards from an elegant ultra-modern tasting room. Some will find it slightly corporate, others perhaps even a shade intimidating, but designers and serious wine connoisseurs will love this place, run by the much respected and liked Léonard and Olivier Humbrecht. The towering Olivier is married to a Scot, so he has an excellent command of English.

These are superb wines, although, apart from the Sylvaner

93 at 37F and a Riesling Wintzenheim 92 at 47F, they are not inexpensive. One of the best Alsace wines you can buy is Zind-Humbrecht's Gewürztraminer Clos Windsbuhl 90, spicy, creamy, elegant and superbly made. Buy this vintage if you can (it is sold in the UK for £15) or the 94 at the vineyard (132F). Taste the peerless delicacy of the Riesling grand cru Brand 94 (136F), the stunning mineral qualities of grand cru Rangen Clos-Saint-Urbain 94 (198F), the Gewürztraminer Clos Windsbuhl 94 (132F), and the Tokay-Pinot Gris Rotenberg 93 vendanges tardives (395F). The exquisite Gewürztraminer Goldert vendanges tardives 89 at 255F is more expensive than in the UK. Whilst the Gewürztraminer Goldert 93 is exceptionally palatable, there is little saving on the UK price.

How to get there: With its discreet sign and modern low-lying building, it is not easy to come across, unless you are specifically looking for the vineyard. Drive out of Turckheim on the road to Colmar, pass the JM factory on your left, then you will see a grey wall on your right, with a gate into Zind-Humbrecht.

Cave de Turckheim

16 rue des Tuileries
68230 Turckheim
Tel: (03) 89 27 06 25
Open daily including holidays

Ignore the housing blocks down the hill from the *cave*, and enjoy the views uphill over the vineyards from the rather elegant tasting room, which is more a bar than a traditional tasting room. The staff are very charming, and this a good place to taste (and buy) wine.

There are a couple of very good wines under 35F: a dry, spicy Gewürztraminer 94 at 33F (just under £6 in the UK) and a refreshing Tokay-Pinot Gris Réserve 94 at 34F. You might enjoy their fresh, concentrated Gewürztraminer Réserve 93 at 37F (just under £7 in the UK). The Riesling grand cru Brand 90 (65F) and Gewürztraminer grand cru Brand 92 (70F) are both well worth tasting.

Josmeyer

76 rue Clémenceau, 68920 Wintzenheim
Tel: (03) 89 27 91 90
Open Monday–Friday only
This grey 1802 building with white shutters and brown window surrounds is easy to find on the busy main street through town; it is opposite the Hôtel Cristal and by bus stop 5 Poincaré. Park in the cobbled courtyard, pretty with its half-timbered buildings, the pastel blue tasting room and the mustard yellow offices.

These are not inexpensive wines. The lovely Gewürztraminer Les Archenets 90, with its intense flavours and delightful nose, costs 85F. A very fine selection of *vendanges tardives* and *sélection de grains nobles*, again from 98F.

Relatively less expensive wines between 50F and 60F include a Tokay-Pinot Gris 94 Le Fromenteau, a Muscat d'Alsace 95 and a Riesling 93.

Pierre Frick

5 rue de Baer, 68250 Pfaffenheim
Tel: (03) 89 49 62 99
Passionate about the environment and organic methods of growing grapes, the Fricks produce wine that will appeal to many on different grounds. The Sylvaner 94 is well balanced, understated and has a pretty colour (29F) and the Riesling grand cru Steinert 93 is a fine example of a delicious Riesling (48F). Don't miss their unusually fresh Muscat 93, complex and full of discrete flavours, a favourite.

Léon Beyer

2 rue de la 1re-Armée
Tasting at 8 place du Château St-Léon
68420 Eguisheim
Tel: (03) 89 41 41 05
Open Monday–Friday
Eguisheim is a stunning mediaeval town, with cobbled streets,

a fountain on the main square, carefully restored buildings and an ancient church. The estate office is easy to find; it is the half-timbered building with a cobbled courtyard on a corner opposite the post office. Or you might prefer to taste these wines in the Léon Beyer shop in town, overlooking the fountain at 8 place du Château St-Léon (not to be confused with Emile Beyer at 7). Whilst their Riesling starts at 52F, the Muscat at 56F and the Gewürztraminer at 59F (the Cuvée des Comtes from 95F is particularly good), it is the *vendanges tardives* that are outstanding, most of which come in half-bottles from 68F.

Maison Léon Baur

71 rue du Rempart-Nord
68420 Eguisheim
Tel: (03) 89 41 79 13

One of the oldest houses in Eguisheim, Baur have been making wine since the 18th century. The current owner, Jean-Louis Baur, lives across the road at 22 rue du Rempart-Nord. Don't hesitate to buy the well made Riesling 94 Cuvée Elisabeth Stumpf, winner of a gold medal in Paris, at 30F or the equally well made Gewürztraminer Kaefferkopf 95 at 48F.

Another very enjoyable Gewürztraminer is the grand cru Pfersigberg 94 at 45F. The 1994 Sylvaner is good value at 21F, as is the Muscat 94 at 32F.

Cave de Pfaffenheim

5 rue du Chai, 68250 Pfaffenheim
Tel: (03) 89 78 08 08

Open Monday–Saturday 8–12am and 2–6pm (and during lunch May–October); Sunday 10–12am and 2–6pm; public holidays except Christmas and New Year's Day

Visible from the main road, well signposted and easy to find, the Cave de Pfaffenheim makes the effort to be open when customers would like it to be open. It also happens to make some very good wines. Particularly fine are the Tokay-Pinot Gris, the Hatschbourg grand cru 93, an elegant Pinot Gris, creamy and slightly peachy, at 69F, and the Cuvée Rabelais 94, fresh and spicy at 46F. The Gewürztraminer 94 is fragrant and appley, great value at 39F, whilst another Gewürztraminer at 65F, the Goldert grand cru 93, is full and spicy. The Sylvaner is the least expensive wine, from 24F.

This a very good place to come and taste in a relaxed atmosphere, without feeling you are taking up too much of the winemakers' time, since the staff are there solely to help you enjoy tasting (and of course buying) the wine. The tasting room is very spacious, with plenty of tables, suffused with a golden yellow light from the stained glass windows.

Domaine Joseph Rieflé

11 place de la Mairie
68250 Pfaffenheim
Tel: (03) 89 49 62 82

The Tokay-Pinot Gris Côte de Rouffach 93 is a very well made wine, interesting with a smoky aroma, and a spicy baked apple taste (39F at the winemaker, £6.80 in the UK). The Riesling Gaentzbrunnen 93 is very typical of its *terroir*, with a delicate smell of flowers (41F). Taste the delicious Tokay-Pinot Gris 89 sélection de grains nobles, 130F for 50cl.

Kuentz-Bas

14 route du Vin
68420 Husseren-les-Châteaux
Tel: (03) 89 49 30 24
Open Monday–Friday and Saturday morning

The drive up to Husseren opens out onto splendid views of the valley below. With its long cobbled courtyard, window boxes and half-timbered buildings in pastel blue and light ochre, this estate looks like a small street in an old village. The estate of Kuentz-Bas, just over 200 years old, has developed a good reputation for winemaking.

The fragrant Gewürztraminer 92 at 52F and rich Riesling 93 at 55F are typical of Kuentz-Bas wines. One of the finest wines is the astonishingly concentrated Gewürztraminer Pfersigberg sélection de grains nobles 89, unfortunately 300F a bottle, or 153F a half-bottle.

René Muré
Clos St-Landelin
68250 Rouffach
Tel: (03) 89 78 58 00
Open Monday–Saturday (and Sunday from Easter to October)
At the southern edge of Rouffach, the ochre and mustard estate buildings of this vineyard are easy to spot from the main highway. The tasting room overlooks the vineyard.

Côte de Rouffach wines start at 30F, Clos St-Landelin wines at 40F. Try the dry but fruity Riesling 94 Clos St-Landelin grand cru Vorbourg (71F) and the oak matured Pinot Noir Clos St-Landelin 93, nicely spicy and quite potent (94F). The apple pie Gewürztraminer Côte de Rouffach 93 is great drinking and is more affordable at 40F.

Léon Heitzmann
2 Grand'Rue
68770 Ammerschwihr
Tel: (03) 89 47 10 64
Very reasonably priced wines here for the quality: try the very good Riesling Ammerschwihr, the Pinot Noir and a delicious Muscat, all under 36F. My favourite wine would be his Gewürztraminer Kaefferkopf 93, more expensive at 53F.

Vins Kuehn
3 Grand'Rue
68770 Ammerschwihr
Tel: (03) 89 78 23 16
Another reliable house in a grand building with splendid cellars. I particularly liked the Muscat, a reasonable 31F, the Tokay-Pinot Gris Réserve Particulière 93 and the Riesling grand cru Sommerberg 93.

Where to stay in the southern vineyards

A l'Arbre Vert
7 rue des Cigognes
68770 Ammerschwihr
Tel: (03) 89 47 12 33
Closed Tuesday; end November, February and March
Double 270–350F

Just off the main square with the Hôtel de Ville, part of the hotel is painted cream, with red canopies over the windows, part pink with white shutters. Look up at the beautiful wrought iron sign that hangs on the corner by the fountain.

One single room with shared bath and loo is only 130F, otherwise single rate is 200F.

The hotel is surrounded by winemakers: next door is **Henri Girardin** at 4 Grand'Rue, and **Léon Heitzmann** at 2. Opposite are the rather grand offices and 18th-century cellars of **Vins Kuehn** at 3 Grand'Rue, and **Vins Henri Erhart** at 7.

A la Ville de Lyon
1 rue Poincaré
68250 Rouffach
Tel: (03) 89 49 65 51
Double 270–420F
Closed end February to mid-March

This hotel is recommended for its location in the heart of the vineyards. It is a bland, ordinary building, but it has a couple of 420F rooms at the back with glorious views of the vineyards and Château d'Isenbourg. And you get a decent breakfast in the dining room overlooking the courtyard.

It is also attached to the **Restaurant Philippe Bohrer** and **Bierstub Chez Julian** (tel: 89 49 69 80), which does a simple three course 48F menu, although the 85F menu offers an appealing *carpaccio* of salmon, *choucroute* as the main course, and a *mousse au kirsch*. Sunday brunch, served from 11–2, is particularly useful for those with children under seven, whose lunch is entirely free.

Hostellerie du Château

2 place du Château
68420 Eguisheim
Tel: (03) 89 23 72 00
Double 480F

Painted pale green with darker green shutters, this hotel looks out onto the small main square in the pretty mediaeval town of Eguisheim with its ancient castle, and half-timbered houses with their wooden balconies and pointed gables.

Rooms are comfortable with white linen and duvets, and prettily tiled bathrooms. Everything is sparkling new, and the design conscious will appreciate the eye for detail. Décor is minimalist 90s, far from provincial traditional. For 590F double you only get a room (and breakfast), there is little else in the way of hotel facilities.

The proprietors also own the **Caveau d'Eguisheim**, the restaurant on the other side of the square.

Berceau du Vigneron

10 place Turenne
68230 Turckheim
Tel: (03) 89 27 23 55
Closed November to March
Offers simple rooms in a half-timbered building from 210F.

Auberge du Cheval Blanc

20 rue de Rouffach
68250 Westhalten
Tel: (03) 89 47 01 16
Closed February, last week in June and first week of July
Double 400F
Very comfortable and has views over the Vosges and a restaurant conveniently next door.

Hôtel du Bollenberg

Domaine du Bollenberg, 68250 Bollenberg
Tel: (03) 89 49 62 47
Double 320–350F

Wine lovers seeking a (mostly) peaceful place in the heart of the countryside and vineyards, with views over the mountains and across the valley below, will be delighted with the location of this hotel, although the rooms themselves are unexceptional and on the small side. The hotel is quite a long drive off the main road, so try to get here during the day. Very convenient after a splendid meal at **Au Vieux Pressoir** (see opposite).

Visit the tasting room of the Domaine, with its magnificent 1787 Joseph Becher timber *pressoir* and old casks.

Where to eat in the southern vineyards

A l'Arbre Vert

7 rue des Cigognes, 68770 Ammerschwihr
Tel: (03) 89 47 12 23
Closed Tuesdays; mid-Feb to end March and part November
menus from 70F
For good value regional cooking.

Restaurant Le Butterfly

1 rue du Romarin, 68770 Ammerschwihr
Tel: (03) 89 47 15 97
Stroll across Grande'Rue for a 58F lunch of *quiche lorraine* or onion tart with a plate of *crudités* and a glass of Pinot Blanc at the bar, or a grill from the wood fire in the dining room.

Aux Armes de France (the Gaertner's restaurant)

1 Grand'Rue, 68770 Ammerschwihr
Tel: (03) 89 47 10 12
Closed Wednesday and Thursday lunchtime
Only come here if you are interested in spending a minimum of 360F at this highly rated and highly expensive restaurant.

Aux Trois Merles (tel: 89 78 24 35) offers a good value 80F menu, with the added pleasure of wine by the glass.

Auberge du Veilleur

12 place Turenne
68230 Turckheim
Tel: (03) 89 27 32 22
Closed Wednesday
Menus from 49F

Located right by the entrance to the old town, you can't miss this *auberge*, but tourist trap it isn't. Brilliant value Alsace specialities, along with reputable local wines by the glass or jug. At lunchtime there is a simple but satisfying 49F *menu du jour*, in the evening choose from a 90F menu offering *salade vigneronne*, *choucroute garnie* and dessert, or blackboard specials such as *boudin chaud sur compote de pommes*.

Wines by the glass are remarkably good value at about 10F, up to 25F for a Muscat 93 by Rolly Gassmann. Many good local wines from Zind-Humbrecht, Josmeyer, Gustave Lorenz and Léon Beyer from 80F.

The interior is cosy and warm, with comfortable banquettes, pink tablecloths and lace lampshades. Children will marvel at the flowers, dolls and puppets adorning the walls.

Au Vieux Pressoir

68250 Bollenberg
Tel: (03) 89 49 60 04

Enter through front doors with magnificent old carved shutters, and walk down a splendid corridor to the dining room, a long room with beautiful panelling on both the walls and ceiling. White linen, large plates and heavy cutlery on the tables. The 85F menu changes regularly, but on this occasion, as part of La Fête de Monsieur Cochon, offered *presskopf* and *sauküss* with pickled grapes and local bread, *civet de porcelet* in Spaetzle as main course, dessert and *petits fours*. Wine is available by the glass, carafe or bottle.

La Grangelière

59 rue du Rempart-Sud
68420 Eguisheim
Tel: (03) 89 23 00 30
Closed Thursday and February
Menus from 120F

This half-timbered restaurant, peach coloured with pale blue shutters, is on the corner of a narrow cobbled street of magnificent mediaeval houses.

Imaginative and high quality cooking: the 120F menu consisted of a *gâteau de lapereau aux lentilles vertes*, a *filet de cabillaud* with leeks or *jambonette de vollaille à la moutarde*, finishing with a *tarte sucrée au fromage blanc* with an apricot *coulis*.

La Taverne Alsacienne

99 rue de la République
68040 Ingersheim
Tel: (03) 89 27 08 41
Closed Sunday evening, Monday; mid-July to early August
Menus from 70F

This restaurant is on a corner overlooking the bridge across the River Fecht. Of the three dining areas, the cosiest with its wooden floor, looks out onto the rue de la République; and the liveliest is the bar.

A 75F menu offered a *terrine de canard et gésiers*, *jambonneau sur choucroute*, and a *tarte*.

Champagne

Champagne is very different from the other wine producing regions in France. It may not have the picture postcard looks of Alsace or the gentle charm of the Loire, and the villages may not have the warmth, life or vibrancy found elsewhere; there may be fewer hotels, cafés and restaurants in the countryside, but it does have very welcoming winemakers, and a marvellous wine called champagne.

Getting there

The easiest and fastest route is straight down the motorway from Calais to Reims. Of course it is more interesting to meander down the almost traffic free E roads, but that becomes a trip in itself. After many trips via the scenic route, I prefer to cover the distance quickly to arrive in Reims in time to relax in a bath or shower before going out for a drink and dinner, and a good night's rest.

ABOUT CHAMPAGNE

Vintages

Great vintages now on the market are the 1985 and 1988. The 1990 has started to be released, but is not necessarily ready to drink in some cases.

Grape varieties

Chardonnay produces a fragrant and sometimes honeyed champagne. Pinot Noir and Pinot Meunier are the black grapes (normally used in making red wine) which are pressed very carefully for champagne.

The wines

Most champagne is made with a blend of white and black grapes. However, there are some 'pure' styles:

199

Blanc de Blancs is made solely from the Chardonnay grape, producing a fresh, lighter style of wine that can be extremely elegant.

Blanc de Noir is made from black grapes only.

See Méthode Champenoise (page 232) for more on making champagne.

There are also the still red, white and rosé wines of Champagne, known as Coteaux Champenois which include Bouzy Rouge, and Rosé des Riceys from the Aube region to the south of Champagne. These should be drunk young.

Where to buy champagne

For some of the more well-known *marques* at competitive prices, and for champagne that is particularly cheap, hypermarkets, whether at the ports or elsewhere in France, are as good a place as any to buy your champagne. Hard nosed corporate buying results in champagne from as little as 50F per bottle, and some of it (not all, though) is good value, depending on what you are looking for. This is because some reputable champagne makers will also produce 'BOB' champagnes, as they are known in the trade, that is 'buyer's own brand'. In general, the maker's name is considerably less evident than the brand name. An example of one such maker producing an inexpensive champagne is Robert Dufour et Fils of Landreville, whose Cuvée Prestige is well known and appreciated, yet produces a champagne called Charles de Celville, selling at 55F at a major supermarket.

The big surprise is that supermarkets in Champagne itself do not carry a larger range of champagne than those elsewhere in the country. Nothing, however, compares with a visit to Champagne itself where there is an unrivalled range of the *Grandes Marques* and an opportunity to visit the great champagne houses. Most exciting of all is the possibility of tasting and buying champagne from small houses, unavailable elsewhere and offering superb value at prices under 80F.

THE *GRANDES MARQUES*

The *Grandes Marques* are situated almost exclusively in the urban centres of Reims (pronounced *rance*) and Epernay.

Several of the major champagne houses will welcome you without any appointment. Just arrive and they will show you around, generally when they have gathered a few English speaking visitors together. Others request that you phone a couple of days in advance, as they may not have full time staff dedicated to looking after visitors.

I have included only a few of the great champagne houses; there are, of course, many others as distinguished.

Reims
In the east end of Reims there are a couple of houses where you will be welcome without an appointment:

Taittinger
9 place St-Niçaise
51100 Reims
Tel: (03) 26 85 45 35

Piper Heidsieck (part of the Rémy group)
51 boulevard Henri-Vasnier
51100 Reims
Tel: (03) 26 85 01 94

Phone in advance to arrange a visit to any one of the following houses:

Pommery
5 place du Gal-Gouraud
51100 Reims
Tel: (03) 26 61 62 63
This is one of my favourites. The buildings may look more like an English Victorian institution than a gracious French cham-

pagne house, but once inside, one hundred glorious steps down to the cellars will transport you into another world.

If you are planning a wedding, you should look at Pommery's particularly attractive Flacon de Fête. This is a bottle with an inscription hand painted in gold leaf for special occasions. A magnum (equivalent to two bottles) will cost 800F and a jeroboam (four bottles) costs 1600F. Either of these would make a treasured present. All their champagnes, however, are elegantly presented.

And across the road is the entrance to one of France's most well known restaurants, Les Crayères (see below).

Ruinart (part of the LMVH empire)
4 rue des Crayères
51100 Reims
Tel: (03) 26 85 40 29

Veuve Clicquot Ponsardin
12 rue du Temple
51100 Reims
Tel: (03) 26 40 25 42

In the north of the city, nearer the centre and most of the hotels, the following is open without appointment:

Mumm (owned by Seagram)
29 rue du Champ-de-Mars, 51100 Reims
Tel: (03) 26 49 59 69

By appointment (phone or write at least a couple of days ahead) you are welcome at:

Jacquart
5 rue Gosset
51100 Reims
Tel: (03) 26 07 20 20

Champagne

What to see
Cathédrale Notre-Dame
Reims

This really is one of the most beautiful cathedrals in the world even though it suffered greatly in the two world wars. Painstaking restoration of the 13th-century stained glass, and the addition of modern windows by Marc Chagall, make a late-afternoon visit here particularly memorable when the low light picks up the brilliant colours in all their glory.

Palais du Tau
Reims

Many of the cathedral's treasures are housed here in this former archbishop's palace built in 1690. The collection includes sculpture, tapestries and coronation robes, as well as chalices and reliquaries.

Cathédrale St-Etienne
Chalons-sur-Marne (28 miles/45km southeast of Reims)

The beautiful Romanesque tower of the cathedral looks out over the banks of the Marne, and the superb stained glass windows date from the 13th century.

Cathédrale St-Pierre-et-St-Paul
Troyes

Joan of Arc visited this cathedral on her way to the crowning of Charles VII. Troyes, famous for its beautiful stained glass, is known as the 'sacred city of windows' and there is a magnificent rose window here.

Musée d'Art Moderne
Troyes
In a renovated bishop's palace next door to the cathedral, the museum has a significant collection of 19th and 20th century art including works by Bonnard, Cézanne, Gauguin, Matisse and Picasso.

Quartier St-Jean
Troyes
The mediaeval quarter of the city, across the canal from the cathedral, has been restored and revitalized, its cobbled streets and 16th-century buildings now housing shops and restaurants.

Krug (part of the Rémy group)
5 rue Coquebert, 51100 Reims
Tel: (03) 26 88 24 24

Heidsieck-Monopole
83 rue Coquebert, 51100 Reims
Tel: (03) 26 07 39 34

Lanson
12 boulevard Lundy, 51100 Reims
Tel: (03) 26 78 50 50

Louis Roederer
21 boulevard Lundy
51100 Reims
Tel: (03) 26 40 42 11
Owners of Château Picard-Beauséjour in Saint-Estèphe, and with a controlling interest in Champagne Deutz.

Epernay

Drive up the appropriately named avenue de Champagne. After passing the tourist office on your left, you will see **Moët et Chandon**, their elegant offices and Orangerie opposite, then **Perrier-Jouët**'s pretty pink-washed premises around a cobbled courtyard. **Venoge** is next door, alongside **Pol Roger**, opposite are **Charbaut et Fils**, built around another pretty cobbled courtyard, and elegant **Besserat de Bellefon**. More famous names follow: **Vranken**, **De Castellane**, **Boizel** and **Mercier**.

You will be welcomed in several of the champagne houses without appointment in Epernay. Several offer particularly interesting tours of their cellars, along with multi-media presentations, which you may find rather commercial and sales oriented, but are nevertheless well worth experiencing.

Mercier (part of the Moët group)
68 avenue de Champagne, 51200 Epernay
Tel: (03) 26 54 75 26

Leclerc Briant
67 Claude-Ruelle, 51200 Epernay
Tel: (03) 26 54 45 33

Pol Roger
1 rue Henri-Lelarge, 51200 Epernay
Tel: (03) 26 55 41 95

De Castellane (part of the Laurent-Perrier group)
57 rue de Verdun, 51200 Epernay
Tel: (03) 26 55 15 33

Phone in advance to arrange a visit to:
Moët et Chandon (owned by the luxury empire of LMVH)
20 avenue de Champagne, 51200 Epernay
Tel: (03) 26 54 71 11

André Charbaut
17 avenue de Champagne, 51200 Epernay
Tel: (03) 26 54 37 55

Besserat de Bellefon
19 avenue de Champagne, 51200 Epernay
Tel: (03) 26 59 51 00

Perrier-Jouët (owned by Seagram)
28 avenue de Champagne, 51200 Epernay
Tel: (03) 26 55 20 53

Demoiselle Vranken (owns Barancourt in Bouzy)
42 avenue de Champagne, 51200 Epernay
Tel: (03) 26 54 91 86

Haut-Villers

Just outside Epernay is the picture postcard village of Haut-Villers, steeped in the history of champagne. Don't be put off by the tourist coaches parked in the place de la République, the village is charming. The church now standing in the village was built in 1518, and is the third building on the site since the church was founded in 650. Here are the tombs of two of the most famous names in Champagne: Dom Petrus Pérignon 1638–1715 and l'Erudit Dom Ruinart 1657–1709.

Opposite the church at 38 rue de l'Eglise is a small tasting and sales room for **J.M. Gobillard** (Tel: (03) 26 51 00 24), whose main office and warehouse is in the considerably less attractive industrial suburb of Dizy, and is open only at weekends from Easter until Christmas. There will be a warm welcome for tasters in a light, vaulted room. The least expensive of their champagnes is the fragrant Brut Tradition (74F) – a favourite, with plenty of bubbles, colour and taste. Chill a bottle and enjoy it on a picnic in Champagne. Superb Blanc de Blancs 91, with marvellous aromas and flavours.

Where to stay in Reims
Hôtel Univers
41 boulevard Foch
51100 Reims
Tel: (03) 26 88 68 08
Double 310F

In true tradition, the ground floor entrance to the hotel is brighter and fresher than the more worn upstairs floors. Although rooms are unexceptional, they are reasonably priced for Reims, and the hotel does have much to recommend it.

Although virtually at the heart of the city, the hotel is easy to find, there is convenient parking right outside the front door, and it is a short stroll to some excellent restaurants and the shopping centre. Front rooms have a leafy view over the trees and gardens between two major boulevards.

The hotel has a good atmosphere; staff are cheerful and helpful, and when something goes wrong, it is fixed quickly, and when you need something, it is provided. A convenient and good value base.

The following three hotels, with rooms under 500F, are comfortable, well looked after, and offer the high standards maintained by all three chains:

Holiday Inn Garden Court
46 rue Buirette
51100 Reims
Tel: (03) 26 47 56 00

Only one block away from boulevard Général Leclerc, the Holiday Inn Garden Court is easily accessible from the motorway, and yet it is close to the city centre.

Rooms are good Holiday Inn standard. The restaurant on the seventh floor (reached by a panoramic glass lift) is bright and cheerful with great views of the city, especially in the summer from the outdoor terrace.

Mercure-Cathédrale

31 boulevard Paul-Doumer, 51100 Reims
Tel: (03) 26 84 49 49
Restaurant closed Saturday and Sunday lunchtimes
Easy to get to from the motorway, yet close to the city centre.
Comfortable rooms, always immaculately clean, and pleasant
staff. Consistently good.

Quality Hotel

37 boulevard Paul-Doumer
51100 Reims
Tel: (03) 26 40 01 08
Restaurant closed Saturday lunchtime and Sunday
Not an attractive building from the outside, but once inside,
rooms are of a good standard, with sparkling bathrooms, a
fridge for your half-bottles, and a light snack all night room service. Charming and friendly staff. Ask for a room overlooking
the Canal d'Aisne. Easy to reach from the motorway.

Where to eat in Reims

Le Drouet

96 place Drouet-d'Erlon
51100 Reims
Tel: (03) 26 88 56 39
Menus from 90F including wine
My favourite restaurant in Reims used to be Le Florence which
is sadly no more. But the owners have moved to the magnificent building next door on the corner of boulevard Foch and
place Drouet d'Erlon to open this more informal, very 90s bar-
diner restaurant. Packed with customers at lunchtime, either ordering just a main course (58–68F) with a 15F glass of wine at
the tables in the bar area, or relaxing in the modern, understated
dining room. Here you can have a delicious two course lunch
for 90F. There is also a terrific value wine list, with house
champagne at 150F and *Grandes Marques* from 190F. Open
until 11.30pm at the weekend.

Champagne

Wine Fairs and Festivals
Cumières, Epernay, Haut-villers, Reims
Festival of St-Jean on the Saturday nearest to the 24th June

Aube
Champagne festival of the Aube vineyards on the last Sunday in August once every three years

Bar-sur-Aube
Champagne wine fair on the second Sunday in September

Le Continental
95 place Drouet-d'Erlon
51100 Reims
Tel: (03) 26 47 01 47
Menus from 79F
Opposite Le Drouet, this more old fashioned restaurant, with its splendid old ceiling and pink linen tablecloths, is packed at lunchtime with business people enjoying the good cooking and good value menus.

Kristea's
8 rue de Thillois
51100 Reims
Tel: (03) 26 88 62 11
Closed Sunday and Monday
Menus from 69F
The large tinted glass front of this restaurant, with curtains that prevent you from looking in, makes it less inviting than it is. Once inside, it's a relaxing place, with minimalist décor of par-

quet floors, light wood panelling, steel and beech chairs, and a few *objets*, including large pots with pretty paper flowers.

Kristea is a daughter of the Larmandier-Bernier winemaking family in Vertus, so inevitably the wine list offers their own champagne (148F) alongside Ruinart (204F). The list of other local champagnes and wines is rather limited, but other wines are well chosen, such as a Sancerre 93 from Bernard Reverdy (134F) and a Bonnezeaux 91 from Gaston Lenôtre.

At lunch the 69F menu consists of a green salad, *blanquette de veau* with wild rice or a *panache de poisson, sauce oseille*, and cheese or dessert.

In the evenings, menus start at 100F, although some à la carte dishes are appealing: *carpaccio* of duck with olive oil or marinated salmon to start, and roast tuna or duck breast as main course. Mostly good value, but a bottle of mineral water at 28F and a cappuccino for 25F are not.

La Vigneraie
14 rue de Thillois
51100 Reims
Tel: (03) 26 88 67 27
Closed Sunday evening and Monday; 1–15 January and 1–21 August. Menus from 90F
For a more formal atmosphere, a couple of doors down from Kristea's, La Vigneraie offers a lunchtime menu of poached eggs with a tomato *coulis* and parmesan, an *émincé de volaille crème*, and cheese or dessert. In the evening, the 130F menu consisted of *croustade de moules, gigot de volaille, sauce diable*, a *brie de Meaux* and a dessert of *poire tiède aux épices*.

Au Petit Bacchus
11 rue de l'Université
51100 Reims
Tel: (03) 26 47 10 05
Menus from 85F
Another restaurant worth visiting, if you are near the cathedral.

Boyer-Les Crayères
64 boulevard Henry-Vasnier
51100 Reims
Tel: (03) 26 82 80 80
Menus from 600F
Closed all day on Monday and Tuesday lunchtime; mid-December to mid-January
One of the most famous restaurants in France, situated in a pretty château in 15 acres (6ha) of grounds, and only a few minutes drive from the city centre. It is a Reims institution, where heads of the large champagne houses entertain their important clients. Rather grand for some – it is essential to book well ahead.

Also offers the ultimate rooms in Reims (with a convenient helipad) from 1000–1800F for a double room, breakfast almost 100F each. When booking, check on the location and size of your room to ensure you are getting exactly what you want.

THE SMALLER CHAMPAGNE HOUSES

Some of the smaller houses are producing superb champagnes. Of course they do not have the resources of the large houses, nor the same stocks of old vintages with which to make their champagne, but the value they offer can be tremendous.

Some of the houses are a delight to visit and almost without exception, the winemakers go out of their way to be welcoming and informative, despite the pressures of time.

A visit to the smaller champagne houses falls into two natural geographical circuits: the northern and southern circuits.

The Northern Circuit
The northern circuit takes in the villages of Ambonnay, Bouzy, Verzenay, Ludes, Chigny-les-Roses and Rilly-la-Montagne. This could be tackled either from a base in Reims or we have suggested Tours-sur-Marne as an out-of-town centre.

Ambonnay

R.H. Coutier

7 rue Henri III and
10 boulevard des Fosses de Ronde
51150 Ambonnay
Tel: (03) 26 57 02 55

Open Monday–Saturday; Sunday and public holidays by appointment; closed February

Drive through green steel gates down a cobbled and gravel driveway into an old farmyard shaded by a fir tree. The original entrance on the other side is through ancient wooden gates to the old house with its huge oak beams and wooden shutters. The farm has been in the family for four generations, although the renovation is fairly recent.

By the original gates, in an old stone building including a small cellar, are a small museum of old viticulture implements and the old tasting room.

Taste the Brut Tradition (74F), particularly good value in half-bottles at 39F, as well as the Brut 90 at 95F.

Bouzy

A much loved name, renowned as well for its still wine, Bouzy Rouge. A rather quiet village, but it does have a *pâtisserie* selling mini-quiches and almond croissants. The only bar is very typical, with a Wurlitzer and photograph of the Bouzy football team proudly displayed above the bar.

Pierre Paillard

2 rue du XXe Siècle
51150 Bouzy
Tel: (03) 26 57 08 04

Open Monday–Saturday; Sunday by appointment

Not to be confused with Bruno Paillard, who is based in Reims, Pierre Paillard is a much smaller producer based in the country. His elegant home looks over a large courtyard and the winemaking buildings in the opposite corner. The tasting room, with its dark ochre walls, and coir floor covering, is partly a museum, filled with many interesting exhibits, a very pleasant and congenial place to taste Paillard's champagnes. And Pierre Paillard is very charming and helpful.

The brut, made mainly from Chardonnay and Pinot Noir, is very fresh and has a light delicate *mousse*, the perfect breakfast champagne, as opposed to an aggressive party champagne. It is the colour of pale straw and has a delicate bouquet. Great value for 78F, half-bottles at 43F. The half-bottles of Brut Rosé are slightly more expensive at 48F. There are still a few bottles of his splendid Brut 1985 left at 112F, or enjoy the excellent 89.

André Clouet
8 rue Gambetta
51150 Bouzy
Tel: (03) 26 57 00 82
All visits by appointment

This is an elegant home, with white shutters and a slate roof, around a large gravel courtyard dotted with tree planters. I first encountered André Clouet's grand cru classé champagnes in a small wine merchant's cellar in England.

The Brut Grande Réserve, made up from the 1990 and 1991 vintages, at 86F is only a couple of francs more expensive than the Brut. The magnums of Brut Grande Réserve would make a splendid gift at 174F. The Brut 90 is available at 112F.

Jean Vesselle
2 place J-B Barnaut
51150 Bouzy
Tel: (03) 26 57 01 55
Open daily

Here is a winemaker who makes wine that expresses its origins, the place and ground whence it came.

The most distinctive of Jean Vesselle's champagnes is his Brut Oeil de Perdrix, a Blanc de Noir, at 89F, with pretty colour and complex tastes. Probably the best value is the Brut Réserve, at 85F (half-bottles 44F).

E. Barnaut

2 rue Gambetta
51150 Bouzy
Tel: (03) 26 57 01 54
Open Monday–Saturday, Sunday by appointment

Now run by the Secondé family, Barnaut produces some very interesting champagnes. The Grande Réserve Brut (85F), two-thirds Pinot Noir, one-third Chardonnay, had a nice colour and would make a good fizzy celebratory champagne. The Sélection Extra Brut (91F), mainly Pinot Noir, is exceptionally good. Taste the 1990 vintage (120F) and the Bouzy Rouge 90 (85F).

Paul Bara

4 rue Yvonne
51150 Bouzy
Tel: (03) 26 57 00 50
Open Monday–Friday
Closed August

This family has been making champagne for six generations. Their Brut Réserve (88F), mainly Pinot Noir, partly Chardonnay, is impeccably made, with a distinctive fruit aroma. The Brut 89 (102F) is well worth tasting. The Grand Rosé de Bouzy is also made mainly from Pinot Noir, with delicious fruit (99F).

Verzenay, Ludes, Chigny-les-Roses and Rilly-la-Montagne

Cattier

6 rue Dom Pérignon
51500 Chigny-les-Roses
Tel: (03) 26 03 42 11

On the main road to Rilly, a simple modern office building with good parking. Well made and good value Brut at 85F, the 90 vintage at 93F.

214

Michel Arnould
28 rue de Mailly
51360 Verzenay
Tel: (03) 26 49 40 06
Open Monday–Friday; by appointment at weekends
An illuminated round yellow sign for this winemaker makes it easy to spot. The tasting room is in the main house.

All the champagne is produced from their own vines. The Brut has good fruit and costs 69F. The same champagne is sold under the label of Patrick Arnould at Tesco in Calais and in the UK, where it sells for £14, making savings quite substantial. The Brut Réserve at 74F is also worth tasting.

Thierry Blondel
Domaine des Monts-Fournois
51500 Ludes
Tel: (03) 26 03 43 92
One mile (1.5 km) north of Ludes, and 6 miles (10 km) south of Reims on the D9. Driving from Ludes, you will see a large farmhouse in open countryside on the left, an elegant building in rough stone, with a red tiled roof and white shutters, and a large barn at the rear. The tasting room is at his new house, well signposted, to the rear.

Blondel produces premier cru champagne from just under 25 acres (10ha) of vines in the *montagne de Reims*. His Carte Or Brut, two-thirds Pinot Noir, one-third Chardonnay, has a slightly peachy aroma, is a well made and delicious champagne in every way; particularly good value at 76F. Taste his Blanc de Blancs 90 at 96F and for comparison, his excellent Vieux Millesime 85 (106F), toasty, buttery and fresh.

If you are interested in a rosé champagne, then Blondel's beautifully coloured and fruity rosé is one to go for.

Where to stay and eat

Tours-sur-Marne makes a particularly convenient base for visiting the villages on the northern circuit.

In the village itself there are a couple of good champagne houses: **Laurent-Perrier** (Tel: (03) 26 58 91 22) which produces still wines as well as champagne (from 137F), and **Lamiable** (8 rue de Condé, Tel: (03) 26 58 92 69).

La Touraine Champenoise
51150 Tours-sur-Marne
Tel: (03) 26 58 91 93
Closed at Christmas
Double room 295F
Menus from 95F

This small hotel by the canal has a bright bar where light lunches (ham sandwich 22F or *plat du jour* for 40F) are served, and a restaurant for more formal dining. The 96F menu consisted of a *mousse de foie de canard* with toast, a *sauté de veau à l'orange* and cheese or dessert.

Rooms at 295F are not the same standard as the 320F rooms at the Mont-Aimé in Vertus, or the 295F rooms at the Central in Saumur, but are still pleasant and well located.

Auberge St-Vincent
rue St-Vincent, 51150 Ambonnay
Tel: (03) 26 57 01 98
Double 300–370F
Menus from 95F
Closed Sunday evening and Monday

St Vincent is the patron saint of winegrowers, so this could be a well-chosen venue for wine lovers. Chef and owner Jean-Claude Pelletier's cooking has a good reputation. A 95F menu consists of a *marbre de lapin* to start, *petit jambonneau aux lentillons rosés de Champagne* for the main course, and *gâteau de pain aux pommes* for dessert.

But you may find the regional dishes using local produce and wines on the 150F *menu Champenois* more interesting. To start, a ham and chervil terrine; the *deuxième plat* (an extra 40F) a rabbit sausage, or pike poached in red butter. As main course, tongue preserved in *ratafia* (a *vin de liqueur* of Champagne) or pheasant in wine with mushrooms. The cheese dish was puff pastry filled with *maroilles*, a cheese which is fairly aggressive in both taste and smell. The most delicious dessert is a *sorbet* made from *marc de champagne*, an *eau de vie* or brandy distilled from the pressed grapes left over after the wine has been made. Drinks, especially locally produced, are on the pricey side.

Ten rooms are available, but check whether demi-pension is obligatory if you are staying during the season, and if so, the additional cost.

The Southern Circuit

The Southern Circuit takes in the villages of Vertus, Mesnil-sur-Oger and Avize.

Vertus

The drive from Montmort to Vertus via Chaltrait is very pretty. Miss breakfast at the Cheval Blanc in Montmort, and stop at the Mont-Aimé for a super value breakfast for 50F (see below). A short drive will bring you to Vertus where there are many champagne houses you might like to drop into.

Guy Larmandier

30 rue du Général Koenig, 51130 Vertus
Tel: (03) 26 52 12 41
Open Monday–Saturday, preferably by appointment
The house is in peaceful old Vertus, at the heart of the village with its cobbled pavements and wooden shutters. Larmandier is across the street from the village pond and old church.

The Brut Premier Cru (75F) is a substantial champagne, very typical of the wines of Vertus, as is the flowery Rosé Brut (81F). Taste the fruity and round Cramant Brut grand cru Blanc de Blancs, at 82F. Buy the award winning 89 and 90 vintages whilst they are still available (105F). Good all round value.

217

Larmandier-Bernier

43 rue du 28 Août
51130 Vertus
Tel: (03) 26 52 13 24
Open Monday–Saturday and Sunday morning
Taste the Brut Tradition premier cru 82F and Brut Blanc de
Blancs premier cru 89F, elegant, well made, restrained but ever
so slightly creamy, certainly different. The Crémant grand cru
90 (100F) has a delightful complex nose, a very satisfying well
balanced wine.

Mesnil-sur-Oger

There are an unusual number of fine champagne houses in
Mesnil-sur-Oger, a charming village further enhanced by a first
rate restaurant, **Le Mesnil**. The champagne houses are well
signposted in town.

J.L. Vergnon

1 Grand'Rue
51190 Mesnil-sur-Oger
Tel: (03) 26 57 53 86
Open Monday–Friday; weekends by appointment
Taste the grand cru Blanc de Blancs, creamy but dry, a distinc-
tive flavour and character; a superb *aperitif* champagne.

Launois Père et Fils

3 avenue de la République
or 2 avenue Eugène Guillaume
51190 Mesnil-sur-Oger
Tel: (03) 26 57 50 15
The round white tower on the street corner is difficult to miss.
There is always a warm welcome from Monsieur Launois,
whose family has been making champagne since 1872, and is
someone who not only knows his business, but also obviously
enjoys it. Not much of this champagne is exported, so you may
come across an impressive line-up of cars that have come from

other European countries to effect their own personal imports of this wonderful wine.

Excellent value champagnes start at 70F, but particularly good is the Blanc de Blancs Cuvée Réservée at 75F, and the vintage Champagne 1988 is well worth the extra at 83F. Look out too for the vintage 90.

Tastings are held in the comfortable front office. However, if you are travelling with a small group of friends, Monsieur Launois would be only too happy to arrange for a more formal tasting out in the courtyard garden or in his museum filled with old champagne making equipment.

Pierre Moncuit

11 rue Persault-Mahen
51190 Mesnil-sur-Oger
Tel: (03) 26 57 52 65
Open daily including holidays

This is an elegant small champagne house. To get there, once in the village of Mesnil-sur-Oger, take the road in the direction of Montmort, and Champagne Pierre Moncuit is to be found on the left.

The handsome white shuttered house looks out over a well tended courtyard, through steel gates to a busy street. Nicole Montcuit, who has taken over running the champagne house from her parents with her brother Yves, is now a highly regarded winemaker. Her mother, Odile, is also involved in this family business and showed me around the immaculate winemaking rooms and cellars.

Unusually, they have available a vintage from every year between 1985 and 1990, except an 87, from 100–127F. Their two least expensive champagnes, Cuvée Hugues de Coulmet at 73F (half-bottle 39F) and Cuvée de Réserve (81F) are very good value. The Cuvée de Réserve is particularly fine, with lots of flavour – this is a champagne of great finesse. Of the vintage champagnes, the Blanc de Blancs 88 is superb with a very delicate aroma.

Claude Cazals
28 rue du Grand Mont
51190 Mesnil-sur-Oger
Tel: (03) 26 57 52 26
Open Monday–Friday
By appointment at weekends

Claude Cazals is the man who revolutionized the champagne industry with his invention of the gyropalette in 1969, which automates the process of tipping and turning champagne bottles, a step which is still not universally appreciated in this previously labour-intensive industry where every bottle had to be turned by hand.

Although the winemaking takes place at this address, the *caves* are under their private home in a neighbouring village. This is a small family business run by charming people. It would be as well to call in advance to arrange a tasting, particularly if you would like to speak English.

All the champagne is Blanc de Blancs – perfect *apéritif* or luncheon champagnes. Especially good when chilled, on a warm day, are the light and well balanced non-vintage Cuvée Extra (75F) and the Carte Or at 82F, which has a little more age. Half-bottles from 41F. Try too to taste the 90 vintage (92F).

Guy Charlemagne
4 rue de la Brèche d'Oger
51190 Mesnil-sur-Oger
Tel: (03) 26 57 52 98
Open Monday–Friday and Saturday morning

Consistently fine champagnes are produced by this house, with a splendid Brut Extra Blanc de Blancs, a delicate, elegant champagne at 75F. Taste the Réserve Brut at 82F for a comparison.

The Cuvée Charlemagne 90 grand cru Blanc de Blancs should be one to add to your collection of the 1990 vintage.

Avize

The vineyards which grow the grapes for the *Grandes Marques* houses of Pommery and Roederer hug the village of Avize from the surrounding slopes, but there is also a good selection of smaller winemakers thriving in this productive country.

Michel Gonet
196 avenue Jean-Jaurès
51190 Avize
Tel: (03) 26 57 50 56
Open Monday–Saturday
Sunday by appointment
The headquarters of Michel Gonet are in a large suburban 19th-century building; the elaborate fence is impossible to miss from the street. Tasting actually takes place in the office block behind the main building.

The Blanc de Blancs grand cru (82F), 100 per cent Chardonnay, is *brut* indeed, lively to the point of being frothy. The Blanc de Blancs 89 is perfectly balanced, an excellent example quality winemaking (92F).

De Sousa et Fils
12 place Léon Bourgeois
51190 Avize
Tel: (03) 26 50 53 29
Open Monday–Saturday
This small and friendly house produces a distinguished Blanc de Blancs, a grand cru Brut (81F), and a Brut Tradition at 79F. Although pale in colour, this is quite a substantial, complex wine, and has a beautiful fresh lemony bouquet. The 90 vintage sold out within months, so keep an eye out for the 92, which should be very good indeed.

Charming people. Their house, with white shutters and hanging flower baskets, is on a square – look for dark green gates leading onto the courtyard.

Where to stay
Hôtel Mont-Aimé
51130 Bergères-les-Vertus
Tel: (03) 26 52 21 31
Closed Sunday evening except by reservation
Double room 320F

This is a cheerful hotel that you will be happy to walk into after a long day's driving. You'll find the hotel on the main road (the D9) to Vertus; park at the front and pop in for directions on how to get to the car park at the rear.

My room was bright, colourful and comfortable, properly lit and decently equipped. Any hotel which provides two electrical sockets at desk height (a very rare occurrence except in international business hotels) will endear itself to a computer toting client. The mini-bar fridge is a big plus, you will be able to enjoy a chilled bottle of champagne picked up at one of the vineyards earlier in the day on your balcony at sunset. There are some smaller rooms. An open air swimming pool is for the hardy during the summer.

The 50F breakfast is such good value compared to the miserable offerings of some hotels at 35F, that for those staying elsewhere, it is worth considering coming here just for breakfast (served until 10am). The buffet offers fruit juices, muesli, yoghurt, honey and fruit, cheese and cold meats, and of course coffee, tea, croissants and bread. Good, if rather formal, restaurant in the hotel, well patronized by non-residents, especially at Sunday lunch.

Le Cheval Blanc
51270 Montmort-Lucy
Tel: (03) 26 59 10 03
Double rooms from 280F; menus from 78F
Restaurant closed on Fridays in winter

This is a typical rural *auberge*, situated at the busy crossroads of a small village known for its attractive château. A pretty exterior, with a large dining room, grand in the provincial sense for weddings and other celebratory occasions.

Noisier, older and brighter rooms at the front of the hotel, newer, quieter ones at the back; these are less bright, but they have pleasant rural views. Comfortable, good value rooms, in attractive countryside and convenient for visiting the champagne vineyards.

Cuisine is rich; slightly old-fashioned. The 78F menu consists of four courses, a *terrine de gibier aux pistaches*, followed by a *noix d'entrecôte, brie de Meaux* and dessert. Servings are vast, noticeable if you are yearning for a plain, light supper. Breakfast, however, at 35F, could not be more of a contrast – see above (Hôtel Mont-Aimé).

Where to eat
Le Mesnil
2 rue Pasteur, 51190 Mesnil-sur-Oger
Tel: (03) 26 57 95 57
Menus from 100F
Closed Monday evenings, Wednesday; mid-August–September
Don't be put off by the early 70s exterior or entrance doors. The cooking here is absolutely of its time, and fine too. The dining room is an oasis of calm, its cream marble floor and pale green walls cool and restful.

The 100F menu provides a light and delicious lunch, with an *amuse-bouche* of gravad lax in a dill sauce served at a table immaculately laid with crisp linen and fresh flowers. To start, a *foie de volaille* which included pheasant, rabbit in aspic and duck with pistachio nuts; then, as main course, a simple roast turkey with lightly cooked vegetables, finishing with a choice of desserts prepared by a *pâtissier* of consummate skill.

The 200F menu includes several glasses of wine (as well as a cheese course) selected by chef-proprietor Claude Jaillant. A local *ratafia* was served as an *apéritif*, a Coteaux Blanc by Claude Cazals (whose vineyard is up the road, and whose champagne is recommended), and a glass of bordeaux, although a glass of Bouzy would have made it a perfect *champenois* meal. The little chocolate champagne corks filled with champagne liqueur that are served with coffee were causing Madame Jaillant some problem, as every table wanted to buy a few to take away as gifts.

Hôtel-Restaurant Mont-Aimé
4–6 rue de Vertus
51130 Bergères-les-Vertus
Tel: (03) 26 52 21 31
Closed Sunday evening
Menus from 100F

Quite formal dining, but still comfortable and relaxing. The dining room is spacious, chairs have tapestry-style covers, and tables are set in pink linen. Very popular with the locals, especially at Sunday lunchtime.

Whilst there is a weekday lunch menu at 100F, the 150F menu offers a choice of dishes. To start, a *cassolette de pétoncles safranés*, a *gâteau de lapereau aux pruneaux* with a *confiture d'oignons tièdes* (which was dense and lush in flavour, outstanding in fact) or a *tartare de saumon aux pomelos rosés*, as main course duck breast cooked in Bouzy wine or a grilled *entrecôte*, cheeses and a dessert from the trolley (*le chariot*).

Good list of champagnes, many at 190F, with some favourites like Guy Larmandier, Pierre Moncuit and De Souza, with half-bottles from 100F. Try a red Bouzy from either Georges Vesselle or Laurent Perrier (190F).

La Comédia
2 rue de Chalons
in the centre of Vertus

If you have had too many four-course meals, and would simply love a pizza and beer, head for La Comédia. Far removed from the fussy décor of many French provincial restaurants, it is urbane, cool and very Italian. Terrific pizzas from the wood-fired oven from 40–50F.

More about Wine and Food

Buying from a vineyard

When you arrive at a vineyard, you'll usually be welcomed into a tasting room (which may also double up as an office), or simply into the winemaking, bottling, storage area. In the small vineyards, the winemaker or someone in their family will usually be more than happy for you to taste their wine. Obviously they can't open a sample of every wine they produce, and it would be unfair of you to expect them to, unless you're a wine merchant's buyer or a customer who buys in quantity – if so, you'll have made an appointment. But if you're just walking in, tasting from about three or four bottles is appropriate. For example, in Sancerre, you might taste the current year's red, white and rosé wines, and perhaps another from the previous year, out of interest and for comparison. Obviously, if you like what you're tasting and are intending to buy, you might ask to taste any special wines the producer makes.

Winemakers will usually be very pleased to answer your questions, and if your French is wobbly, try asking them to speak more slowly – you might find at this point that they'll pick up enough courage to speak English, which might quite possibly be much more fluent than your French. Please remember that a winemaker's shyness or modesty might sometimes come across as disinterest, but it isn't. No question is too simple: if you know very little about wine or a particular region, don't feel embarrassed, even some winemakers remember the time when they too perhaps knew little about wine.

HOW TO BUY OR NOT BUY

Even though this book has tried to direct you to the vineyards which make good wine and offer great value, what happens if you have tasted the wine and you don't like it? Remember that it's a matter of personal taste – after all, you're looking for wine that you'll enjoy drinking yourself when you return home. You

225

don't have to criticize the wine, you simply have to say or indicate that, sorry, unfortunately it's not to your taste or not quite what you wanted, but thank you for your time, for talking to us, and for giving us an opportunity to taste your wines.

If you do like the wine and you'd like to buy some, there are two things to note. Firstly, buying one bottle is rather like buying a single cigarette as opposed to a packet. In France, with the exception of very expensive wines, the unit of purchase is a *carton*, which is six bottles. The producers are generally so amiable and polite that they'd never show any disapproval if you bought only a couple of bottles. Secondly, you'll regret buying only a bottle or two of a wine you like. Do what the French do, and that is, buy six or 12 bottles, and drink them over a couple of years, less if it's a wine that should be drunk young, say in the first year after vintage.

To pay for your purchases at a vineyard, take French cash or French franc travellers' cheques. Some producers will accept Eurocheques, but recent problems with these at French banks may affect their acceptance. Few vineyards can afford to set up credit card facilities, much as they would like to, given that they sometimes lose business if they haven't got the facility. Of course the large, more commercial producers take credit cards.

As for **transporting your wine**, if you're going to be leaving your car out in the hot summer sun for a couple of weeks with your purchases sitting in the boot, it would be better to try and buy towards the end of your trip. When you get back home, your wine will have been shaken around considerably. Young wines should be fine, but older wines with sediment will need to settle, perhaps for a couple of weeks, before drinking.

Wine tasting

The purpose of tasting a wine is simply to see if you like it. You don't have to be an expert to taste wines and discern the various flavours. You can start to tell a lot about a wine by simply looking at its colour, swirling it around a glass and breathing in the smells it gives off, and by taking a large sip and rolling it around your mouth.

You might be intimidated by watching people taste wine, and you might think they're being a little pretentious when they start talking about 'hints of gooseberry in the nose' or 'sweaty horses' (used more in Australia than France). But the interesting thing is that once you start to taste wine, you'll very quickly start to distinguish smells and flavours that you never thought of before. Use your own words to describe them. In the same way that you can probably tell (especially with your eyes closed) the difference between Bramley and Granny Smith apples, you'll soon be able to distinguish wine from different grapes – it just takes practice.

COLOUR

Look at the colour, against a white background if possible, tipping your glass away from you slightly. With white wines, the paler the colour, probably the younger the wine. A pale colour may indicate that the wine is from a cooler climate (see the difference in depth of colour between a Loire white and an Australian white). Some fine Chardonnays will acquire more colour over time, and sweet wines can be golden. With red wines, the colour reflects where the wine comes from more than the wine's age. Purple is from a southern sunny climate, ruby a lighter wine from a more northerly climate.

SMELL

Usually pleasant. Swirl the wine around the glass (if the glass is only half full, the wine's less likely to spill, and it has a chance to give off the most smell within the glass), place your nose in the top of the glass, and take a deep breath.

A couple of exceptions to the 'usually pleasant' rule are the Sauvignon Blanc grape, for example in Sancerre, which may not smell as delightful as you might expect (a hint of tomcat), and old red burgundy, which can smell not all that pleasantly of farmyard.

TASTE

Take a sip, swirl it gently around your mouth, and try to suck
some air into your mouth, which aerates the wine in the same
way as swirling it around your glass does. Do you like the
taste? It may not be your kind of wine, but can you, nevertheless, taste whether it's a good wine?

TASTING TERMS AND WHAT THEY REALLY MEAN

The language of tasting can seem arcane, or plain daft when it's
overdone. Here are some helpful simple terms which are often
used in describing the tastes and smells of wine. Keep them in
mind when you smell or taste wine, and see if you can apply
any.

Each term is followed by examples of wines or grapes that
might have the qualities described, or by an explanatory note.
But don't forget that your own words to describe what you
smell or taste are as valid as the standard vocabulary.

apple	fresh, crisp apple flavours in the young white wines of the Loire and some Chardonnays; cooked apple flavours in Riesling
apricot	look for this in wines from the Viognier grape
aromatic and spicy	Gewürztraminer or Tokay-Pinot Gris
biscuity	some champagnes, rather like shortbread
blackcurrant	Cabernet Sauvignon and Pinot Noir
cat's pee	disgusting, maybe, but used of Sauvignon Blanc to describe a slight tartness
cherry	smelling of cherries; Beaujolais
dirty socks	you won't want to drink this wine
farmyard	a good earthy smell, usually red wine
flinty	a slightly metallic taste, found in Pouilly-Fumé and some Chardonnays
gooseberry	smelling of gooseberries, sometimes in Loire Sauvignons

228

grassy	smells like a recently mowed lawn: Pouilly-Fumé, Sancerre, Sauvignon de Touraine
honey	Sauternes, Monbazillac, especially Loire *moelleux* (sweet wines)
pepper	Grenache or Syrah and some bordeaux
petrol	not negative: Riesling
smoky	Pouilly-Fumé
spicy	wines from the Rhône, and white wine from Gewürztraminer
toffee	Merlot
vanilla	wines aged in new oak
violets	red burgundy

Some other wine tasting terms, and what they mean:

acidity	not a negative term; gives life and freshness
backward	underdeveloped for its age
balanced	a harmonious, well-made wine
bite	a lot of acidity
body	full of flavour
bouquet	the smell
breathing	letting air into a bottle of wine before drinking; some wines do taste better if you uncork the bottle half an hour before drinking, though this is sometimes disputed
closed	not yet showing its qualities
cloying	stickily sweet with no acidity
coarse	rough
corked	wine that's gone off because of a bad cork
crisp	fresh with acidity
depth	the taste stays with you (pleasant)
dry	no hint of sweetness
earthy	when you taste this, you'll know it
elegant	as in any other product
finish	what happens to the taste when you've swallowed the wine: does it linger (a long finish) or disappear immediately (a short finish)?

forward	a wine well developed for its age
length	how long the taste of the wine stays in your mouth
lees	sediment that settles whilst wine is ageing
mellow	well-matured, well-rounded
nose	the smell
oxidized	wine exposed to air
quaffing	for everyday drinking; not special
rough	if it's rough, let it breathe (see above), and if it still doesn't improve, don't bother drinking it
round	smooth
short	the taste disappears quickly
silky	very smooth
tannin	the element in red wine that feels as though it's cleaning your teeth

Also see the French/English wine glossary on page 240.

WINE TEMPERATURE

The optimum temperature at which to serve wine is one which brings out its best qualities and flavours. White and rosé wines are often served far too cold. Whilst this may be refreshing on a hot day, it does hide the qualities of a well-made wine. It also happens to be a way of covering up the poorer qualities of less well-made wine.

Red wines are often served too warm: light reds can be served slightly chilled, or at cellar temperature, with bordeaux best able to take warmer temperatures. Don't chill champagne too much as this dulls its flavours, which will recover, though, once the wine has warmed a little in your glass. Suitable serving temperatures:

Rosé	9–11°C
Dry white	9–11°C
Sweet white	9–13°C
Reds from the Loire, Beaujolais and Alsace	11–15°C
Red bordeaux	17–19°C
Red burgundy	15–17°C

White burgundy	11–15°C
Champagne	9–13°C

Winemaking

Whilst winemaking may appear to be the process of pressing grapes and then fermenting the juice, with the winemaker applying all his skills to produce the best wine, the process starts well before this phase. The eventual flavour of the wine will depend on what grape was grown, in what soil, in which climate, the particular weather during the year, and the specific conditions of the vineyard.

At harvest time (autumn), the grapes are picked, rotten ones removed, and the good ones transported to the winery. The quicker they get there the better; exposure to the air can lead to oxidization. The grapes need to be pressed – the more gentle the pressing, the clearer the juice, hence the use of expensive pneumatic presses. The juice may be left to settle for a day (for heavier wines) or filtered and passed into a tank for fermenting. The tank could be stainless steel or wood. Stainless steel is state-of-the-art, with precise temperature control. Wood is the old way, allowing the wine to breathe, but giving the winemaker less control than with modern methods. New wood imparts a distinctive flavour, which might be described as oaky vanilla (after a few years the wood loses its 'flavour').

Fermentation can be caused by natural or cultured yeasts. Red wines are fermented at a higher temperature, whilst a lower temperature, used for white wines and some reds, results in a fresher, fruitier wine. Not too low a temperature, though, or there will be no fermentation, and not too high, or the yeasts will be destroyed.

After fermentation, different processes occur: the wine is either left on its lees to intensify its flavour, or it is put in a fresh vat; it may be filtered, or it may be subjected to a malolactic fermentation (a secondary fermentation which makes the wine 'softer').

METHODE CHAMPENOISE

By law, the only region allowed to use the term champagne for its sparkling wines is Champagne itself. As a result, until recently other regions used the term *méthode champenoise* to describe sparkling wine made in exactly the same way as champagne. Then the people of Champagne, worried by how good these sparkling wines were, managed to have the term banned for use on labels, so now winemakers use the term *méthode traditionelle*, or *méthode classique*. They also use the name *crémant* for such sparkling wines. Elsewhere in the world, beyond the reach of French bureaucrats, you still find *méthode champenoise* in use.

Still wine is made sparkling through a secondary fermentation. This occurs by bottling the wine with the addition of *liqueur de tirage*, sugar dissolved in wine with yeast added. The best fermentation takes place slowly and should produce a large number of small bubbles when the wine is eventually poured. The process starts with the bottles of wine stored horizontally, which causes dead yeasts to gather on one side of the bottle. The bottles are then moved to specially designed racks, where, by being turned a little every day, they end up vertical and upside down, with the neck of the bottle at the bottom. The turning process involves a gentle shake, and is known as *remuage* (riddling, or shaking, stirring). It used to be done by hand, but there are now machines called *gyropalettes* that do the equivalent mechanically.

As a result of gentle *remuage*, all the deposits settle on the cork. The bottles are then cellared in their upside-down position, until they're put in a conveyor which passes the neck of the bottle through a freezing liquid, turning the sediment into a solid lump. The cork is removed, the lump of sediment pops out under pressure, the bottle is topped up with the same wine, a measure of liquid sugar is added (a process known as *dosage*), the bottle is corked again, and at last it's ready for labelling and sale.

232

GRAPE VARIETIES

Black (or Red) Grapes

Cabernet Franc: when you smell blackcurrants in a wine, it may be made from Cabernet Franc. Chinon and Bourgueil in the Loire use this grape alone. Elsewhere it's often blended with Merlot.

Cabernet Sauvignon: found mainly in bordeaux.

Carignan: you may not have heard of this grape, but you will have heard of Fitou, Minervois and Corbières, which are made from it.

Gamay: should usually be drunk young. Mainly in Beaujolais.

Grenache: blended to make Côtes du Rhône.

Merlot: found in St-Emilion and Pomerol, both bordeaux. (Château Petrus, the most famous Pomerol, is made mainly from Merlot.)

Pinot Noir: associated with burgundy, it is also used in Champagne, where it is blended with Chardonnay.

Syrah: found in Hermitage.

White Grapes

Aligoté: makes the fresh acidic Bourgogne Aligoté.

Chardonnay: there isn't a wine drinker who hasn't heard of this grape. It's blended in Champagne, or used alone to make a lighter Blanc de Blancs. It also flourishes in Burgundy.

Chasselas: a rather run-of-the-mill grape, producing less than exciting wines like Pouilly-sur-Loire (not to be confused with the wonderful Pouilly-Fumé).

Chenin Blanc: much used in the Loire, especially in the region's sparkling and sweet wines.

Colombard:	found in Cognac and Provence.
Gewürztraminer:	one of the great grapes of Alsace.
Marsanne:	grown in the Rhône Valley.
Muscat:	famous for its use in luscious sweet wines like Beaumes-de-Venise.
Pinot Blanc:	Alsace.
Riesling:	Alsace.
Sauvignon Blanc:	at its best in Sancerre and Pouilly-Fumé.
Sylvaner:	produces probably the least exciting wine in Alsace.
Tokay-Pinot Gris:	makes one of the great wines of Alsace.
Viognier:	the rare and now highly fashionable grape used in Condrieu.

GRAPE VARIETIES AND WINE PRODUCING AREAS

Here's a summary of the main grape varieties grown in each of France's main wine producing areas.

Alsace

Red   Pinot Noir
White Gewürztraminer, Muscat, Pinot, Tokay-Pinot Gris, Riesling, Sylvaner

Bordeaux

Red   Cabernet Sauvignon, Cabernet Franc Merlot, Malbec
White Sauvignon Blanc, Sémillon

Burgundy

Red   Pinot Noir, Gamay
White Chardonnay, Aligoté

Mâconnais-Beaujolais

Red   Gamay
White Chardonnay

234

Champagne

Red   Pinot Meunier (or Meunier), Pinot Noir
White Chardonnay

Loire

Red   Cabernet Sauvignon, Cabernet Franc Gamay, Pinot Noir
White Chardonnay, Chasselas, Chenin Blanc Melon de Bourgogne, Sauvignon Blanc

Rhône

Red   Grenache, Syrah
White Grenache Blanc, Marsanne, Muscat, Viognier

CLASSIFICATIONS

Vin de Table (literally, table wine) is the cheapest and most ordinary wine with the least amount of regulation.

Vin de Pays (country or regional wine) meets certain criteria: it's made from a recognizable grape in a particular region. This gives the consumer a guarantee of the wine's origin, which can be regional, such as Vin de Pays du Jardin de la France from the Loire Valley, or Vin de Pays d'Oc, which could come from anywhere in Languedoc-Roussillon, or a narrower *département* origin, such as Vin de Pays de l'Ardèche.

The most tightly regulated in terms of region of origin, grapes used and permissible yields are **Appellation Contrôlée** wines (AC, or sometimes AOC: Appellation d'Origine Contrôlée). Whilst in theory these should be the best wines in France, this isn't always the case. You may find certain Vins de Pays that are of much greater quality than some rogue Appellation Contrôlée wines. Just to complicate matters, some regions, such as Bordeaux, have further distinctions and layers in quality (**Crus Classés** of Bordeaux, and the lesser **Crus Bourgeois**) as does Burgundy with its **Grands Crus** and **Premiers Crus**.

Vin Délimité de Qualité Supérieure (VDQS) is a classification somewhere between Vin de Pays and Appellation Contrôlée, that is used for wines from small areas that are improving and may eventually reach Appellation Contrôlée status. This happens very rarely these days, but you may still see examples, particularly around the edges of the Loire.

VINTAGES

Vintage usually refers to the year in which a wine is produced. People talk about a good or bad vintage, according to the weather experienced in that year.

Good winemakers can make very good wine even in a poor year – they simply have to call on all their creative and technical skills, and use their ingenuity. And whilst a year may be regarded as poor in general in an area, local climatic differences have a big impact. 1986 was a much better year for white burgundy than it was for red burgundy.

Each vintage has its own distinct character, and sometimes it can be difficult comparing the quality of one vintage of a wine with another, they are just different. The main point is that a good winemaker will often produce a decent wine even in an indifferent year, whilst a poor winemaker may not produce a wine in a good year as pleasurable as you might expect.

There was a run of extraordinarily good vintages in the 80s, ending in 1990. This was followed by a few difficult years in some regions. The good news is that 1995 was, in general, the best vintage in every region since 1990, so there should be some excellent wines available.

In addition, champagnes from the splendid 1990 vintage are now being released, and 1989 and 1990 sweet wines from the Loire are almost ready for drinking. This is a good time to buy.

Alsace

Best years:

1983   exceptional, especially for *vendanges tardives* wines.

1985   a very dry summer, with virtually no rain for four months, so the wines are rich and concentrated. Another superb year.

1988	a good year that was on its way to being even better until rain fell just before picking.
1989	another fine hot year. Very good for late-picked wines.
1990	last of the run of superb years in the 80s.
1995	the best year since 1990.

Loire

Best years in the Anjou region (western Loire):

1985	a sunny harvest, superb *moelleux*.
1988	a good vintage.
1989	the best vintage in living memory (since 1947), especially for sweet wines.
1990	not quite as fine as 89, but still produced great wines.
1995	very good.

Champagne

Different producers declare vintages in different years, depending on whether they think a year was particularly good.

In general, you'll find the following years consistently fine: 1983, 85, 89, and 90, which is the most recently released, and will be of the greatest interest to you.

Rhône

Whilst there were variations for reds and whites from the northern and southern Rhône, the following vintages were all good to superb: 1983, 85, 88, 89, 90, 95.

Red burgundy has some variation in the quality of its vintages, but in general terms, the following years produced good to superb wines: 1985, 88, 89, 90 and 95. An example of this variation is evident when you look at the 86 vintage for white burgundy. Whilst it was not a particularly interesting year for red burgundy, it was a good year for the whites.

Bordeaux

Red bordeaux had a string of great vintages in the 80s. However, a good year on a plain generic bordeaux doesn't compare in any way to the wines from the best châteaux. Remember, too, that there are many different regions covered by the term bordeaux. 1982 was a particularly fine year for St-Emilion and Pomerol, 1983 the best year for Margaux in this decade. Apart from 1984 and 87, all the years until 1990 were rather good. Keep an eye out for the 95s.

White bordeaux are generally fine from 83 till 90 with the exception of 84 and 87. The sweet white bordeaux vintages to go for are 83, 86, 88, 89, and 90

Matching wine and food

Most French wine is made to be drunk with food. It's intended to complement food, and certain foods bring out the best in some wines. The old rule that you should drink white with fish, red with meat, and a red with cheese, is mostly fine (with the exception of the red with cheese) if you want to follow it. But it does limit your range of choice, and there's a great adventure in going well beyond this view. I like drinking what I feel like with whatever food I'm eating, with no hard and fast rules.

However, there are some useful parameters: choose a wine that matches your food and doesn't overpower it, one that enhances your enjoyment of the food. At the same time, where a food is strongly flavoured, choose a wine big enough to balance it. Beware of highly spiced foods from cultures that don't drink much wine. They may simply vanquish the flavours in a wine, and you'll sometimes have to accept there's no wine to match.

FOOD AND WHAT TO DRINK WITH IT

Fish and seafood

Oysters:	very dry whites (Sancerre, Chablis or Muscadet).
Lobster:	Tokay-Pinot Gris from Alsace.
Poached salmon:	wine that's not too acidic, such as Mâcon-Villages or white Châteauneuf-du-Pape.
Smoked salmon:	Tokay-Pinot Gris or a Gewürztraminer.

| Trout, sea bass: | Chardonnay or a burgundy. |

Meat

Roast or grilled red meat:	bordeaux, burgundy.
Casserole:	bordeaux, Gevrey-Chambertin (rich burgundy), Châteauneuf-du-Pape.
Meat in cream sauce:	some acidity (Beaujolais).
Pork:	light red (Loire or Beaujolais) or white (Alsace Tokay-Pinot Gris).
Chicken, goose, turkey:	light red (Loire or Beaujolais) or white (Alsace Riesling or Chardonnay).
Poultry and cream:	wine with some acidity (Alsace Riesling, Vouvray or Sauvignon).
Duck:	red (Loire or Beaujolais).
Pheasant, partridge, grouse, pigeon:	St-Emilion, Pomerol, red burgundy, or if strong tasting, Crozes Hermitage.
Venison:	lively, spicy red like Cahors or Madiran.

Dessert

| Fruit tart: | Beaumes-de-Venise, late harvest Alsace Muscat. |
| Creamy puddings: | Sauternes, sweet Loire wines. |

Cheese

Goat's cheese:	Sancerre, Pouilly-Fumé.
Soft cheese:	red.
Blue cheese:	quality mature sweet wine (Sauternes).

WINES AND WHAT TO EAT WITH THEM

You might have the wines, and want to create a meal around them. Here are some wines from various regions, and suggestions for suitable dishes to go with them:

Alsace

Sweet Tokay or Gewürztraminer *vendanges tardives* for an *apéritif*.

Riesling is good with fish, seafood or *choucroute* (sauerkraut).
  Sylvaner goes with *ballottine* or *galantine* (delicate boned
  and stuffed poultry dishes).
Pinot Noir or Pinot Blanc with poultry or veal.
A powerful Gewürztraminer or Tokay goes well with cheeses
  like Munster, or blue cheese like Roquefort.

Anjou

A Crémant de Loire or a sweet white wine (Coteaux du Layon,
  Coteaux de Saumur, Savennières demi-sec,
Bonnezeaux or Quarts de Chaume) as an *apéritif*.
The sweet (*moelleux* and *liquoreux*) wines are superb with *pâté
  de foie gras* or indeed with blue cheese.
Saumur blanc and Savennières go with fish, seafood or oysters.
Rosés from the Loire are delightful with summer dishes like
  quiche or light *crudités* (raw vegetable starters).
Anjou rouge, Saumur rouge, Saumur-Champigny and Chinon
  are served cooler than, say, a bordeaux, with simply prepared
  red meats, or, since these are light red wines, poultry.

Bordeaux

Graves sec or Entre-deux-Mers with shellfish and seafood.
Sauternes with *foie gras* (and Roquefort cheese).
Pauillac, Margaux or Saint-Julien with grilled meat.
Saint-Emilion, Canon-Fronsac, Pomerol, Saint-Estèphe or
  Graves with roasts.

Burgundy

A kir (*crème de cassis* mixed into Bourgogne Aligoté) or a Cré-
  mant de Bourgogne as an *apéritif*.
Chablis and Pouilly-Fuissé with oysters.
Chassagne-Montrachet and Puligny-Montrachet with seafood
  and fish.
Montrachet and Meursault also with fish, but good with chick-
  en in a cream sauce.
Nuit-St-Georges, Vougeot or Vosne-Romanée with red meat.

Volnay, Chambolle-Musigny, Aloxe-Corton, Monthelie or Beaune with white meat.

Pommard, Santenay, Clos-de-Vougeot and Corton with *boeuf bourguignon* (beef cooked in red burgundy).

Chambertin, Fixin or Musigny with cheese.

Languedoc
Crémant or Blanquette de Limoux as an *apéritif*.

White Corbières or Minervois with fish.

A young and light red Corbières or Coteaux-du-Languedoc with *charcuterie* (ham, pâtés, *saucisson* – French salami – and so on).

Fitou, or a powerful Corbières or Minervois, go particularly well with venison.

Sancerre and Pouilly-Fumé
Sancerre blanc as an *apéritif*, with fish or *andouillette* or with the local speciality, goat's cheese.

Sancerre rosé with starters like omelette, or meat-filled galettes.

Red Sancerre with meat or fish.

Pouilly-Fumé with fish.

Wines from the South
Bergerac with goose.

Madiran and Cahors with *confit de canard* (duck preserve).

Muscat with *foie gras*.

Maury and Banyuls as an *apéritif*.

A young red Côtes du Roussillon with *charcuterie* (see Languedoc above).

White Côtes du Roussillon with shellfish and fish.

Rhône wines
Condrieu and Hermitage with fish.

Tavel and Lirac with white meat.

Châteauneuf-du-Pape, Cornas, Côte-Rotie with game.

Red Hermitage with meat.

French/English Wine Glossary

apéritif	a drink which you have before a meal; may be wine or fortified wine
appellation/ appellation contrôlée	see page 236
blanc de blancs	white wine made from white grapes
bouchon	cork
bouteille	bottle
brut	very dry (to describe champagne)
cave	winery, cellar
cave coopérative	cooperative winemaker
cépage	grape/vine variety
chais	wine store
chambré	at room temperature
crémant	lightly sparkling wines
cru	used for some top quality vineyards
cuve	vat, tank
degré alcoolique	alcohol content
dégustation	tasting
demi-bouteille	half-bottle
demi-sec	medium-dry
doux	sweet
eau-de-vie	spirit
en vrac	loose, not bottled
étiquette	label
fermentation	fermentation
fût	cask
jus de raisin	grape juice
fort	strong
frais	fresh (taste), cool (temperature)
goût	flavour
grappe	bunch (of grapes)
léger	light
lie	lees (sediments)
liquoreux	sweet wine high in alcohol

madérisé	oxidized
maturité	ripeness
mis en bouteille	bottled
moelleux	medium sweet (used of whites)
mousseux	sparkling wine
négociant (en vin)	(wine) merchant
nouveau	under a year old (used of reds)
pépin	seed
pétillant	slightly sparkling
pourriture (noble)	(noble) rot, botrytis
précoce	early maturing
raisin	grape(s)
raisin blanc	green grapes
raisin noir	black (or red) grapes
raisin de cuve	wine grapes
raisin de table	eating grapes
sec	dry
sucre	sugar
tanin	tannin
terroir	a piece of land and its particular, natural characteristics for wine growing
tonneau	cask
tuffeau	known as 'tufa' in English, a type of rock found in the central Loire Valley
vendange	grape harvest, (grape) crop, vintage
vendange tardive	late harvest (used in Alsace)
verre (à dégustation)	(tasting) glass
vieillissement (en bouteille/fût)	(bottle/cask) ageing
vigne	vine (also vineyard)
vigneron	winegrower
vignoble	vineyard
vin	wine
viticulteur	winegrower

French/English Food Glossary

The **Berlitz European Menu Reader** gives invaluable assistance with everyday menus. The following is a translation of the more exotic dishes given in French throughout the text of this book.

boeuf à la minute	steak shown the grill for one minute; or prepared while you wait
boeuf tartare	chopped raw steak served with capers, onion, parsley and a raw egg yolk
à la fondue de poireaux	leek fondue
abricots secs macérés aux épices	spiced apricots
ail rôti	roast garlic
amuse-bouche, amuse-gueule	appetizers
andouille(tte)	tripe sausage
aux coques	in their shells; or with cockles
bavette poêlée à l'échalote	steak with shallots
Bayonne	ham from Bayonne
blanquette	in a white sauce
bleu	very rare
boudin (blanc)	black pudding (white – without blood)
cabillaud	cod
carpaccio au basilic	carpaccio with basil
cassolette d'escargots au persil plat	snails with parsley
cassolette de pétoncles safranés	scallops with saffron
cassoulet	stew of goose, pork and beans
céleri-rave	celeriac
chausson de pétoncles	scallops in pastry

244

chou frisé	curly cabbage
choucroute Alsacienne	Alsation sauerkraut
cidre bouché Normandie brut	dry Normandy cider
civet de lièvre	jugged hare
civet de porcelet	stewed pork
clafoutis aux cerises aigres	sour-cherry batter cake
collet fumé	smoked neck
compote	fruit cooked in syrup
confit de joue de porc piqué d'ail	preserved pork cheek spiked with garlic
confiture d'oignons tièdes	warm onion conserve
coq au Riesling	chicken cooked in Riesling
cornichons	gherkins
coulis d'orange	orange purée/sauce
crème anglaise	egg custard
crème brûlée	baked custard with crisp caramel
crème caramel	baked custard with caramel
crème fraîche	sour cream
crêpes suzettes	pancake with orange sauce
crépinette de lotte	monkfish sausage
croûtons	crisply fried bread
crudités	mixed raw vegetable starter
cuissot de canard confit	leg of preserved duck
cuites à l'assiette	cooked on the plate
dos de lapereau rôti	roast rabbit
effilochée de cabillaud	flaked cod
émincé de boeuf aux nouilles	sliced beef with noodles
entrecôte	rib/rib-eye steak
entrecôte béarnaise	steak with sauce of egg, wine, vinegar, onion and tarragon
escalope de saumon à l'oseille	salmon with sorrel
estouffade de boeuf	beef stew

245

feuilleté	puff or flaky pastry
filet de cabillaud au coulis de crevettes	filet of cod with prawn sauce
filet de truite rôti	roast filet of trout
filet julienne flambée	sliced vegetables flamed with brandy
filet mignon de porc	pork filet
filets de rouget grillés	grilled fillets of red mullet
foie gras (pâté de)	goose liver with truffles
foie de canard	duck liver
fond de poireaux et jus de lapereau	leeks with rabbit sauce
fondue de tomate	tomato purée
fricassée de volaille	chicken in a white sauce made with eggs and cream
frisée	curly lettuce
fromage blanc en sorbet	sorbet made with white cheese
garni(e)	garnished
gâteau de lapereau aux lentilles vertes, aux pruneaux	flan of young rabbit with green lentils and prunes
gâteau de pain aux pommes	apple cake
gâteau de riz	dense rice pudding
gibier aux pommes	game with apples
gigolette de volaille	small poultry legs
gigot d'agneau	leg of lamb
girolle	chanterelle mushrooms
glacée à la grande champagne	glazed with champagne
gratin de cuisses de grenouilles tièdes	quiche of frogs' legs topped with cheese and grilled
jambonnette de canard	duck
jambonnette de volaille à la moutarde	chicken with mustard
jus de céleri vert	green celery sauce
jus de volaille au thé	chicken stock with tea

kir	aperitif of white wine with a drop of blackcurrant liqueur
lait de chèvre	goat's milk
langoustines mayonnaise	large prawns in mayonnaise
lardons	bacon pieces
le lieu jaune	pollack
le pot au feu faitout	beef stew
marbre de lapin	marbled rabbit
maroilles	dark, rich cheese
médaillons de chocolat	rounds of chocolate
médaillons de crème de foie d'oie	rounds of creamed goose liver
méli-mélo des poissons	selection of fish
moules marinières	mussels cooked in wine
mousse de foie de canard	duck liver mousse
mousse de fromage de chèvre frais	goat's cheese mousse
noisettes d'agneau sautées	sautéed filet of lamb
noix de veau	rounds of veal
normande	white sauce made with fish, mushroom stock and cream
pavé	thick piece of steak
persillé de cuisse de canard	duck legs with parsley
petit jambonneau aux lentillons	pig's knuckle with lentils
petits fours	little cakes served with coffee
pintade forestière	guinea fowl with morels and bacon
poêlée de calamars	squid fried in butter
poire meringuée au Grand Marnier	pear meringue with Grand Marnier
poitrine de canard fumée	smoked duck breast
potiron et jambon sec	pumpkin and cured ham
presskopf	brawn (head cheese)

rates au safran	spleen with saffron
ravioles de saumon	salmon ravioli
rillettes de cabillaud	rich cod paste
rillettes de saumon	rich salmon paste
rognons blanc en persillade	veal kidneys with parsley salad
rouget	red mullet
rouille	garlic and chilli paste
salade aux foies de volailles	chicken liver salad
salade aux lardons	salad with bacon
salade champêtre	country salad
salade de boudin	salad with black pudding
salade de calamars	salad with squid
salade de gésiers confits	salad of preserved gizzards
salade de magret de canard avec copeaux de foie gras	salad of duck breast with shavings of goose liver
salade de moules au safran et coeur de laitue	salad of mussels with saffron and lettuce hearts
salade du pêcheur	fisherman's salad
salade vigneronne	winemaker's salad
saucisson	French salami
sauté de biche	fried venison
sauté de veau à l'orange	fried veal with orange
savarin	yeast cake soaked in rum
sirop de cacao	chocolate syrup
sorbet citron au marc de Gewürztztraminer	lemon sorbet made with wine spirit
soupe aux bouchots	seafood soup
soupe de poissons	fish soup
sauce aux cèpes	mushroom sauce
tartare de saumon aux pomelos rosés	raw salmon with pink grapefruit
tarte a l'orange	orange tart
tarte au fromage blanc	white cheese tart

tarte aux pommes	apple tart
tarte fine à la nougatine mignardises	small tart filled with praline cream
tarte flambée (flammenkuche)	tart flamed in brandy
tarte maison	house speciality
tarte normande	tart with cream filling
tarte sucrée au fromage blanc	tart with a sweet cheese filling
tarte Tatin	upside down apple tart
terrine de canard et gésiers	coarse pâté of duck and gizzards
terrine de foie	coarse liver pâté
terrine de lapin	rabbit pâté
terrine maison aux cèpes	homemade mushroom pâté
tomates vertes confit	preserved green tomatoes
tourte vigneronne	winemaker's torte (covered tart)
truite meunière	trout in brown butter, parsley, lemon

UK specialist importers

Where merchants offer free delivery on one or two cases, and where the total value of the order does not need to be over £100 to qualify, the area to which they will deliver free is shown in brackets. (UK) means any reasonably accessible part of the mainland.

Avon	Averys (UK) 0117 921 4141
	Châteaux Wines (UK) 01454 613 959
	Harvey, John (UK) 0117 927 5009
	Reid (Central London & Bristol) 01761 452 645
Berks	Bordeaux Direct & Sunday Times Wine Club (UK) 01734 481 718
Bucks	Philip Eyres (Amersham) 01494 433 823
Cambs	Byrne, Anthony 01487 814 555
Cheshire	Portland (Sale) 0161 962 8752

Devon	Nobody Inn 01647 52394
	Piper, Christopher 01404 812 100
	Wylie, Peter 01884 277 555
Dorset	Eldridge Pope 0800 378 757
Essex	Lay & Wheeler (UK) 01206 764 446
Glos	Bennetts (England & Wales) 01386 840 392
	Karn & Son (Glos) 01242 513 265
	Windrush (Central London, Cheltenham, Oxford, Hungerford) 01451 860 680
Herts	Majestic (Watford) 01923 816 999
	Wine Society (UK, Northern Ireland) 01438 741 177
Lancs	Whitesides 01200 22281
	Booths 01772 251 701
London	Amis (Les) du Vin 0181 451 0469
	Armit (John) Wines 0171 727 6846
	Barnes Wine Shop (London) 0181 878 8643
	Berry Bros & Rudd (UK) 0171 396 9600
	Bibendum (England) 0171 722 5577
	Bute Wines 0171 937 1629
	Corney & Barrow (M25) 0171 251 4051
	Farr Vintners 0171 828 1960
	Fuller's (Chiswick) 0181 996 2000
	Goedhuis & Co (London) 0171 793 7900
	Harcourt (London) 0171 723 7202
	Hayes Hanson & Clark (Central London & Glos) 0171 259 0102
	Lea & Sandeman 0171 376 4767
	Morris & Verdin (Central London) 0171 357 8866
	Nez (Le) Rouge (UK) 0171 609 4711
	Réserve (La) (Central London) 0171 589 2020
	Ripley, Howard 0181 360 8904
	Roberson (Kensington) 0171 371 2121
	Vigneronne (La) (Central London) 0171 589 6113
	Waterloo Wine 0171 403 7967
	Wine (Central London) 0171 351 6856
Norfolk	Harris, Roger 01603 880 171

	Satchells (Norfolk) 01328 738 272
	T & W (UK) 01842 765 646
Northants	Summerlee (Northants, Oxford, Cambridge, Central London) 01933 682 221
Notts	Gauntleys (Nottingham) 01159 417 973
Oxon	Hampden 01844 213 251
Salop	Halves (UK) 01584 877 866
	Tanners (UK) 01743 232 400
Suffolk	Adnams (UK) 01502 727 220
	Amey's Wines (Sudbury) 01787 377144
	Peatling, Thos. (UK) 01284 755 948
	Seckford (Ipswich) 01473 626681
Surrey	Davisons 0181 760 0390
Sussex	Butlers (Brighton) 01273 698 724
Yorks	Wright Wine (Skipton) 01756 700 886
Wilts	Yapp (UK) 01747 860 423
Scotland	Forth Wines 01577 862 513
	Gelston Castle (Castle Douglas) 01556 503 012
	Green (Peter) (Edinburgh) 0131 229 5925
	Hogg JE (Edinburgh) 0131 556 4025
	Raeburn 0131 332 5166
	Ubiquitous Chip 0141 334 5007
Wales	Platt, Terry (Gwynedd) 01492 592 971
	Towy Valley (South Wales) 01267 290 808

Channel Islands

Sommelier (CI) 01481 721 677

Northern Ireland

Direct Wine (Northern Ireland) 01232 243 906
Nicholson, James (Northern Ireland) 01396 830 091

Republic of Ireland

Febvre & Co (Dublin) 1 -295 9036
Grants (Dublin 1-626 4680
Cassidy Wines (Dublin) 1-295 4497
Edward Dillon (Dublin) 1-874 1064

251

Index

Other Berlitz titles to help you enjoy your visit to France

Pocket Guides
Brittany
Châteaux of the Loire
Côte d'Azur
Disneyland Paris
Dordogne
France
Normandy
Paris
Provence

Discover Guides
Brittany
France
Loire Valley
Normandy
Pyrenees

Travellers' Guides
France

Language help for the traveller
Berlitz French Phrase Book

Berlitz French Cassette Pack
Berlitz French CD Pack
Berlitz French/English Dictionary
Pardon My French! Video and CD ROM

Self-study language courses
Berlitz Basic French
Berlitz Basic French Deluxe
Berlitz French Workbook
Berlitz Advanced French Workbook
Think and Talk French

Language reference materials
Berlitz Language Handbooks:
French Grammar
French Verbs
French Vocabulary

For children
Just for Kids: French

For the business traveller
Berlitz Business French Phrase Book and Cassette Pack